Think
Act Anew

In this temple
as in the hearts of the people
for whom he saved the Union
the memory of Abraham Lincoln
is enshrined forever

—*Inscription on the Lincoln Memorial, Washington, D.C.*

Think Anew, Act Anew

Abraham Lincoln
on Slavery, Freedom,
and Union

Brooks D. Simpson
Editor

 Harlan Davidson, Inc.
Wheeling, Illinois 60090-6000

Grateful acknowledment is hereby given to the Abraham Lincoln Association and the Illinois Historic Preservation Agency for permission to reprint the text from Abraham Lincoln documents. All other parts of this book © 1998 by Harlan Davidson, Inc. All Rights Reserved.

Library of Congress Cataloging-in-Publication Data

Lincoln, Abraham, 1809–1865.
    Think anew, act anew : Abraham Lincoln on slavery, freedom, and union / Brooks D. Simpson, editor.
          p.   cm.
    Includes bibliographical references and index.
          ISBN 0-88295-975-1
    1. United States–Politics and government, 1849–1861. 2. United States–Politics and government–1861–1865. 3. Illinois–Politics and government–To 1865. 4. Lincoln, Abraham, 1809–1865–Political and social views.   I. Simpson, Brooks D.   II. Title.
E457.2.L753   1998
973.7'092–dc21   97-51541
                                                                          CIP

Cover image: Courtesy of The Newberry Library, Chicago
Cover design: DePinto Graphic Design.

Manufactured in the United States of America
01 00 99 98 1 2 3 4 TS

FOR ANDREW AND LINDA

Acknowledgments

I HAVE LONG THOUGHT it might be useful to assemble a concise selection of Abraham Lincoln's writings on race, slavery, emancipation, and reconstruction. What reinforced the idea was a series of encounters with Europeans during a stint as a Fulbright Scholar at Leiden University in the Netherlands in the spring of 1995. Statues of Lincoln in Edinburgh and London, across from Parliament, reminded me that Lincoln's fame is not limited to America's shores; I listened as Eastern European scholars struggled to explain a man they sought to appreciate all the more in light of recent events. At the same time, it became evident to me that many Americans do not possess a sound understanding of Lincoln's positions on these key issues, while a mischievous few distort his words by quoting them out of context to serve various unworthy ends or to craft a view of the American past that does great violence to the historical record. It seemed that all involved could benefit, much as I had, by reading what Lincoln himself said about the crucial questions of liberty and union.

Thomas F. Schwartz of the Abraham Lincoln Association provided valuable assistance and welcome advice, both of which went far to make this volume possible. So, in a different way, did my parents, John and Adelaide, who gave me at an early age a multivolume edition of Lincoln's collected writings, and my sister, Joy, who patiently stood by as her brother explored the worlds of Washington, D.C., and Gettysburg, unaware that the closest she would get to Disneyland as a child was when she watched the talking Lincoln figure at Illinois's exhibit during the 1964–65 World's Fair. At Harlan Davidson, Linda Gaio-Davidson and Claudia Siler worked long and hard at preparing large portions of the manuscript, and Lucy Herz designed the text and saw this book through production; without such assistance this volume would have been far longer in the making.

My wife Jean has, as always, helped facilitate my work while offering her own insights. And my daughters Rebecca and Emily both know something about the sixteenth president, but their main contribution was in dragging me away from my word processor to engage in games of hide-and-seek and yard hockey in order to remind me what is really important in life. All three are probably secretly relieved that this is not yet another book about that bearded fellow in the blue uniform puffing away at a cigar.

Finally, I would like to thank Andrew and Linda Davidson. At an early point in my career Andrew made possible an opportunity few would have offered me; since then he has listened to my ideas and suggestions with patience, even enthusiasm. So has Linda. Both of them have made writing and publishing more fun than it ought to be.

Table of Contents

CHAPTER FIVE: **The Winding Road to Emancipation, 1862–1863** 109

CHAPTER SIX: **A New Birth of Freedom, 1863** 146

1809   Born on February 12 in Hardin County, Kentucky, son of Thomas Lincoln, a farmer and carpenter, and Nancy Hanks Lincoln.

1816   Family moves to Perry County, Indiana.

1830   Family moves to Macon County, Illinois.

1831   Travels to New Orleans on a flatboat; upon return to Illinois, moves to New Salem.

1832   Fights in Black Hawk War as an Illinois militiaman; loses first political contest for state house of representatives.

1834   Wins election to state house of representatives as a Whig for first of four terms (1834–1842); begins study of law.

1836   Admitted to bar.

1837   Moves to Springfield, the new state capital.

1842   Marries Mary Todd on November 4. They have four sons: Robert (b. 1843), Edward (1846–1850), William, (1850–1862), and Thomas (b. 1853).

1846   Elected to the House of Representatives as a Whig for the Thirtieth Congress; serves one term.

1849   Rejects offers of federal posts in Oregon from the Taylor administration, and decides to concentrate on law practice.

1854   Reenters active political life upon passage of Kansas-Nebraska Act.

1855   Loses bid for United States Senate.

1858   Delivers "House Divided" speech in accepting Republican nomination for the Senate; debates Democratic incumbent Stephen A. Douglas in seven confrontations; loses election.

1860   Travels east and delivers address at New York's Cooper Union; secures Republican presidential nomination on third ballot at Chicago, May 18; triumphs in four-way race, with 180 electoral votes to 72 for John C. Breckinridge (Southern Democrats), 39 for John Bell (Constitutional Unionists) and 12 for Stephen A. Douglas (Democrats), despite winning just under 40 percent of the popular vote. On December 20, 1860, South Carolina secedes from the Union.

1861   Inaugurated sixteenth president of the United States on March 4, by which time six other states (Georgia, Florida, Alabama, Mississippi, Louisiana, and Texas) have joined South Carolina to form the Confederate States of America; Confederate forces open fire on Fort Sumter on April 12; four more states (Virginia, North Carolina, Tennessee, and Arkansas) join the Confederacy when Lincoln issues a call for soldiers; four other slave states (Delaware, Kentucky, Missouri, and Maryland) eventually stay in the Union. Confederacy triumphs at First Bull Run July 21, although by end of year Union forces are poised to invade the Confederate interior.

1862   Union victories at Forts Henry and Donelson (February 6–16), Shiloh (April 6–7) and elsewhere balanced by defeat of George B. McClellan by Robert E. Lee (June 25–July 1); in July, Lincoln drafts preliminary Emancipation Proclamation; issues document on September 22 after Union victory at Antietam; major Union defeat at Fredericksburg December 13.

1863   Final Emancipation Proclamation issued January 1; after a setback at Chancellorsville (May 1–6), Union victories at Gettysburg (July 1–3), Vicksburg (surrenders July 4), and Chattanooga (November 23–25) turn back Confederate high tide; delivers Gettysburg Address November 19; on December 8 outlines plan of amnesty and reconstruction.

1864   Appoints Ulysses S. Grant general-in-chief of the United States Army in March; watches as Grant launches overall offensive in May; wins renomination in June; vetoes congressional plan of reconstruction (the Wade-Davis bill) in July; series of Union victories in Georgia and Virginia secure his reelection victory in November over Democratic candidate George B. McClellan, 212–21 in electoral votes with a 55 percent popular majority.

1865   Inaugurated for second term March 4; fall of Confederate capital at Richmond April 3 and surrender of Robert E. Lee to Grant at Appomattox on April 9 signal close of war imminent; Lincoln shot April 14 by Confederate sympathizer John Wilkes Booth while watching a play at Ford's Theater, Washington, D.C.; dies April 15.

Introduction

❦

THE SPEECHES AND WRITINGS of Abraham Lincoln inspire and instruct today as much as they did during his lifetime—sometimes more so. Thus it should come as no surprise that there exist numerous compilations of his collected works, from the rather comprehensive edition offered us by Roy Basler and his associates to countless selections in various editions, most of which offer glimpses into Lincoln's entire public career as well as his private life. In contrast, this volume focuses on the interrelated themes of slavery, union, emancipation, and reconstruction—the issues on which Lincoln's claim to everlasting fame rests. By reading and comparing the documents that follow, one can gain a much better understanding of the evolution of Lincoln's thinking about slavery, politics, and the fate of the American republic, as well as on the establishment and justification of war aims, the transformation of the struggle to save the Union to incorporate a quest for freedom, and the problem of reuniting the nation in the aftermath of war and emancipation.

The documents reproduced herein offer an introduction to Lincoln's own explanation of his thoughts, positions, and actions concerning slavery and freedom, the Union and the Constitution, war and peace. They shed light on various issues that are still debated by historians, students of Lincoln, and the general public. How did Lincoln define equality? How did he harmonize his rejection of slavery as immoral with his toleration of it where it existed? How did he reconcile his celebration of democracy and self-government with his rejection of popular sovereignty and secession? What were his views on race? Did they change over time? How did he justify accepting war as the price of preserving the Union while at first seeking to avoid attacking the very institution that he thought lay at the center of the conflict? What did freedom mean to him?

Lincoln's role in the emergence of emancipation during the war continues to spark discussion among scholars searching for an answer

1

to the question, "who freed the slaves?" Many people–slaves, free blacks, soldiers, generals, politicians, citizens, and even Confederate authorities and slaveholders (however unwittingly)–as well as the course of the war contributed to what remains one of the most revolutionary events in American history. Nevertheless, Lincoln remains a key player in the drama, for no single person played a more important role in the process. The documents reprinted here help us understand how and why he came to embrace emancipation as a war aim and the many ways in which, depending on circumstances, he sought to achieve it and secure a lasting basis for it. The documents also remind us that Lincoln had to view emancipation in the broader context of saving the Union and that he had to balance and address various concerns and constituencies as he framed policy–considerations often minimized or ignored altogether by some of his more impatient critics, then and now. As he later told Michigan Republican Zachariah Chandler, "I hope to 'stand firm' enough not to go backward, and yet not go forward fast enough to wreck the country's cause."[1]

Some of the documents that follow are private letters in which Lincoln set forth, elaborated, or clarified his thinking, although in writing to other public figures Lincoln understood the political impact his words might have even when expressed in such a letter. Other documents, ranging from speeches and debates to state documents and public letters, must be understood as instruments of persuasion as well as expressions of his position. Over time Lincoln became far more particular about how he expressed himself in public, carefully choosing both his words and his audience; he usually spoke from prepared texts or employed reasoning he had long rehearsed in his mind, foregoing truly extemporaneous remarks because of their potential for mischief. Even what seemed to be turns of phrase inspired by the moment were often products of deliberation, and he often employed them more than once. Therefore, in evaluating what Lincoln wrote or said, it is important to recall the circumstances and context in which he expressed himself and his intended audience.

This selection of Lincoln's own words offers you, the reader, a chance to explore how he understood the prevailing political issues of his America. You may choose to celebrate or to criticize his responses, or both, but this volume provides you with some of the essential material to realize how he wrestled with the fundamental issues of his time. If it contributes to a more informed discussion of the man and the challenges he faced, it will have served a useful purpose.

IN THE 1850S, Abraham Lincoln struggled to fashion an antislavery stand within the framework of American political institutions. He hated slavery and argued for the fundamental humanity of African Americans, although he could not rid himself of racial prejudices and failed to expand his definition of equality beyond civil rights under the law. Moreover, his opposition to the peculiar institution respected the protections extended to slaveholders under the Constitution. Short of persuading slaveholders to voluntarily give up their slaves or through constitutional amendment, Lincoln saw no way to destroy slavery outright. By embracing the idea of exporting free and newly freed blacks to colonies outside the United States, he hoped he had found a way to encourage slaveowners to renounce their property claims and to counter white fears about the consequences of emancipation and the influx of freed blacks into American society. Thus he sought to reconcile human freedom with racial prejudice—although he was oblivious to the wishes of the black persons involved.

When it came to the possible expansion of slavery, Lincoln had no qualms about attacking it. Willing to tolerate slavery where it existed, he saw no need to restrain himself when it came to its introduction into new territories, for that was a legitimate topic for political debate. Thus he could acknowledge both his moral indignation and his commitment to the democratic process, republican institutions, and the rule of law. Yet it is well to remember that this position was also politically advantageous, for it placed him in opposition to Illinois's most prominent political leader, Democrat Stephen A. Douglas, a United States senator and long-time rival of Lincoln, who had been a Whig and initially was a somewhat reluctant Republican. Douglas's proposed solution to the problem of slavery in the territories, "popular sovereignty," posed problems for Lincoln. By allowing the residents of a territory to decide for themselves whether they would permit the establishment of slavery within the territory, popular sovereignty appeared to remove the issue of the fate of slavery in the territories from the arena of national political deliberation while embodying the democratic principle of letting the people rule. Douglas would allow those people to decide for themselves whether slavery was immoral, refusing to impose his own judgment on others—the root of his claim that he did not care whether slavery was voted up or down.

In articulating a response to this position, Lincoln had to devise a position that observed democratic processes and principles while affirming the need and right to take moral stands in politics. There were also more practical political considerations to consider. In 1857, the Supreme Court's controversial ruling in *Dred Scott* v. *Sandford* appeared to guarantee the right of slavery in the territories–thus upsetting both Lincoln's principle of containment and Douglas's approach of popular sovereignty. Not surprisingly, most Southern Democrats welcomed the ruling, as did the new president, James Buchanan. Some Republicans, enthusiastic about Douglas's increasing uneasiness with some of his fellow Democrats, entertained thoughts that Douglas might well be an ideal fusion anti-South candidate. Reaffirming that slavery was fundamentally a moral issue and that Republicans opposed it because they believed it was immoral, Lincoln argued that to support Douglas, who explicitly refused to treat slavery as a moral issue, would betray Republican principles. Aware of the racism of many northern white voters, especially in Illinois, Lincoln rejected Douglas's assertion that he favored the social or political equality of blacks even as he made it clear that he thought slavery was wrong and that blacks were equally entitled to enjoy the freedoms and liberties promised to "all men" in the Declaration of Independence. Render the question of slavery purely in terms of property rights, he warned, and the pose of moral indifference assumed by Douglas would open the way for slavery to expand into existing free states as well as the territories, sacrificing the economic prospects of whites and the principles of free labor to the property rights of slaveholders. At the same time Lincoln took pains to argue that his position on slavery and its future was consistent with that taken up by the founding generation of the American republic as well as more recent political icons, notably his own hero, Henry Clay.

In such ways Lincoln sought middle ground consistent with both his personal beliefs and political ambitions. Although he barely lost to Douglas in the 1858 senatorial contest, the campaign brought him national attention as someone who could hold his own against the Northern Democrat; speaking tours in 1859 and early 1860 added to his reputation and won him a broader audience. Thus he was not quite the unknown pictured by some accounts of how the Republican party chose him as its standard bearer in 1860. Nor, in light of some of his public statements, can it be persuasively argued that Republicans chose him instead of Senator William H. Seward of New York because of the latter's description of the debate over slavery as "an irrepressible conflict," for Lincoln had sounded similar themes in his House Divided speech of 1858 (indeed, his remarks predated those of Seward). Rather, Lincoln carried fewer political liabilities than did Seward, no small consideration as Republicans sought to maintain the majorities they had achieved in the previous years in order to lay claim to the presidency.

Lincoln's victory in November 1860 changed the political landscape and presented the incoming president with a transformed agenda when he assumed office in March 1861. The expansion of slavery was no longer a major issue: the possible dismemberment of the Union now dominated discussion and demanded decision. Lincoln tried to avoid war and preserve the Union without caving in to secession. Unable to fashion a settlement based upon those principles and forced to chose between disunion and war, he accepted that the latter might result from his decision to replenish the dwindling supplies of the federal garrison at Fort Sumter. In the year of war that followed he reminded Americans, North and South, that his primary objective was to save the Union. He did not embrace emancipation as a war aim, however much he privately might have desired the end of slavery, because to do so at that time would render far more difficult the task of preserving the American republic. Northern whites divided over the wisdom, necessity, method, and consequences of emancipation; whites in the slaves states still in the Union and in pockets of loyalty throughout the Confederacy were at best uneasy and more often opposed to emancipation, a step which might well bolster support for the Confederacy to the point of adding to the number of seceded states; and Lincoln still believed that he might cultivate a resurgence of unionism among reluctant Confederates if he kept to his initial pledge not to touch slavery where it existed—although the friction of war itself was beginning to erode the bonds of captivity in various ways. Nevertheless, the president provided incentives for slaveholders to emancipate their slaves, and he continued to press for colonization as the best way to avoid the problems of race relations in post-emancipation society.

Changing circumstances offered new possibilities and presented new challenges for Lincoln. The persistence of Confederate resistance, the failure of Union armies to achieve decisive victories, and the resulting pressure from portions of the Northern public for a more vigorous prosecution of the war made emancipation both possible and necessary. Republican lawmakers began fashioning legislative weapons to strike blows at slavery. At the same time, the limp and uncertain efforts of the vast majority of Southern unionists to fashion loyal alternatives to the Confederacy convinced Lincoln that his reliance on them had been mistaken. Thus, by July 1862, the president had decided in his mind that he would have to act aggressively against slavery. Still, it was important for him to move deliberately, warning white Southerners that escalation was in the offing, preparing Northern public opinion for the measure and its consequences, and establishing the justification of military necessity. Once more he sought to mitigate against white racism by holding forth the possibility of colonization, only to learn that blacks found that unacceptable as a solution. In issuing the preliminary proclamation on September 22, he left open the possibility that white Southerners might still escape the impact of immediate emancipation by returning to the Union; his December annual message once more set forth his preference for gradual and compensated emancipation followed by colonization.

With the issuance of the Emancipation Proclamation on January 1, 1863, the nature of the struggle to save the Union changed, for now it portended a revolution in Southern and, to a lesser extent, American society. During 1863 Lincoln pressed for the raising of black regiments and the reestablishment of loyal civil regimes, while in the Gettysburg Address he offered a short yet eloquent statement of the purpose of the war, embracing freedom and union even as it omitted explicit mention of slavery. In December 1863 he gave a more concrete outline of the process of reconstruction he preferred; during the following year, as he sought reelection, he battled Republicans in Congress over the best way to achieve the restoration of legitimate civil governments. At the same time, he began to ponder the question of the place of blacks in post-emancipation America; he also had to respond to warnings that his support of emancipation might cost him reelection. All in all, Lincoln's struggles with the means and ends of reconstruction illustrate the fundamental truth of his claim that it was "the greatest question ever presented to practical statesmanship."[2]

Winning reelection in November 1864, Lincoln worked to secure both emancipation and reconstruction. He pushed for the passage of a constitutional amendment abolishing slavery; still, he was in other ways willing to do what he could to help facilitate a lasting reunion based upon lenient treatment of the defeated if that would help hurry along Confederate collapse. As the war drew to a close, he began to adjust his notions of reconstruction in accordance with new circumstances, going so far as to make public his preference that at least some blacks be granted the vote. Assassination silenced whatever other plans he had in mind; to ponder what would have happened had Lincoln lived must in the end be relegated to the field of speculation, however informed, for simply to project his wartime actions into the postwar world would wrench them out of context.

1. Lincoln to Zachariah Chandler, November 20, 1863, Fehrenbacher, *Lincoln: Speeches and Writings*, 2:537.
2. Tyler Dennett, ed., *Lincoln and the Civil War in the Diaries and Letters of John Hay* (New York, 1939), 73.

The Monstrous Injustice, 1854–1857

CHAPTER ONE

ALTHOUGH IN LATER YEARS Abraham Lincoln stated that he had always hated slavery, prior to 1854 he rarely discussed the issue in public. In 1836, he had been one of only six members of the Illinois state legislature to vote against resolutions that condemned abolition and supported slavery as constitutional; the following year he cosponsored a protest that characterized slavery as "founded on both injustice and bad policy" and insisted that Congress could abolish slavery in the District of Columbia–although adding that abolitionism was more likely to exacerbate than to settle the issue. Eleven years later, as Illinois's lone Whig congressman, he supported the Wilmot Proviso, which barred slavery from lands acquired as a result of the war with Mexico; in 1849 he announced that he would introduce a resolution calling for the adoption of a plan of gradual and compensated emancipation in the District of Columbia–although in the end he decided not to do so after learning that his idea had little chance of adoption.

These antislavery acts, while noteworthy, were not at the core of Lincoln's career as a Whig political leader, which featured the theme of fostering economic development and opportunity; as a congressman, he was far better known for his opposition to President James K. Polk's use of presidential war powers. Rather, they reflect his beliefs that slavery was wrong; that it must be tolerated where it existed; that it should not expand; that emancipation should be gradual and with compensation to owners; that abolitionist agitation would spark more trouble; and that it would be best to couple emancipation with colonization of the freed blacks outside the United States. Returning to Springfield, Illinois, in 1849 to practice law, he did not seek elective office for several years, although he dispensed advice to his fellow Whigs. However, in delivering a eulogy about one of his political idols, Henry Clay, he took the opportunity to endorse Clay's views on slavery as a necessary evil that should be terminated with the colonization of freed blacks,

7

reminding listeners that Clay acted in the spirit of the Declaration of Independence's assertion that "all men are created equal."

It was the introduction of legislation to organize the territories of Kansas and Nebraska by Senator Stephen A. Douglas of Illinois, a Democrat and long-time rival, that spurred Lincoln's return to public prominence. Douglas's proposal, framed in part to gain the support of Southerners in Congress for legislation to organize western territories, delegated to the residents of those territories the power to decide whether to allow the introduction of slavery—a principle Douglas called "popular sovereignty." After much struggle, Congress passed the legislation; the act, known thereafter as the Kansas-Nebraska Act, declared void the so-called Missouri Compromise of 1820, which barred slavery in the territories possessed by the United States at that time above 36°30' latitude—the vast majority of which was acquired as part of the Louisiana Purchase in 1803. That the man most associated with the passage of the Missouri Compromise was none other than Henry Clay added to Lincoln's anger, as did Douglas's pose of moral indifference to the possible spread of slavery. Although he had always refrained from attacking slavery in the states where it existed, Lincoln was committed to bar its expansion, believing that it was wrong to support the spread of the peculiar institution. That Douglas was from Illinois enabled Lincoln to make him the primary target of his attacks with an eye toward building an anti-Democratic coalition in the state. Although at first Lincoln thought that a revived Whig party could best serve as the nucleus of that coalition, eventually he came to accept that it would be the Republican party, born in the fury caused by the Kansas-Nebraska Act, that would emerge as the vehicle of both his principles and political ambitions.

Disturbed by efforts of Southern thinkers to prove that slavery was justifiable and a positive good, Lincoln poked holes in their logic [Document 1-1]. But his main target was Douglas and popular sovereignty. At Peoria, Illinois, on October 16, 1854, after Douglas had set forth his own policy in the afternoon, Lincoln responded in his first sustained public attack on popular sovereignty [Document 1-2]. In the elections several weeks later, the anti-Nebraska forces gained a majority of the seats in the state legislature, leading Lincoln to entertain notions of winning election as United States senator. Eventually, he had to give way to another anti-Nebraska man, Lyman Trumbull, with the understanding that the next time (1858) he would be the coalition's choice—against none other than Douglas himself.

As Lincoln looked forward to the 1858 election, he wondered whether the eventual extinction of slavery through peaceful processes was still as viable a hope as it was in the days of the founding of the republic–a concern he shared with a family lawyer [Document 1-3]. He also realized that in opposing the expansion of slavery, he might lose old friends, such as fellow lawyer Joshua F. Speed, who now lived in Kentucky [Document 1-4]. By 1856, he clearly identified himself as a Republican, and campaigned that fall on behalf of that party's candidates; the following year, in a speech at Springfield, he made clear his displeasure with the Supreme Court's *Dred Scott* decision, which declared that Congress could not prohibit slavery in the territories [Document 1-5]. The decision rendered it impossible for either Congress or a territorial government to prohibit slavery's expansion westward prior to a territory's application for statehood–and, as Lincoln would later argue, the logic of Chief Justice Roger B. Taney's opinion opened the door to another court case to challenge a state's right to bar slavery. What Douglas had made possible with the principle of popular sovereignty–the spread of slavery into territories where it was previously prohibited–the *Dred Scott* decision made difficult to stop altogether.

[DOCUMENT 1–1]
FRAGMENT ON SLAVERY (C. 1854–1859)

Although Lincoln's private secretaries and later biographers John Hay and John Nicolay later speculated that this undated fragment was composed in 1854, it may have been prepared anytime during the 1850s. Nevertheless, it reflects Lincoln's private thinking as he challenged traditional justifications for the enslavement of African Americans; the note is typical of his tendency to work out his thoughts on paper.

If A. can prove, however conclusively, that he may, of right, enslave B.–why may not B. snatch the same argument, and prove equally, that he may enslave A.?–

You say A. is white, and B. is black. It is *color,* then; the lighter, having the right to enslave the darker? Take care. By this rule, you are to be slave to the first man you meet, with a fairer skin than your own.

You do not mean *color* exactly?–You mean the whites are *intellectually* the superiors of the blacks, and, therefore have the right to enslave them? Take care again. By this rule, you are to be slave to the first man you meet, with an intellect superior to your own.

But, say you, it is a question of *interest;* and, if you can make it your *interest,* you have the right to enslave another. Very well. And if he can make it his interest, he has the right to enslave you.

[DOCUMENT 1-2]
SPEECH AT PEORIA, ILLINOIS, OCTOBER 16, 1854 (EXCERPTS)

In 1854 Congress passed the Kansas-Nebraska Act, which allowed white settlers in the territories of Kansas and Nebraska to decide for themselves whether to allow slavery to be established there. The act's passage rescinded the Missouri Compromise of 1820, which held that slavery would be barred from all of the territory acquired as part of the Louisiana Purchase above the latitude of 36° 30' (except for Missouri itself); the land currently being organized into the territories of Kansas and Nebraska was included in that agreement. The act's sponsor, Illinois senator Stephen A. Douglas, returned to his home state after its passage, aware of the furor the legislation had raised in the North. Among his critics was Lincoln, a long-time political rival whose interest in politics was revitalized by the controversy. On October 16 the two men met in Peoria, Illinois; what follows are excerpts from Lincoln's reply to Douglas's speech delivered earlier that day.

The repeal of the Missouri Compromise, and the propriety of its restoration, constitute the subject of what I am about to say.

As I desire to present my own connected view of this subject, my remarks will not be, specifically, an answer to Judge Douglas; yet, as I proceed, the main points he has presented will arise, and will receive such respectful attention as I may be able to give them.

I wish further to say, that I do not propose to question the patriotism, or to assail the motives of any man, or class of men; but rather to strictly confine myself to the naked merits of the question.

I also wish to be no less than National in all the positions I may take; and whenever I take ground which others have thought, or may think, narrow, sectional and dangerous to the Union, I hope to give a reason, which will appear sufficient, at least to some, why I think differently.

And, as this subject is no other, than part and parcel of the larger general question of domestic-slavery, I wish to MAKE and to KEEP the distinction between the EXISTING institution, and the EXTENSION of it, so broad, and so clear, that no honest man can misunderstand me, and no dishonest one, successfully misrepresent me.

[here Lincoln offers his account of federal policy concerning the territorial expansion of slavery from 1787 to 1854]

This is the *repeal* of the Missouri Compromise. The foregoing history may not be precisely accurate in every particular; but I am sure it is sufficiently so, for all the uses I shall attempt to make of it, and in it, we have before us, the chief material enabling us to correctly judge whether the repeal of the Missouri Compromise is right or wrong.

I think, and shall try to show, that it is wrong; wrong in its direct effect, letting slavery into Kansas and Nebraska—and wrong in its prospective principle, allowing it to spread to every other part of the wide world, where men can be found inclined to take it.

This *declared* indifference, but as I must think, covert *real* zeal for the spread of slavery, I can not but hate. I hate it because of the monstrous injustice of slavery itself. I hate it because it deprives our republican example of its just influence in the world—enables the enemies of free institutions, with plausibility, to taunt us as hypocrites—causes the real friends of freedom to doubt our sincerity, and especially because it forces so many really good men amongst ourselves into an open war with the very fundamental principles of civil liberty—criticising the Declaration of Independence, and insisting that there is no right principle of action but *self-interest.*

Before proceeding, let me say I think I have no prejudice against the Southern people. They are just what we would be in their situation. If slavery did not now exist amongst them, they would not introduce it. If it did now exist amongst us, we should not instantly give it up. This I believe of the masses north and south. Doubtless there are individuals, on both sides, who would not hold slaves under any circumstances; and others who would gladly introduce slavery anew, if it were out of existence. We know that some southern men do free their slaves, go north, and become tip-top abolitionists; while some northern ones go south, and become most cruel slave-masters.

When southern people tell us they are no more responsible for the origin of slavery, than we; I acknowledge the fact. When it is said that the institution exists; and that it is very difficult to get rid of it, in any satisfactory way, I can understand and appreciate the saying. I surely will not blame them for not doing what I should not know how to do myself. If all earthly power were given me, I should not know what to do, as to the existing institution. My first impulse would be to free all the slaves, and send them to Liberia,—to their own native land. But a moment's reflection would convince me, that whatever of high hope, (as I think there is) there may be in this, in the long run, its sudden execution is impossible. If they were all landed there in a day, they would all perish in the next ten days; and there are not surplus shipping and surplus money enough in the world to carry them there in many times ten days. What then? Free them all, and keep them among us as underlings? Is it quite certain that this betters their condition? I think I would not hold one in slavery, at any rate; yet the point is not clear enough for me to denounce people upon. What next? Free them, and make them politically and socially, our equals? My own feelings will not admit of this; and if mine would, we well know that those of the great mass of white people will not. Whether this feeling accords with justice and sound judgment, is not the sole question, if indeed, it is any part of it. A universal feeling, whether well or ill-founded, can not be safely disregarded. We can not, then, make them equals. It does seem to me that systems of gradual emancipation might be adopted; but for their tardiness in this, I will not undertake to judge our brethren of the south.

When they remind us of their constitutional rights, I acknowledge them, not grudgingly, but fully, and fairly; and I would give them any legislation for the reclaiming of their fugitives, which should not, in its stringency, be more likely to carry a free man into slavery, than our ordinary criminal laws are to hang an innocent one.

But all this; to my judgment, furnishes no more excuse for permitting slavery to go into our own free territory, than it would for reviving the African slave trade by law. The law which forbids the bringing of slaves *from* Africa; and that which has so long forbid the taking them *to* Nebraska, can hardly be distinguished on any moral principle; and the repeal of the former could find quite as plausible excuses as that of the latter.

The doctrine of self government is right–absolutely and eternally right–but it has no just application, as here attempted. Or perhaps I should rather say that whether it has such just application depends upon whether a negro is *not* or *is* a man. If he is *not* a man, why in that case, he who *is* a man may, as a matter of self-government, do just as he pleases with him. But if the negro *is* a man, is it not to that extent, a total destruction of self-government, to say that he too shall not govern *himself*? When the white man governs himself that is self-government; but when he governs himself, and also governs *another* man, that is *more* than self-government–that is despotism. If the negro is a *man*, why then my ancient faith teaches me that "all men are created equal;" and that there can be no moral right in connection with one man's making a slave of another.

Judge Douglas frequently, with bitter irony and sarcasm, paraphrases our argument by saying "The white people of Nebraska are good enough to govern themselves, *but they are not good enough to govern a few miserable negroes*!!"

Well I doubt not that the people of Nebraska are, and will continue to be as good as the average of people elsewhere. I do not say the contrary. What I do say is, that no man is good enough to govern another man, *without that other's consent.* I say this is the leading principle—the sheet anchor of American republicanism. Our Declaration of Independence says:

"We hold these truths to be self evident: that all men are created equal; that they are endowed by their Creator with certain inalienable rights; that among these are life, liberty and the pursuit of happiness. That to secure these rights, governments are instituted among men, DERIVING THEIR JUST POWERS FROM THE CONSENT OF THE GOVERNED."

I have quoted so much at this time merely to show that according to our ancient faith, the just powers of governments are derived from the consent of the governed. Now the relation of masters and slaves is, PRO TANTO, a total violation of this principle. The master not only governs the slave without his consent; but he governs him by a set of rules altogether different from those which he prescribes for himself. Allow ALL the governed an equal voice in the government, and that, and that only is self government.

Let it not be said I am contending for the establishment of political and social equality between the whites and blacks. I have already said the contrary. I am not now combating the argument of NECESSITY, arising from the fact that the blacks are already amongst us; but I am combating what is set up as MORAL argument for allowing them to be taken where they have never yet been—arguing against the EXTENSION of a bad thing, which where it already exists, we must of necessity, manage as we best can.

In support of his application of the doctrine of self-government, Senator Douglas has sought to bring to his aid the opinions and examples of our revolutionary fathers. I am glad he has done this. I love the sentiments of those old-time men; and shall be most happy to abide by their opinions. He shows us that when it was in contemplation for the colonies to break off from Great Britain, and set up a new government for themselves, several of the states instructed their delegates to go for the measure PROVIDED EACH STATE SHOULD BE ALLOWED TO REGULATE ITS DOMESTIC CONCERNS IN ITS OWN WAY. I do not quote; but this in substance. This was right. I see nothing objectionable in it. I also think it probable that it had some reference to the existence of slavery amongst them. I will not deny that it had. But had it, in any reference to the carrying of slavery into NEW COUNTRIES? That is the question; and we will let the fathers themselves answer it.

This same generation of men, and mostly the same individuals of the generation, who declared this principle—who declared independence—who fought the war of the revolution through—who afterwards made the constitution under which we still live—these same men passed the ordinance of '87, declaring that slavery should never go to the northwest territory. I have no doubt Judge Douglas thinks they were very inconsistent in this. It is a question of discrimination between them and him. But there is not an inch of ground left for his claiming that their opinions—their example—their authority—are on his side in this controversy.

Again, is not Nebraska, while a territory, a part of us? Do we not own the country? And if we surrender the control of it, do we not surrender the right of self-government? It is part of ourselves. If you say we shall not control it because it is ONLY part, the same is true of every other part; and when all the parts are gone, what has become of the whole? What is then left of us? What use for the general government, when there is nothing left for it to govern?

But you say this question should be left to the people of Nebraska, because they are more particularly interested. If this be the rule, you must leave it to each individual to say for himself whether he will have slaves. What better moral right have thirty-one citizens of Nebraska to say, that the thirty-second shall not hold slaves, than the people of the thirty-one States have to say that slavery shall not go into the thirty-second State at all?

But if it is a sacred right for the people of Nebraska to take and hold slaves there, it is equally their sacred right to buy them where they can buy them cheapest; and that undoubtedly will be on the coast of Africa; provided you will consent to not hang them for going there to buy them. You must remove this restriction too, from the sacred right of self-government. I am aware you say that taking slaves from the States to Nebraska, does not make slaves of freemen; but the African slave-trader can say just as much. He does not catch free negroes and bring them here. He finds them already slaves in the hands of their black captors, and he honestly buys them at the rate of about a red cotton handkerchief a head. This is very cheap, and it is a great abridgement of the sacred right of self-government to hang men for engaging in this profitable trade!

Another important objection to this application of the right of self-government, is that it enables the first FEW, to deprive the succeeding MANY, of a free exercise of the right of self-government. The first few may get slavery IN, and the subsequent many cannot easily get it OUT. How common is the remark now in the slave States—"If we were only clear of our slaves, how much better it would be for us." They are actually deprived of the privilege of governing themselves as they would, by the action of a very few, in the beginning. The same thing was true of the whole nation at the time our constitution was formed.

Whether slavery shall go into Nebraska, or other new territories, is not a matter of exclusive concern to the people who may go there. The whole nation is interested that the best use shall be made of these territories. We want them for the homes of free white people. This they cannot be, to any considerable extent, if slavery shall be planted within them. Slave States are places for poor white people to remove FROM; not to remove TO. New free States are the places for poor people to go to and better their condition. For this use, the nation needs these territories.

Still further; there are constitutional relations between the slave and free States, which are degrading to the latter. We are under legal obligations to catch and return their runaway slaves to them—a sort of dirty, disagreeable job, which I believe, as a general rule the slave-holders will not perform for one another. Then again, in the control of the government—the management of the partnership affairs—they have greatly the advantage of us. By the constitution, each State has two Senators—each has a number of Representatives; in proportion to the number of its people—and each has a number of presidential electors, equal to the whole number of its Senators and Representatives together. But in ascertaining the number of the people, for this purpose, five slaves are counted as being equal to three whites. The slaves do not vote; they are only counted and so used, as to swell the influence of the white people's votes. The practical effect of this is more aptly shown by a comparison of the States of South Carolina and Maine. South Carolina has six representatives, and so has Maine; South Carolina has eight presidential electors, and so has Maine. This is precise equality so far; and, of course they are equal in Senators, each having two. Thus in the control of the government, the two States are equals precisely. But how are they in the number of their white people? Maine has 581,813—while

South Carolina has 274,567. Maine has twice as many as South Carolina, and 32,679 over. Thus each white man in South Carolina is more than the double of any man in Maine. This is all because South Carolina, besides her free people, has 384,984 slaves. The South Carolinian has precisely the same advantage over the white man in every other free State, as well as in Maine. He is more than the double of any one of us in this crowd. The same advantage, but not to the same extent, is held by all the citizens of the slave States, over those of the free; and it is an absolute truth, without an exception, that there is no voter in any slave State, but who has more legal power in the government, than any voter in any free State. There is no instance of exact equality; and the disadvantage is against us the whole chapter through. This principle, in the aggregate, gives the slave States, in the present Congress, twenty additional representatives–being seven more than the whole majority by which they passed the Nebraska bill.

Now all this is manifestly unfair; yet I do not mention it to complain of it, in so far as it is already settled. It is in the constitution; and I do not, for that cause, or any other cause, propose to destroy, or alter, or disregard the constitution. I stand to it, fairly, fully, and firmly.

But when I am told I must leave it altogether to OTHER PEOPLE to say whether new partners are to be bred up and brought into the firm, on the same degrading terms against me, I respectfully demur. I insist, that whether I shall be a whole man, or only, the half of one, in comparison with others, is a question in which I am somewhat concerned; and one which no other man can have a sacred right of deciding for me. If I am wrong in this–if it really be a sacred right of self-government, in the man who shall go to Nebraska, to decide whether he will be the EQUAL of me or the DOUBLE of me, then after he shall have exercised that right, and thereby shall have reduced me to a still smaller fraction of a man than I already am, I should like for some gentleman deeply skilled in the mysteries of sacred rights, to provide himself with a microscope, and peep about, and find out, if he can, what has become of my sacred rights! They will surely be too small for detection with the naked eye.

Finally, I insist, that if there is ANY THING which it is the duty of the WHOLE PEOPLE to never entrust to any hands but their own, that thing is the preservation and perpetuity, of their own liberties, and institutions. And if they shall think, as I do, that the extension of slavery endangers them, more than any, or all other causes, how recreant to themselves, if they submit the question, and with it, the fate of their country, to a mere hand-full of men, bent only on temporary self-interest. If this question of slavery extension were an insignificant one–one having no power to do harm—it might be shuffled aside in this way. But being, as it is, the great Behemoth of danger, shall the strong gripe of the nation be loosened upon him, to entrust him to the hands of such feeble keepers?

I have done with this mighty argument, of self-government. Go, sacred thing! Go in peace.

But even if we fail to technically restore the compromise, it is still a great point to carry a popular vote in favor of the restoration. The moral weight of such a vote can not be estimated too highly. The authors of Nebraska are not at all satisfied with the destruction of the compromise—an endorsement of this PRINCIPLE, they proclaim to be the great object. With them, Nebraska alone is a small matter—to establish a principle, for FUTURE USE, is what they particularly desire.

That future use is to be the planting of slavery wherever in the wide world, local and unorganized opposition can not prevent it. Now if you wish to give them this endorsement—if you wish to establish this principle—do so. I shall regret it; but it is your right. On the contrary if you are opposed to the principle—intend to give it no such endorsement—let no wheedling, no sophistry, divert you from throwing a direct vote against it.

Some men, mostly whigs, who condemn the repeal of the Missouri Compromise, nevertheless hesitate to go for its restoration, lest they be thrown in company with the abolitionist. Will they allow me as an old whig to tell them good humoredly, that I think this is very silly? Stand with anybody that stands RIGHT. Stand with him while he is right and PART with him when he goes wrong. Stand WITH the abolitionist in restoring the Missouri Compromise; and stand AGAINST him when he attempts to repeal the fugitive slave law. In the latter case you stand with the southern disunionist. What of that? you are still right. In both cases you are right. In both cases you oppose the dangerous extremes. In both you stand on middle ground and hold the ship level and steady. In both you are national and nothing less than national. This is good old whig ground. To desert such ground, because of any company, is to be less than a whig—less than a man—less than an American.

I particularly object to the NEW position which the avowed principle of this Nebraska law gives to slavery in the body politic. I object to it because it assumes that there CAN be MORAL RIGHT in the enslaving of one man by another. I object to it as a dangerous dalliance for a free people—a sad evidence that, feeling prosperity we forget right—that liberty, as a principle, we have ceased to revere. I object to it because the fathers of the republic eschewed, and rejected it. The argument of "Necessity" was the only argument they ever admitted in favor of slavery; and so far, and so far only as it carried them, did they ever go. They found the institution existing among us, which they could not help; and they cast blame upon the British King for having permitted its introduction. BEFORE the constitution, they prohibited its introduction into the north-western Territory—the only country we owned, then free from it. AT the framing and adoption of the constitution, they forbore to so much as mention the word "slave" or "slavery" in the whole instrument. In the provision for the recovery of fugitives, the slave is spoken of as a "PERSON HELD TO SERVICE OR LABOR." In that prohibiting the abolition of the African slave trade for twenty years, that trade is spoken of as "The migration or importation of such persons as any of the States NOW EXISTING, shall think proper to admit," &c. These are the only provisions alluding to slavery. Thus, the thing is hid away, in the constitution, just as an afflicted man hides away a wen or a cancer, which he dares not cut out at once, lest he bleed to death; with the promise, nevertheless, that the cutting may begin at the end of a given time. Less than this our fathers COULD not do; and MORE they WOULD not do. Necessity drove them so far, and farther, they would not go. But this is not all. The earliest Congress, under the constitution, took the same view of slavery. They hedged and hemmed it in to the narrowest limits of necessity.

In 1794, they prohibited an out-going slave-trade—that is, the taking of slaves FROM the United States to sell.

In 1798, they prohibited the bringing of slaves from Africa, INTO the Mississippi Territory—this territory then comprising what are now the States of Mississippi and Alabama. This was TEN YEARS before they had the authority to do the same thing as to the States existing at the adoption of the constitution.

In 1800 they prohibited AMERICAN CITIZENS from trading in slaves between foreign countries—as, for instance, from Africa to Brazil.

In 1803 they passed a law in aid of one or two State laws, in restraint of the internal slave trade.

In 1807, in apparent hot haste, they passed the law, nearly a year in advance, to take effect the first day of 1808—the very first day the constitution would permit—prohibiting the African slave trade by heavy pecuniary and corporal penalties.

In 1820, finding these provisions ineffectual, they declared the trade piracy, and annexed to it, the extreme penalty of death. While all this was passing in the general government, five or six of the original slave States had adopted systems of gradual emancipation; and by which the institution was rapidly becoming extinct within these limits.

Thus we see, the plain unmistakable spirit of that age, towards slavery, was hostility to the PRINCIPLE, and toleration, ONLY BY NECESSITY.

But NOW it is to be transformed into a "sacred right." Nebraska brings it forth, places it on the high road to extension and perpetuity; and, with a pat on its back, says to it, "Go, and God speed you." Henceforth it is to be the chief jewel of the nation—the very figure-head of the ship of State. Little by little, but steadily as man's march to the grave, we have been giving up the OLD for the NEW faith. Near eighty years ago we began by declaring that all men are created equal; but now from that beginning we have run down to the other declaration, that for SOME men to enslave OTHERS is a "sacred right of self-government." These principles can not stand together. They are as opposite as God and mammon; and whoever holds to the one, must despise the other. When Pettit, in connection with his support of the Nebraska bill, called the Declaration of Independence "a self-evident lie" he only did what consistency and candor require all other Nebraska men to do. Of the forty odd Nebraska Senators who sat present and heard him, no one rebuked him. Nor am I apprized that any Nebraska newspaper, or any Nebraska orator, in the whole nation, has ever yet rebuked him. If this had been said among Marion's men, Southerners though they were, what would have become of the man who said it? If this had been said to the men who captured André, the man who said it, would probably have been hung sooner than André was. If it had been said in old Independence Hall, seventy-eight years ago, the very door-keeper would have throttled the man, and thrust him into the street.

Let no one be deceived. The spirit of seventy-six and the spirit of Nebraska, are utter antagonisms; and the former is being rapidly displaced by the latter.

Fellow countrymen—Americans south, as well as north, shall we make no effort to arrest this? Already the liberal party throughout the world, express the apprehension "that the one retrograde institution in America, is undermining the principles of progress, and fatally violating the noblest political system the world ever saw." This is not the taunt of enemies, but the warning of friends. Is it quite safe to disregard it—to despise it? Is there no danger to liberty itself, in discarding the earliest practice, and first precept of our ancient faith? In our greedy chase to make profit of the negro, let us beware, lest we "cancel and tear to pieces" even the white man's charter of freedom.

Our republican robe is soiled, and trailed in the dust. Let us repurify it. Let us turn and wash it white, in the spirit, if not the blood, of the Revolution. Let us turn slavery from its claims of "moral right," back upon its existing legal rights, and its arguments of "necessity." Let us return it to the position our fathers gave it; and there let it rest in peace. Let us re-adopt the Declaration of Independence, and with it, the practices, and policy, which harmonize with it. Let north and south—let all Americans—let all lovers of liberty everywhere—join in the great and good work. If we do this, we shall not only have saved the Union; but we shall have so saved it, as to make, and to keep it, forever worthy of the saving. We shall have so saved it, that the succeeding millions of free happy people, the world over, shall rise up, and call us blessed, to the latest generation. . . .

[DOCUMENT 1-3]
TO GEORGE ROBERTSON, AUGUST 15, 1855

Judge George Robertson, who practiced law in Lexington, Kentucky, had represented Lincoln and others in litigation to determine the rightful owner of Todd family property. Visiting Springfield in July 1855 while Lincoln was in Chicago, he had left behind a copy of his collected speeches and papers. Robertson had served in Congress during the debates over the Missouri Compromise.

Hon: Geo. Robertson   Lexington, Ky.
Springfield, Ills.   Aug. 15. 1855

My dear Sir: The volume you left for me has been received. I am really grateful for the honor of your kind remembrance, as well as for the book. The partial reading I have already given it, has afforded me much of both pleasure and instruction. It was new to me that the exact question which led to the Missouri compromise, had arisen before it arose in regard to Missouri; and that you had taken so prominent a part in it. Your short, but able and patriotic speech upon that occasion, has not been improved upon since, by those holding the same views; and, with all the lights you then had, the views you took appear to me as very reasonable.

You are not a friend of slavery in the abstract. In that speech you spoke of *"the peaceful extinction of slavery"* and used other expressions indicating your belief that the thing was, at some time, to have an end. Since then we have had thirty six years of experience; and this experience has demonstrated, I think, that there is no peaceful extinction of slavery in prospect for us. The signal failure of Henry Clay, and other good and great men, in 1849, to effect any thing in favor of gradual emancipation in Kentucky, together with a thousand other signs, extinguishes that hope utterly. On the question of liberty, as a principle, we are not what we have been. When we were the political slaves of King George, and wanted to be free, we called the maxim that "all men are created equal" a self evident truth; but now when we have grown fat, and have lost all dread of being slaves ourselves, we have become so greedy to be *masters* that we call the same maxim "a self-evident lie" The fourth of July has not quite dwindled away; it is still a great day—*for burning firecrackers*!!!

That spirit which desired the peaceful extinction of slavery, has itself become extinct, with the *occasion,* and the *men* of the Revolution. Under the impulse of that occasion, nearly half the states adopted systems of emancipation at once, and it is a significant fact, that not a single state has done the like since. So far as peaceful, voluntary emancipation is concerned, the condition of the negro slave in America, scarcely less terrible to the contemplation of a free mind, is now as fixed, and hopeless of change for the better, as that of the lost souls of the finally impenitent. The Autocrat of all the Russias will resign his crown, and proclaim his subjects free republicans sooner than will our American masters voluntarily give up their slaves.

Our political problem now is "Can we, as a nation, continue together *permanently—forever*—half slave, and half free?" The problem is too mighty for me. May God, in his mercy, superintend the solution. Your much obliged friend, and humble servant   A. Lincoln

[DOCUMENT 1-4]
TO JOSHUA F. SPEED, AUGUST 24, 1855

Joshua F. Speed was a Kentucky-born lawyer who moved to Springfield in 1835; two years later he met Lincoln, who had just arrived in Springfield, and for the next four years the men roomed together. Speed returned to Kentucky in 1841; the two men, once close friends, drifted apart and disagreed over slavery.

Andrew Reeder was Kansas's first territorial governor; Dr. John Stringfellow, who served as speaker of the territorial legislature, was a leading supporter of the proslavery forces in the territory who advocated committing acts of violence against antislavery voters.

Dear Speed: Springfield, Aug: 24, 1855
    You know what a poor correspondent I am. Ever since I received your very agreeable letter of the 22nd. of May I have been intending to write you in answer to it. You suggest that in political action now, you and I would differ. I suppose we would; not quite as much, however, as you may think. You know I dislike slavery; and you fully admit the

abstract wrong of it. So far there is no cause of difference. But you say that sooner than yield your legal right to the slave—especially at the bidding of those who are not themselves interested, you would see the Union dissolved. I am not aware that *any one* is bidding you to yield that right; very certainly *I* am not. I leave that matter entirely to yourself. I also acknowledge *your* rights and *my* obligations, under the constitution, in regard to your slaves. I confess I hate to see the poor creatures hunted down, and caught, and carried back to their stripes, and unrewarded toils; but I bite my lip and keep quiet. In 1841 you and I had together a tedious low-water trip, on a Steam Boat from Louisville to St. Louis. You may remember, as I well do, that from Louisville to the mouth of the Ohio there were, on board, ten or a dozen slaves, shackled together with irons. That sight was a continual torment to me; and I see something like it every time I touch the Ohio, or any other slave-border. It is hardly fair for you to assume, that I have no interest in a thing which has, and continually exercises, the power of making me miserable. You ought rather to appreciate how much the great body of the Northern people do crucify their feelings, in order to maintain their loyalty to the constitution and the Union.

I do oppose the extension of slavery, because my judgment and feelings so prompt me; and I am under no obligation to the contrary. If for this you and I must differ, differ we must. You say if you were President, you would send an army and hang the leaders of the Missouri outrages upon the Kansas elections; still, if Kansas fairly votes herself a slave state, she must be admitted, or the Union must be dissolved. But how if she votes herself a slave state *unfairly*—that is, by the very means for which you say you would hang men? Must she still be admitted, or the Union be dissolved? That will be the phase of the question when it first becomes a practical one. In your assumption that there may be a *fair* decision of the slavery question in Kansas, I plainly see you and I would differ about the Nebraska-law. I look upon that enactment not as a *law,* but as *violence* from the beginning. It was conceived in violence, passed in violence, is maintained in violence, and is being executed in violence. I say it was *conceived* in violence, because the destruction of the Missouri Compromise, under the circumstances, was nothing less than violence. It was *passed* in violence, because it could not have passed at all but for the votes of many members, in violent disregard of the known will of their constituents. It is *maintained* in violence because the elections since, clearly demand it's repeal, and this demand is openly disregarded. *You* say men ought to be hung for the way they are executing that law; and *I* say the way it is being executed is quite as good as any of its antecedents. It is being executed in the precise way which was intended from the first; else why does no Nebraska man express astonishment or condemnation? Poor Reeder is the only public man who has been silly enough to believe that any thing like fairness was ever intended; and he has been bravely undeceived.

That Kansas will form a Slave constitution, and, with it, will ask to be admitted into the Union, I take to be an already settled question; and so settled by the very means you so pointedly condemn. By every principle of law, ever held by any court, North or South, every negro taken to Kansas is free; yet in utter disregard of this—in the spirit of violence merely—that beautiful Legislature gravely passes a law to hang men who shall venture to inform a negro of his legal rights. This is the substance, and real object of the law. If, like Haman, they should hang upon the gallows of their own building, I shall not be among the mourners for their fate.

In my humble sphere, I shall advocate the restoration of the Missouri Compromise, so long as Kansas remains a territory; and when, by all these foul means, it seeks to come into the Union as a Slave-state, I shall oppose it. I am very loth, in any case, to withhold my assent to the enjoyment of property *acquired,* or *located,* in good faith; but I do not admit that *good faith,* in taking a negro to Kansas, to be held in slavery, is a *possibility* with any man. Any man who has sense enough to be the controller of his own property, has too much sense to misunderstand the outrageous character of this whole Nebraska business. But I digress. In my opposition to the admission of Kansas I shall have some company; but we may be beaten. If we are, I shall not, on that account, attempt to dissolve the Union. On the contrary, if we succeed, there will be enough of us to take care of the Union. I think it probable, however, we shall be beaten. Standing as a unit among yourselves, you can, directly, and indirectly, bribe enough of our men to carry the day—as you could on an open proposition to establish monarchy. Get hold of some man in the North, whose position and ability is such, that he can make the support of your measure—whatever it may be—a *democratic party necessity,* and the thing is done. *Appropos* of this, let me tell you an anecdote. Douglas introduced the Nebraska bill in January. In February afterwards, there was a call session of the Illinois Legislature. Of the one hundred members composing the two branches of that body, about seventy were democrats. These latter held a caucus, in which the Nebraska bill was talked of, if not formally discussed. It was thereby discovered that just three, and no more, were in favor of the measure. In a day or two Douglas' orders came on to have resolutions passed approving the bill; and they were passed by large majorities!!! The truth of this is vouched for by a bolting democratic member. The masses too, democratic as well as whig, were even, nearer unanamous against it; but as soon as the party necessity of supporting it, became apparent, the way the democracy began to see the *wisdom* and *justice* of it, was perfectly astonishing.

You say if Kansas fairly votes herself a free state, as a christian you will rather rejoice at it. All decent slave-holders *talk* that way; and I do not doubt their candor. But they never *vote* that way. Although in a private letter, or conversation, you will express your preference that Kansas shall be free, you would vote for no man for Congress who would say the same thing publicly. No such man could be elected from any district in any slave-state. You think Stringfellow & Co ought to be hung; and yet, at the next presidential election you will vote for the exact type and representative of Stringfellow. The slave-breeders and slave-traders, are a small, odious and detested class, among you; and yet in politics, they dictate the course of all of you, and are as completely your masters, as you are the masters of your own negroes.

You enquire where I now stand. That is a disputed point. I think I am a whig; but others say there are no whigs, and that I am an abolitionist. When I was at Washington I voted for the Wilmot Proviso as good as forty times, and I never heard of any one attempting to unwhig me for that. I now do no more than oppose the *extension* of slavery.

I am not a Know-Nothing. That is certain. How could I be? How can any one who abhors the oppression of negroes, be in favor of degrading classes of white people? Our progress in degeneracy appears to me to be pretty rapid. As a nation, we began by declaring that *"all men are created equal."* We now practically read it "all men are created equal, *except negroes.*" When the Know-Nothings get control, it will read "all men are created equal, except negroes, *and foreigners, and catholics.*" When it comes to this I should prefer emigrating to some country where they make no presence of loving liberty–to Russia, for instance, where despotism can be taken pure, and without the base alloy of hypocracy.

Mary will probably pass a day or two in Louisville in October. My kindest regards to Mrs. Speed. On the leading subject of this letter, I have more of her sympathy than I have of yours.

And yet let say I am   Your friend forever

                                                            A. Lincoln

[DOCUMENT 1-5]
SPEECH AT SPRINGFIELD, ILLINOIS, JUNE 26, 1857 (EXCERPTS)

In March 6, 1857, the Supreme Court issued its decision in the case of Dred Scott v. Sandford. *Scott, a Missouri slave, and his wife Harriet had sued for their freedom in 1846, arguing that they were now free because their former master, an army surgeon, had taken them into a free state (Illinois) and a free territory (Minnesota), where slavery was illegal. The status of the Scotts' two daughters would be determined by the outcome of the suit. The case found its way into federal courts due to Scott's claim that he and his present owners were citizens of different states. A majority of the Court found that Scott had no standing to sue in federal court because he was a slave (and therefore not a citizen) or simply because he was black; in addition, six of the nine justices agreed that the Missouri Compromise, barring slavery in the Louisiana Purchase above 36° 30' (except for the new state of Missouri), was invalid, thus establishing the legal basis for the expansion of slavery into Kansas, Nebraska, and other territories. The opinion ran counter to Lincoln's determined opposition to the expansion of slavery.*

John McLean and Benjamin Curtis were the two justices on the Supreme Court who dissented from the majority decision; both argued that Scott (and thus his family) was entitled to freedom. Chief Justice Roger B. Taney's lengthy opinion became the focus of much debate, especially his claim that black people "had no rights which the white man was bound to respect" and his argument that the Missouri Compromise infringed upon slaveholders' property rights.

And now as to the Dred Scott decision. That decision declares two propositions—first, that a negro cannot sue in the U.S. Courts; and secondly, that Congress cannot prohibit slavery in the Territories. It was made by a divided court—dividing differently on the different points. Judge Douglas does not discuss the merits of the decision; and, in that respect, I shall follow his example, believing I could no more improve on McLean and Curtis, than he could on Taney.

He denounces all who question the correctness of that decision, as offering violent resistance to it. But who resists it? Who has, in spite of the decision, declared Dred Scott free, and resisted the authority of his master over him?

Judicial decisions have two uses—first, to absolutely determine the case decided, and secondly, to indicate to the public how other similar cases will be decided when they arise. For the latter use, they are called "precedents" and "authorities."

We believe, as much as Judge Douglas, (perhaps more) in obedi¯ ence to, and respect for the judicial department of government. We think its decisions on Constitutional questions, when fully settled, should control, not only the particular cases decided, but the general policy of the country, subject to be disturbed only by amendments of the Constitution as provided in that instrument itself. More than this would be revolution. But we think the Dred Scott decision is erroneous. We know the court that made it, has often over-ruled its own decisions, and we shall do what we can to have it to over-rule this. We offer no *resistance* to it.

Judicial decisions are of greater or less authority as precedents, according to circumstances. That this should be so, accords both with common sense, and the customary understanding of the legal profession.

If this important decision had been made by the unanimous concurrence of the judges, and without any apparent partisan bias, and in accordance with legal public expectation, and with the steady practice of the departments throughout our history, and had been in no part, based on assumed historical facts which are not really true; or, if wanting in some of these, it had been before the court more than once, and had there been affirmed and re-affirmed through a course of years, it then might be, perhaps would be, factious, nay, even revolutionary, to not acquiesce in it as a precedent.

But when, as it is true we find it wanting in all these claims to the public confidence, it is not resistance, it is not factious, it is not even disrespectful, to treat it as not having yet quite established a settled doctrine for the country—

There is a natural disgust in the minds of nearly all white people, to the idea of an indiscriminate amalgamation of the white and black races; and Judge Douglas evidently is basing his chief hope, upon the chances of being able to appropriate the benefit of this disgust to himself. If he can, by much drumming and repeating, fasten the odium of that idea upon his adversaries, he thinks he can struggle through the storm. He therefore clings to this hope, as a drowning man to the last plank. He makes an occasion for lugging it in from the opposition to the Dred Scott decision. He finds the Republicans insisting that the Declaration of Independence includes ALL men, black as well as white; and forthwith he boldly denies that it includes negroes at all, and proceeds to argue gravely that all who contend it does, do so only because they want to vote, and eat, and sleep, and marry with negroes! He will have it that they cannot be consistent else. Now I protest against that counterfeit logic which concludes that, because I do not want a black woman for a *slave* I must necessarily want her for a *wife*. I need not have her for either, I can just leave her alone. In some respects she certainly is not my equal; but in her natural right to eat the bread she earns with her own hands without asking leave of any one else, she is my equal, and the equal of all others.

Chief Justice Taney, in his opinion in the Dred Scott case, admits that the language of the Declaration is broad enough to include the whole human family, but he and Judge Douglas argue that the authors of that instrument did not intend to include negroes, by the fact that they did not at once, actually place them on an equality with the whites. Now this grave argument comes to just nothing at all, by the other fact, that they did not at once, *or ever afterwards,* actually place all white people on an equality with one or another. And this is the staple argument of both the Chief Justice and the Senator, for doing this obvious violence to the plain unmistakable language of the Declaration. I think the authors of that notable instrument intended to include *all* men, but they did not intend to declare all men equal *in all respects*. They did not mean to say all were equal in color, size, intellect, moral developments, or social capacity. They defined with tolerable distinctness, in what respects they did consider all men created equal–equal in "certain inalienable rights, among which are life, liberty, and the pursuit of happiness." This they said, and this meant. They did not mean to assert the obvious untruth, that all were then actually enjoying that equality, nor yet, that they were about to confer it immediately upon them. In fact they had no power to confer such a boon. They meant simply to declare the *right,* so that the *enforcement* of it might follow as fast as circumstances should permit. They meant to set up a standard maxim for free society, which should be familiar to all, and revered by all; constantly looked to, constantly labored for, and even though never perfectly attained, constantly approximated, and thereby constantly spreading and deepening its influence, and augmenting the happiness and value of life to all people of all colors everywhere. The assertion that "all men are created equal" was of no practical use in effecting our separation from Great Britain; and it was placed in the Declaration, not for that, but for future use. Its authors meant it to be, thank God, it is now proving itself, a stumbling block to those who in after times might seek to turn a free people back into the hateful paths of despotism. They knew the proneness of prosperity to breed tyrants, and they meant when such should re-appear in this fair land and commence their vocation they should find left for them at least one hard nut to crack.

The Debate with Douglas, 1858

~~~~~~~~~~~~~~~~~~

CHAPTER TWO

IN 1858 ILLINOIS REPUBLICANS took the highly unusual step of explicitly identifying Abraham Lincoln as their choice for the United States Senate should the party control the state legislature as a result of the fall election. Accepting the party's nomination, Lincoln delivered a speech rendered most notable by his use of a house as a metaphor for the Union [Document 2-1]. In the contest against Douglas that followed, Lincoln agreed to a series of seven debates across the state. Although some political commentators today celebrate these debates as a high point in American political discourse, a reading of the speeches in their entirety suggests that they were more akin to a slugfest on the stump, in which both participants engaged in exaggeration and occasionally misrepresentation.

Both of the excerpts included in this volume reflect these characteristics. At Freeport, Illinois, Lincoln opened by refuting a series of questions set forth by Douglas in their first debate, several of which were framed in ways that misrepresented Lincoln's views. The Republican candidate immediately counterattacked, assailing the application of the principle of popular sovereignty as he endeavored to force Douglas to make admissions damaging to his electoral prospects [Document 2-3]. Of these, the most threatening were the second and third questions: how could citizens follow the principles of popular sovereignty in the aftermath of the *Dred Scott* decision, which rendered unconstitutional congressional attempts to bar slavery in the territories? Would Douglas honor what Lincoln came to call a second *Dred Scott* decision, which reasoned that if slaves were no different than any other sort of property, then efforts by states to prohibit slavery violated constitutional provisions concerning due process? After all, such was the very reasoning Chief Justice Taney employed with respect to slavery and the territories in the first decision. Douglas's response to the former question, thereafter known as the Freeport Doctrine, repeated what he had heretofore stated—that by failing to pass local legislation, such as police regulations, necessary to the protection of slavery, territorial residents could in effect bar the introduction of slavery in their communities by rendering it insecure. This position damaged Douglas's prospects for the presidency in 1860 by arming Southern Democrats with the claim that Douglas was in fact looking for ways to combat the expansion of slavery, which in turn prodded them to seek explicit protection for it in the form of a federal slave code for the territories—thus rendering more plausible Lincoln's fear that slavery might well be nationalized. At Edwardsville, Illinois, in a speech that was not part of the series of debates, Lincoln offered his own understanding of these questions and their consequences [Document 2-4].

The other excerpt from the Lincoln-Douglas debates [Document 2-5] reflects Lincoln's efforts to counter Douglas's charge that he embraced complete equality between blacks and whites, leading to the mixing of the races socially and in marriage. In raising this issue at Jonesboro, located in southern Illinois, Douglas hoped to play to the racial prejudices of both the audience present—many of who either had migrated from slaveholding states or were descended from such migrants—and the Illinois electorate statewide. It was a charge Lincoln had heard before: at Chicago he had attacked "that counterfeit logic which resumes that because I do not want a negro woman for a slave, I do necessarily want her for a wife," while at Springfield he had offered a more extended explanation of his position regarding black equality [Document 2-2].[1] In his response to Douglas at Charleston, Lincoln defined various forms of equality in order to clarify his position in a statement often cited by people anxious to argue that Lincoln was a racist. Many such discussions distort Lincoln's views on race and slavery to serve other agendas, ignoring the context in which he made them. In an effort to summarize his own position and show that it harmonized with that of Henry Clay, he shared several clippings from his speeches, including statements reprinted in Documents 1-2, 1-5, and 1-10, with James N. Brown, a former state legislator. [Document 2-6].

Although the Republicans secured a plurality of the votes cast that fall, they did not secure control of the state legislature, and thus Douglas claimed victory. But in standing toe-to-toe with such a prominent opponent, Lincoln gained a national reputation. Disheartened by defeat, he nevertheless renewed his efforts to play a role in Republican politics with an eye toward securing the party's triumph in the election of 1860.

1. Lincoln, Speech at Chicago, Illinois, July 10, 1858, in Fehrenbacher, *Lincoln: Speeches and Writings,* 1:454–455.

[DOCUMENT 2-1]
SPEECH AT SPRINGFIELD, ILLINOIS, JUNE 16, 1858
(THE "HOUSE DIVIDED" SPEECH)

On June 16, 1858, Illinois Republicans, meeting in convention in Spring-
field, nominated Abraham Lincoln as their candidate for United States senator.
The nomination itself was unusual, for it would be the state legislators, not the
voters of Illinois, who would select the next senator; the nomination was in part
a device to short-circuit efforts to displace Lincoln, the consensus candidate, and
to counter efforts of several eastern Republicans who entertained the notion of
wooing Senator Stephen A. Douglas into their party following his break with
President James Buchanan over the fate of Kansas's bid for statehood under a
proslavery constitution that had been framed in dubious circumstances.

Franklin Pierce was the fourteenth president of the United States (1853–
1857); his successor, James Buchanan, having been tipped off that the Dred
Scott *decision was forthcoming, afterwards supported it. The proslavery consti-*
tution adopted at Lecompton, Kansas, became the source of a dispute between
Buchanan and Douglas, for the senator realized that by failing to offer Kansans
a chance to exclude slavery from Kansas, the document mocked Douglas's prin-
ciple of popular sovereignty, in which the voters in a territory decided for them-
selves whether to allow or prohibit the introduction of slavery. Senator Salmon
P. Chase of Ohio had opposed the Kansas-Nebraska Act; so did Daniel Macy, a
congressman from Indiana; Samuel Nelson was an associate justice on the Su-
preme Court.

If we could first know *where* we are, and *whither* we are tending, we
could better judge *what* to do, and *how* to do it.

We are now far into the *fifth* year, since a policy was initiated, with
the *avowed* object, and *confident* promise, of putting an end to slavery
agitation.

Under the operation of that policy, that agitation has not only, *not
ceased,* but has *constantly augmented.*

In *my* opinion, it *will* not cease, until a *crisis* shall have been reached,
and passed

"A house divided against itself cannot stand."

I believe this government cannot endure, permanently half *slave* and
half *free.*

I do not expect the Union to be *dissolved*–I do not expect the house
to *fall*–but I *do* expect it will cease to be divided.

It will become *all* one thing, or *all* the other.

Either the *opponents* of slavery, will arrest the further spread of it, and place it where the public mind shall rest in the belief that it is in course of ultimate extinction; or its *advocates* will push it forward, till it shall become alike lawful in *all* the States, *old* as well as *new*—*North* as well as *South*.

Have we no *tendency* to the latter condition?

Let any one who doubts, carefully contemplate that now almost complete legal combination—piece of *machinery* so to speak—compounded of the Nebraska doctrine, and the Dred Scott decision. Let him consider not only *what work* the machinery is adapted to do, and *how well* adapted; but also, let him study the *history* of its construction, and trace, if he can, or rather *fail*, if he can, to trace the evidences of design, and concert of action, among its chief bosses, from the beginning.

The new year of 1854 found slavery excluded from more than half the States by State Constitutions, and from most of the national territory by congressional prohibition.

Four days later, commenced the struggle, which ended in repealing that Congressional prohibition.

This opened all the national territory to slavery; and was the first point gained.

But, so far, *Congress* only, had acted; and an *indorsement* by the people, *real* or apparent, was indispensable, to *save* the point already gained, and give chance for more.

This necessity had not been overlooked; but had been provided for, as well as might be, in the notable argument of *"squatter sovereignty,"* otherwise called *"sacred right of self government,"* which latter phrase, though expressive of the only rightful basis of any government, was so perverted in this attempted use of it as to amount to just this: That if any *one* man, choose to enslave *another,* no *third* man shall be allowed to object.

That argument was incorporated into the Nebraska bill itself, in the language which follows: *"It being the true intent and meaning of this act not to legislate slavery into any Territory or State, nor to exclude it therefrom; but to leave the people thereof perfectly free to form and regulate their domestic institutions in their own way, subject only to the Constitution of the United States."*

Then opened the roar of loose declamation in favor of "Squatter Sovereignty," and "Sacred right of self government."

"But," said opposition members, "let us be more *specific*—let us *amend* the bill so as to expressly declare that the people of the territory *may* exclude slavery." "Not we," said the friends of the measure; and down they voted the amendment.

While the Nebraska bill was passing through congress, a *law case,* involving the question of a negroe's freedom, by reason of his owner having voluntarily taken him first into a free State and then a territory covered by the congressional prohibition, and held him as a slave for a long time in each, was passing through the U. S. Circuit Court for the District of Missouri; and both Nebraska bill and law suit were brought to a decision in the same month of May, 1854. The negroe's name was "Dred Scott," which name now designates the decision finally made in the case.

Before the *then* next Presidential election, the law case came *to,* and was argued *in* the Supreme Court of the United States; but the *decision* of it was deferred until *after* the election. Still, *before* the election, Senator Trumbull, on the floor of the Senate, requests the leading advocate of the Nebraska bill to state *his opinion* whether the people of a territory can constitutionally exclude slavery from their limits; and the latter answers, "That is a question for the Supreme Court."

The election came. Mr. Buchanan was elected, and the *indorsement,* such as it was, secured. That was the *second* point gained. The indorsement, however, fell short of a clear popular majority by nearly four hundred thousand votes, and so, perhaps, was not overwhelmingly reliable and satisfactory.

The *outgoing* President, in his last annual message, as impressively as possible *echoed back* upon the people the *weight* and *authority* of the indorsement.

The Supreme Court met again; *did not* announce their decision, but ordered a re-argument.

The Presidential inauguration came, and still no decision of the court; but the *incoming* President, in his inaugural address, fervently exhorted the people to abide by the forthcoming decision, *whatever it might be.*

Then, in a few days, came the decision.

The reputed author of the Nebraska bill finds an early occasion to make a speech at this capitol indorsing the Dred Scott Decision, and vehemently denouncing all opposition to it.

The new President, too, seizes the early occasion of the Silliman letter to *indorse* and strongly *construe* that decision, and to express his *astonishment* that any different view had ever been entertained.

At length a squabble springs up between the President and the author of the Nebraska bill, on the *mere* question of *fact,* whether the Lecompton constitution was or was not, in any just sense, made by the people of Kansas; and in that quarrel the latter declares that all he wants is a fair vote for the people, and that he *cares* not whether slavery be voted *down* or voted *up*. I do not understand his declaration that he cares not whether slavery be voted *down* or voted *up*, to be intended by him other than as an *apt definition* of the *policy* he would impress upon the public mind—the *principle* for which he declares he has suffered much, and is ready to suffer to the end.

And well may he cling to that principle. If he has any parental feeling, well may he cling to it. That principle, is the only *shred* left of his original Nebraska doctrine. Under the Dred Scott decision, "squatter sovereignty" squatted out of existence, tumbled down like temporary scaffolding—like the mold at the foundry served through one blast and fell back into loose sand—helped to carry an election, and then was kicked to the winds. His late *joint* struggle with the Republicans, against the Lecompton Constitution, involves nothing of the original Nebraska doctrine. That struggle was made on a point, the right of a people to make their own constitution, upon which he and the Republicans have never differed.

The several points of the Dred Scott decision, in connection with Senator Douglas' "care not" policy, constitute the piece of machinery, in its *present* state of advancement. This was the third point gained.

The *working* points of that machinery are:

First, that no negro slave, imported as such from Africa, and no descendant of such slave can ever be a *citizen* of any State, in the sense of that term as used in the Constitution of the United States.

This point is made in order to deprive the negro, in every possible event, of the benefit of that provision of the United States Constitution, which declares that—

"The citizens of each State shall be entitled to all privileges and immunities of citizens in the several States."

Secondly, that "subject to the Constitution of the United States," neither *Congress* nor a *Territorial Legislature* can exclude slavery from any United States Territory.

This point is made in order that individual men may *fill up* the territories with slaves, without danger of losing them as property, and thus enhance the chances of *permanency* to the institution through all the future.

Thirdly, that whether the holding a negro in actual slavery in a free State, makes him free, as against the holder, the United States courts will not decide, but will leave to be decided by the courts of any slave State the negro may be forced into by the master.

This point is made, not to be pressed *immediately;* but, if acquiesced in for a while, and apparently *indorsed* by the people at an election, *then* to sustain the logical conclusion that what Dred Scott's master might lawfully do with Dred Scott, in the free State of Illinois, every other master may lawfully do with any other *one,* or one *thousand* slaves, in Illinois, or in any other free State.

Auxiliary to all this, and working hand in hand with it, the Nebraska doctrine, or what is left of it, is to *educate* and *mould* public opinion, at least *Northern* public opinion, to not *care* whether slavery is voted *down* or voted *up.*

This shows exactly where we now *are;* and *partially* also, whither we are tending.

It will throw additional light on the latter, to go back, and run the mind over the string of historical facts already stated. Several things will *now* appear less *dark* and *mysterious* than they did *when* they were transpiring. The people were to be left "perfectly free" "subject only to the Constitution." What the Constitution had to do with it, outsiders could not *then* see. Plainly enough *now,* it was an exactly fitted *niche* for the Dred Scott decision to afterward come in, and declare that *perfect freedom* of the people, to be just no freedom at all.

Why was the amendment, expressly declaring the right of the people to exclude slavery, voted down? Plainly enough *now,* the adoption of it, would have spoiled the niche for the Dred Scott decision.

Why was the court decision held up? Why, even a Senator's individual opinion withheld, till *after* the Presidential election? Plainly enough *now,* the speaking out *then* would have damaged the *"perfectly free"* argument upon which the election was to be carried.

Why the *outgoing* President's felicitation on the indorsement? Why the delay of a reargument? Why the incoming President's *advance* exhortation in favor of the decision?

These things *look* like the cautious *patting* and *petting* of a spirited horse, preparatory to mounting him, when it is dreaded that he may give the rider a fall.

And why the hasty after indorsements of the decision by the President and others?

We cannot absolutely *know* that all these exact adaptations are the result of preconcert. But when we see a lot of framed timbers, different portions of which we know have been gotten out at different times and places and by different workmen—Stephen, Franklin, Roger, and James, for instance—and we see these timbers joined together, and see they exactly make the frame of a house or a mill, all the tenons and mortices exactly fitting, and all the lengths and proportions of the different pieces exactly adapted to their respective places, and not a piece too many or too few—not omitting even scaffolding—or, if a single piece be lacking, we see the place in the frame exactly fitted and prepared to yet bring such piece in—in *such* a case, we find it impossible not to *believe* that Stephen and Franklin and Roger and James all understood one another from the beginning, and all worked upon a common *plan* or *draft* drawn up before the first lick was struck.

It should not be overlooked that, by the Nebraska bill, the people of a *State* as well as *Territory,* were to be left *"perfectly free" "subject only to the Constitution."*

Why mention a *State?* They were legislating for *territories,* and not *for* or *about* States. Certainly the people of a *State are* and *ought to be* subject to the Constitution of the United States; but why is mention of this *lugged* into this merely *territorial* law? Why are the people of a *territory* and the people of a *state* therein *lumped* together, and their relation to the Constitution therein treated as being *precisely* the same?

While the opinion of *the Court,* by Chief Justice Taney, in the Dred Scott case, and the separate opinions of all the concurring Judges, expressly declare that the Constitution of the United States neither permits Congress nor a territorial legislature to exclude slavery from any United States territory, they all *omit* to declare whether or not the same Constitution permits a *state,* or the people of a State, to exclude it.

Possibly, this is a mere *omission;* but who can be *quite* sure, if McLean or Curtis had sought to get into the opinion a declaration of unlimited power in the people of a *state* to exclude slavery from their limits, just as Chase and Macy sought to get such declaration, in behalf of the people of a territory, into the Nebraska bill—I ask, who can be quite *sure* that it would not have been voted down, in the one case, as it had been in the other?

The nearest approach to the point of declaring the power of a State over slavery, is made by Judge Nelson. He approaches it more than once, using the precise idea, and *almost* the language too, of the Nebraska act. On one occasion his exact language is, "except in cases where the power is restrained by the Constitution of the United States, the law of the State is supreme over the subject of slavery within its jurisdiction."

In what *cases* the power of the *states* is so restrained by the U. S. Constitution is left an *open* question, precisely as the same question, as to the restraint on the power of the *territories* was left open in the Nebraska act. Put *that* and *that* together, and we have another nice little niche, which we may, ere long, see filled with another Supreme Court decision, declaring that the Constitution of the United States does not permit a *state* to exclude slavery from its limits.

And this may especially be expected if the doctrine of "care not whether slavery be voted *down* or voted *up,*" shall gain upon the public mind sufficiently to give promise that such a decision can be maintained when made.

Such a decision is all that slavery now lacks of being alike lawful in all the States.

Welcome or unwelcome, such decision *is* probably coming, and will soon be upon us, unless the power of the present political dynasty shall be met and overthrown.

We shall *lie down* pleasantly dreaming that the people of Missouri are on the verge of making their State *free;* and we shall *awake* to the *reality,* instead, that the *Supreme* Court has made *Illinois* a *slave* State.

To meet and overthrow the power of that dynasty, is the work now before all those who would prevent that consummation.

That is *what* we have to do.

But *how* can we best do it?

There are those who denounce us *openly* to their *own* friends, and yet whisper *us softly,* that *Senator Douglas* is the *aptest* instrument there is, with which to effect that object. *They* do *not* tell us, nor has *he* told us, that he *wishes* any such object to be effected. They wish us to *infer* all, from the facts, that he now has a little quarrel with the present head of the dynasty; and that he has regularly voted with us, on a single point, upon which, he and we, have never differed.

They remind us that *he* is a *great man,* and that the largest of us are very small ones. Let this be granted. But "a *living dog* is better than a *dead lion.*" Judge Douglas, if not a *dead* lion *for this work,* is at least a *caged* and *toothless* one. How can he oppose the advances of slavery? He don't *care* anything about it. His avowed *mission is impressing* the "public heart" to *care* nothing about it.

A leading Douglas Democratic newspaper thinks Douglas' superior talent will be needed to resist the revival of the African slave trade.

Does Douglas believe an effort to revive that trade is approaching? He has not said so. Does he *really* think so? But if it is, how can he resist it? For years he has labored to prove it a *sacred right* of white men to take negro slaves into the new territories. Can he possibly show that it is *less* a sacred right to *buy* them where they can be bought cheapest? And, unquestionably they can be bought *cheaper in Africa* than in *Virginia.*

He has done all in his power to reduce the whole question of slavery to one of a mere *right of property;* and as such, how can *he* oppose the foreign slave trade—how can he refuse that trade in that "property" shall be "perfectly free"—unless he does it as a *protection* to the home production? And as the home *producers* will probably not *ask* the protection, he will be wholly without a ground of opposition.

Senator Douglas holds, we know, that a man may rightfully be *wiser to-day* than he was *yesterday*—that he may rightfully change when he finds himself wrong.

But, can we for that reason, run ahead, and *infer* that he *will* make any particular change, of which he, himself, has given no intimation? Can we *safely* base *our* action upon any such *vague* inference?

Now, as ever, I wish to not *misrepresent* Judge Douglas' *position,* question his *motives,* or do aught that can be personally offensive to him.

Whenever, *if ever,* he and we can come together on *principle* so that *our great cause* may have assistance from *his great ability,* I hope to have interposed no adventitious obstacle.

But clearly, he is not *now* with us—he does not *pretend* to be—he does not *promise* to *ever* be.

Our cause, then, must be intrusted to, and conducted by its own undoubted friends—those whose hands are free, whose hearts are in the work—who *do care* for the result.

Two years ago the Republicans of the nation mustered over thirteen hundred thousand strong.

We did this under the single impulse of resistance to a common danger, with every external circumstance against us.

Of *strange, discordant,* and even, *hostile* elements, we gathered from the four winds, and *formed* and fought the battle through, under the constant hot fire of a disciplined, proud, and pampered enemy.

Did we brave all *then,* to *falter* now? —*now*—when that same enemy is *wavering,* dissevered, and belligerent?

The result is not doubtful. We shall not fail—if we stand firm, we shall not fail.

Wise counsels may *accelerate* or *mistakes delay* it, but sooner or later the victory is *sure* to come.

[DOCUMENT 2-2]
SPEECH AT SPRINGFIELD, ILLINOIS, JULY 17, 1858 (EXCERPT)

Lincoln spoke to an assembled crowd in Springfield in the evening; Douglas had spoken that afternoon. The excerpt herein reproduced was in response to Douglas's claim that Lincoln favored the political and social equality of blacks, a charge the senator would often repeat in an effort to arouse the racial prejudices of white voters.

My declarations upon this subject of negro slavery may be misrepresented, but can not be misunderstood. I have said that I do not understand the Declaration to mean that all men were created equal in all respects. They are not our equal in color; but I suppose that it does mean to declare that all men are equal in some respects; they are equal in their right to "life, liberty, and the pursuit of happiness." Certainly the negro is not our equal in color—perhaps not in many other respects; still, in the right to put into his mouth the bread that his own hands have earned, he is the equal of every other man, white or black. In pointing out that more has been given you, you can not be justified in taking away the little which has been given him. All I ask for the negro is that if you do not like him, let him alone. If God gave him but little, that little let him enjoy.

When our Government was established, we had the institution of slavery among us. We were in a certain sense compelled to tolerate its existence. It was a sort of necessity. We had gone through our struggle and secured our own independence. The framers of the Constitution found the institution of slavery amongst their other institutions at the time. They found that by an effort to eradicate it, they might lose much of what they had already gained. They were obliged to bow to the necessity. They gave power to Congress to abolish the slave trade at the end of twenty years. They also prohibited it in the Territories where it did not exist. They did what they could and yielded to the necessity for the rest. I also yield to all which follows from that necessity. What I would most desire would be the separation of the white and black races.

[DOCUMENT 2-3]
SPEECH AT FREEPORT, ILLINOIS, AUGUST 27, 1858; (SECOND
LINCOLN-DOUGLAS DEBATE; EXCERPT)

In August, Lincoln and Douglas agreed to engage in a series of face-to-face debates across Illinois in the seven congressional districts where the two candidates had not appeared together. This excerpt from the second debate at Freeport includes Lincoln's reply to a series of charges Douglas had advanced at the first debate in Ottawa on August 21 and Lincoln's counterattack, designed to force Douglas to reiterate his position on slavery in Kansas territory in the wake of the Dred Scott *decision and subsequent political debate.*

Lyman Trumbull was the Republican senator from Illinois; Representative English's bill proposed to offer Kansas the proceeds from specified public land sales if the territory's voters ratified the Lecompton Constitution; otherwise, Kansas would have to wait until it had attained a population equal to that of the average congressional district (approximately 93,000 people) before applying for statehood.

Having said thus much, I will take up the Judge's interrogatories as I find them printed in the Chicago *Times,* and answer them *seriatim.* In order that there may be no mistake about it, I have copied the interrogatories in writing, and also my answers to them. The first one of these interrogatories is in these words:

Question 1. "I desire to know whether Lincoln to-day stands, as he did in 1854, in favor of the unconditional repeal of the fugitive slave law?"

Answer. I do not now, nor ever did, stand in favor of the unconditional repeal of the fugitive slave law. [Cries of "good," "good."]

Q. 2. "I desire him to answer whether he stands pledged today, as he did in 1854, against the admission of any more slave States into the Union, even if the people want them?"

A. I do not now, nor ever did, stand pledged against the admission of any more slave States into the Union.

Q. 3. "I want to know whether he stands pledged against the admission of a new State into the Union with such a Constitution as the people of that State may see fit to make."

A. I do not stand pledged against the admission of a new State into the Union, with such a Constitution as the people of that State may see fit to make. [Cries of "good," "good."]

Q. 4. "I want to know whether he stands to-day pledged to the abolition of slavery in the District of Columbia?"

A. I do not stand to-day pledged to the abolition of slavery in the District of Columbia.

Q. 5. "I desire him to answer whether he stands pledged to the prohibition of the slave trade between the different States?"

A. I do not stand pledged to the prohibition of the slave trade between the different States.

Q. 6. "I desire to know whether he stands pledged to prohibit slavery in all the Territories of the United States, North as well as South of the Missouri Compromise line."

A. I am impliedly, if not expressly, pledged to a belief in the *right* and *duty* of Congress to prohibit slavery in all the United States Territories. [Great applause.]

Q. 7. "I desire him to answer whether he is opposed to the acquisition of any new territory unless slavery is first prohibited therein."

A. I am not generally opposed to honest acquisition of territory;

and, in any given case, I would or would not oppose such acquisition, accordingly as I might think such acquisition would or would not agravate the slavery question among ourselves. [Cries of good, good.]

Now, my friends, it will be perceived upon an examination of these questions and answers, that so far I have only answered that I was not *pledged* to this, that or the other. The Judge has not framed his interrogatories to ask me anything more than this, and I have answered in strict accordance with the interrogatories, and have answered truly that I am not *pledged* at all upon any of the points to which I have answered. But I am not disposed to hang upon the exact form of his interrogatory. I am rather disposed to take up at least some of these questions, and state what I really think upon them.

As to the first one, in regard to the Fugitive Slave Law, I have never hesitated to say, and I do not now hesitate to say, that I think, under the Constitution of the United States, the people of the Southern States are entitled to a Congressional Fugitive Slave Law. Having said that, I have had nothing to say in regard to the existing Fugitive Slave Law further than that I think it should have been framed so as to be free from some of the objections that pertain to it, without lessening its efficiency. And inasmuch as we are not now in an agitation in regard to an alteration or modification of that law, I would not be the man to introduce it as a new subject of agitation upon the general question of slavery.

In regard to the other question of whether I am pledged to the admission of any more slave States into the Union, I state to you very frankly that I would be exceedingly sorry ever to be put in a position of having to pass upon that question. I should be exceedingly glad to know that there would never be another slave State admitted into the Union; [applause]; but I must add, that if slavery shall be kept out of the Territories during the territorial existence of any one given Territory, and then the people shall, having a fair chance and a clear field, when they come to adopt the Constitution, do such an extraordinary thing as to adopt a Slave Constitution, uninfluenced by the actual presence of the institution among them, I see no alternative, if we own the country, but to admit them into the Union. [Applause.]

The third interrogatory is answered by the answer to the second, it being, as I conceive, the same as the second.

The fourth one is in regard to the abolition of slavery in the District of Columbia. In relation to that, I have my mind very distinctly made up. I should be exceedingly glad to see slavery abolished in the District of Columbia. [Cries of "good, good."] I believe that Congress possesses the constitutional power to abolish it. Yet as a member of Congress, I should not with my present views, be in favor of *endeavoring* to abolish slavery in the District of Columbia, unless it would be upon these conditions. *First,* that the abolition should be gradual. *Second,* that it should be on a vote of the majority of qualified voters in the District, and *third,* that compensation should be made to unwilling owners. With these three conditions, I confess I would be exceedingly glad to see Congress abolish slavery in the District of Columbia, and, in the language of Henry Clay, "sweep from our Capital that foul blot upon our nation." [Loud applause.]

In regard to the fifth interrogatory, I must say here, that as to the question of the abolition of the Slave Trade between the different States, I can truly answer, as I have, that I am *pledged* to nothing about it. It is a subject to which I have not given that mature consideration that would make me feel authorized to state a position so as to hold myself entirely bound by it. In other words, that question has never been prominently enough before me to induce me to investigate whether we really have the Constitutional power to do it. I could investigate it if I had sufficient time, to bring myself to a conclusion upon that subject, but I have not done so, and I say so frankly to you here, and to Judge Douglas. I must say, however, that if I should be of opinion that Congress does possess the Constitutional power to abolish the slave trade among the different States, I should still not be in favor of the exercise of that power unless upon some conservative principle as I conceive it, akin to what I have said in relation to the abolition of slavery in the District of Columbia.

My answer as to whether I desire that slavery should be prohibited in all the Territories of the United States is full and explicit within itself, and cannot be made clearer by any comments of mine. So I suppose in regard to the question whether I am opposed to the acquisition of any more territory unless slavery is first prohibited therein, my answer is such that I could add nothing by way of illustration, or making myself better understood, than the answer which I have placed in writing.

Now in all this, the Judge has me and he has me on the record. I suppose he had flattered himself that I was really entertaining one set of opinions for one place and another set for another place—that I was afraid to say at one place what I uttered at another. What I am saying here I suppose I say to a vast audience as strongly tending to Abolitionism as any audience in the State of Illinois, and I believe I am saying that which, if it would be offensive to any persons and render them enemies to myself, would be offensive to persons in this audience.

I now proceed to propound to the Judge the interrogatories, so far as I have framed them. I will bring forward a new installment when I get them ready. [Laughter.] I will bring them forward now, only reaching to number four.

The first one is—

Question 1. If the people of Kansas shall, by means entirely unobjectionable in all other respects, adopt a State Constitution, and ask admission into the Union under it, *before* they have the requisite number of inhabitants according to the English Bill—some ninety-three thousand—will you vote to admit them? [Applause.]

Q. 2. Can the people of a United States Territory, in any lawful way, against the wish of any citizen of the United States, exclude slavery from its limits prior to the formation of a State Constitution? [Renewed applause.]

Q. 3. If the Supreme Court of the United States shall decide that States can not exclude slavery from their limits, are you in favor of acquiescing in, adopting and following such decision as a rule of political action? [Loud applause.]

Q. 4. Are you in favor of acquiring additional territory, in disregard of how such acquisition may affect the nation on the slavery question? [Cries of "good," "good."]

[DOCUMENT 2-4]
SPEECH AT EDWARDSVILLE, ILLINOIS,
SEPTEMBER 11, 1858 (EXCERPTS)

The Lincoln-Douglas debates represented but a portion of Lincoln's speaking obligations during the 1858 campaign. Here, at Edwardsville, he offered voters his understanding of the issues at stake in the contest.

I have been requested to give a concise statement, as I understand it, of the difference between the Democratic and the Republican parties on the leading issues of this campaign. The question has just been put to me by a gentleman whom I do not know. I do not even know whether he is a friend of mine or a supporter of Judge Douglas in this contest; nor does that make any difference. His question is a pertinent one and, though it has not been asked me anywhere in the State before, I am very glad that my attention has been called to it to-day. Lest I should forget it, I will give you my answer before proceeding with the line of argument I had marked out for this discussion.

The difference between the Republican and the Democratic parties on the leading issue of this contest, as I understand it, is, that the former consider slavery a moral, social and political wrong, while the latter *do not* consider it either a moral, social or political wrong; and the action of each, as respects the growth of the country and the expansion of our population, is squared to meet these views. I will not allege that the Democratic party consider slavery morally, socially and politically *right;* though their tendency to that view has, in my opinion, been constant and unmistakable for the past five years. I prefer to take, as the accepted maxim of the party, the idea put forth by Judge Douglas, that he "don't care whether slavery is voted down or voted up." I am quite willing to believe that many Democrats would prefer that slavery be always voted down, and I am sure that some prefer that it be always "voted up"; but I have a right to insist that their action, especially if it be their *constant and unvarying* action, shall determine their ideas and preferences on the subject. Every measure of the Democratic party of late years, bearing directly or indirectly on the slavery question, has corresponded with this notion of utter indifference whether slavery or freedom shall outrun in the race of empire across the Pacific—every measure, I say, up to the Dred Scott decision, where, it seems to me, the idea is boldly suggested that slavery is *better* than freedom. The Republican party, on the contrary, hold that this government was instituted to secure the blessings of freedom, and that slavery is an unqualified evil to the negro, to the white man, to the soil, and to the State. Regarding it an evil, they will not molest it in the States where it exists; they will not overlook the constitutional guards which our forefathers have placed around it; they will do nothing which can give proper offence to those who hold slaves by legal sanction; but they will use every constitutional method to prevent the evil from becoming larger and involving more negroes, more white men, more soil, and more States in its deplorable consequences. They will, if possible, place it where the public mind shall rest in the belief that it is in course of ultimate peaceable extinction, in God's own good time. And to this end they will, if possible, restore the government to the policy of the fathers—the policy of preserving the new territories from the baneful influence of human bondage, as the Northwestern territories were sought to be preserved by the ordinance of 1787 and the compromise act of 1820. They will oppose, in all its length and breadth, the modern Democratic idea that slavery is as good as freedom, and ought to have room for expansion all over the continent, if people can be found to carry it. All, or very nearly all, of Judge Douglas' arguments about "Popular Sovereignty," as he calls it, are logical if you admit that slavery is as good and as right as freedom; and not one of them is worth a rush if you deny it. This is the difference, as I understand it, between the Republican and the Democratic parties; and I ask the gentleman, and all of you, whether his question is not satisfactorily answered.—[Cries of "Yes, yes."]

My friends, I have endeavored to show you the logical consequences of the Dred Scott decision, which holds that the people of a Territory cannot prevent the establishment of Slavery in their midst. I have stated what cannot be gainsayed—that the grounds upon which this decision is made are equally applicable to the Free States as to the Free Territories, and that the peculiar reasons put forth by Judge Douglas for endorsing this decision, commit him in advance to the next decision, and to all other decisions emanating from the same source. Now, when by all these means you have succeeded in dehumanizing the negro; when you have put him down, and made it forever impossible for him to be but as the beasts of the field; when you have extinguished his soul, and placed him where the ray of hope is blown out in darkness like that which broods over the spirits of the damned; are you quite sure the demon which you have roused *will not turn and rend you?* What constitutes the bulwark of our own liberty and independence? It is not our frowning battlements, our bristling sea coasts, the guns of our war steamers, or the strength of our gallant and disciplined army. These are not our reliance against a resumption of tyranny in our fair land. All of them may be turned against our liberties, without making us stronger or weaker for the struggle. Our reliance is in the *love of liberty* which God has planted in our bosoms. Our defense is in the preservation of the spirit which prizes liberty as the heritage of all men, in all lands, every where. Destroy this spirit, and you have planted the seeds of despotism around your own doors. Familiarize yourselves with the chains of bondage, and you are preparing your own limbs to wear them. Accustomed to trample on the rights of those around you, you have lost the genius of your own independence, and become the fit subjects of the first cunning tyrant who rises. And let me tell you, all these things are prepared for you with the logic of history, if the elections shall promise that the next Dred Scott decision and all future decisions will be quietly acquiesced in by the people.—[Loud applause.]

[DOCUMENT 2-5]
SPEECH AT CHARLESTON, ILLINOIS, SEPTEMBER 18, 1858
(FOURTH LINCOLN-DOUGLAS DEBATE; EXCERPT)

This excerpt from the fourth debate in southern Illinois contains a much-quoted section on Lincoln's racial views.

Colonel Richard M. Johnson, who gained such fame as the killer of the Indian chief Tecumseh that eventually he served as vice president (1837–1841), had a black mistress, with whom he had several children.

While I was at the hotel to-day an elderly gentleman called upon me to know whether I was really in favor of producing a perfect equality between the negroes and white people. [Great laughter.] While I had not proposed to myself on this occasion to say much on that subject, yet as the question was asked me I thought I would occupy perhaps five minutes in saying something in regard to it. I will say then that I am not, nor ever have been in favor of bringing about in any way the social and political equality of the white and black races, [applause]— that I am not nor ever have been in favor of making voters or jurors of negroes, nor of qualifying them to hold office, nor to intermarry with white people; and I will say in addition to this that there is a physical difference between the white and black races which I believe will for ever forbid the two races living together on terms of social and political equality. And inasmuch as they cannot so live, while they do remain together there must be the position of superior and inferior, and I as much as any other man am in favor of having the superior position assigned to the white race. I say upon this occasion I do not perceive that because the white man is to have the superior position the negro should be denied everything. I do not understand that because I do not want a negro woman for a slave I must necessarily want her for a wife. [Cheers and laughter.] My understanding is that I can just let her alone. I am now in my fiftieth year, and I certainly never have had a black woman for either a slave or a wife. So it seems to me quite possible for us to get along without making either slaves or wives of negroes. I will add to this that I have never seen to my knowledge a man, woman or child who was in favor of producing a perfect equality, social and political, between negroes and white men. I recollect of but one distinguished instance that I ever heard of so frequently as to be entirely satisfied of its correctness—and that is the case of Judge Douglas' old friend Col. Richard M. Johnson. [Laughter.] I will also add to the remarks I have made, (for I am not going to enter at large upon this subject,) that I have never had the least apprehension that I or my friends would marry negroes if there was no law to keep them from it, [laughter] but as Judge Douglas and his friends seem to be in great apprehension that they might, if there were no law to keep them from it, [roars of laughter] I give him the most solemn pledge that I will to the very last stand by the law of this State, which forbids the marrying of white people with negroes. [Continued laughter and applause.] I will add one further word, which is this, that I do not understand there is any place where an alteration of the social and political relations of the negro and the white man can be made except in the State Legislature— not in the Congress of the United States—and as I do not really appre-

hend the approach of any such thing myself, and as Judge Douglas
seems to be in constant horror that some such danger is rapidly approaching, I propose as the best means to prevent it that the Judge be
kept at home and placed in the State Legislature to fight the measure.
[Uproarious laughter and applause.] I do not propose dwelling longer
at this time on this subject.

[DOCUMENT 2-6]
TO JAMES N. BROWN, OCTOBER 18, 1858

*Lincoln clarified his views on race and slavery in a letter to Brown, a former
Illinois state representative, emphasizing the harmony of his views on equality
with those of Henry Clay (1777–1852), one of Lincoln's political idols.*

Hon. J. N. Brown   Springfield,
My dear Sir   Oct. 18. 1858
        I do not perceive how I can express myself, more plainly, than I
have done in the foregoing extracts. In four of them I have expressly
disclaimed all intention to bring about social and political equality between the white and black races, and, in all the rest, I have done the
same thing by clear implication

        I have made it equally plain that I think the negro is included in the
word "men" used in the Declaration of Independence.

        I believe the declaration that "all men are created equal" is the great
fundamental principle upon which our free institutions rest; that negro
slavery is violative of that principle; but that, by our frame of government, that principle has not been made one of legal obligation; that by
our frame of government, the States which have slavery are to retain it,
or surrender it at their own pleasure; and that all others–individuals,
free-states and national government–are constitutionally bound to leave
them alone about it.

        I believe our government was thus framed because of the *necessity*
springing from the actual presence of slavery, when it was framed.

        That such necessity does not exist in the teritories, where slavery is
not present.

        In his Mendenhall speech Mr. Clay says

        "Now, as an abstract principle, there is no doubt of the truth of that
declaration (all men created equal) and it is desireable, in the original
construction of society, and in organized societies, to keep it in view, as
a great fundamental principle"

Again, in the same speech Mr. Clay says:

"If a state of nature existed, and we were about to lay the foundations of society, no man would be more strongly opposed than I should to incorporate the institution of slavery among it's elements;"

Exactly so. In our new free teritories, a state of nature *does* exist. In them Congress lays the foundations of society; and, in laying those foundations, I say, with Mr. Clay, it is desireable that the declaration of the equality of all men shall be kept in view, as a great fundamental principle; and that Congress, which lays the foundations of society, should, like Mr. Clay, be strongly opposed to the incorporation of slavery among it's elements."

But it does not follow that social and political equality between whites and blacks, *must* be incorporated, because slavery must *not*. The declaration does not so require. Yours as ever

A. Lincoln

Stand By Your Principles, 1859–1860

IN 1859 ABRAHAM LINCOLN devoted himself to preparing Republicans for the presidential contest of 1860. He urged party leaders in other states to avoid discussing issues that would promote divisions within the party, and remained somewhat concerned that Stephen A. Douglas's break with the Buchanan administration might make him an attractive candidate in the eyes of some Republicans. Time and again he reminded listeners that slavery was a moral issue, and that it was but a step from Douglas's pose of indifference to an acceptance of the peculiar institution as moral. These themes surfaced in a speech he gave Chicago Republicans on the occasion of the party's triumph in city elections [Document 3-1].

In battling Douglas on the stump in 1858, Lincoln had gained a national reputation as a skilled political speaker. Ohio Republicans invited him to visit their state to counter a campaign tour by Douglas; Lincoln took advantage of one of these occasions to defend his "House Divided" speech, cast doubts upon the wisdom of a threatened secession, and reiterate the Republican pledge not to interfere with slavery where it existed [Document 3-2]. These remarks reflected his extensive reading in the intentions of the founding generation about slavery, on which he spoke at greater length at the Cooper Institute in New York City [Document 3-3]. Taking as his point of departure Douglas's rather selective reading of the statements and actions of the founders concerning slavery, Lincoln insisted that the Illinois senator overlooked much in his effort to argue that the founders were not opposed to slavery; in turn, Lincoln's address clearly placed himself and his fellow Republicans as the natural inheritors of their legacy. The speech also offered Lincoln the opportunity to reply to his party's critics, as he emphasized the Republican commitment to seek change legitimately through political action undertaken in accordance with constitutional processes.

The Cooper Institute speech was the high point in a speaking tour that bolstered Lincoln's reputation with eastern Republicans in time for them to mention him as a possible presidential nominee in 1860. Initially reluctant to consider himself as a suitable candidate, Lincoln finally admitted that he found the idea attractive; at worst he would enhance his stature in the party and promote his future political prospects. He worked hard to make sure that if he was not a delegate's first choice, he would be the second choice in case of a deadlock; he did not alienate his rivals. At the Republican national convention in Chicago, no candidate secured a majority on the first ballot; two ballots later Lincoln bested pre-convention frontrunner Senator William H. Seward of New York, and thus entered a contest that pitted him once again against Douglas, the candidate of the Northern Democrats (the Democratic party having split over its inability to agree on a nominee satisfactory to both North and South), John C. Breckinridge, Vice President of the United States and standard bearer of the Southern Democrats, and Tennessee's John Bell, nominated by the newly formed Constitutional Unionists. As the Republican cause was unlikely to draw much support in the South, the party and its candidates had to retain the majorities (and pluralities) it had gained over the last four years against Douglas–Lincoln's primary target for the past six years. As Lincoln realized, Republican prospects rested upon the ability to defeat Douglas and the Northern Democrats; should the Republicans sweep to victory in those contests, the party would secure enough votes in the Electoral College to lay claim to the presidency in only its second national election.

[DOCUMENT 3-1]
SPEECH AT CHICAGO, ILLINOIS, MARCH 1, 1859 (EXCERPT)

Although Lincoln failed in his bid to unseat Douglas, his performance in the fall elections confirmed his standing as one of the state's leading Republicans; what follows is taken from a speech he delivered in Chicago following the party's triumph in that day's municipal election.

This much being said on that point, I wish now to add a word that has a bearing on the future. The Republican principle, the profound central truth that slavery is wrong and ought to be dealt with as a wrong, though we are always to remember the fact of its actual existence amongst us and faithfully observe all the constitutional guarantees–the unalterable principle never for a moment to be lost sight of that it is a wrong and ought to be dealt with as such, cannot advance at all upon

Judge Douglas' ground–that there is a portion of the country in which slavery must always exist; that he does not care whether it is voted up or voted down, as it is simply a question of dollars and cents. Whenever, in any compromise or arrangement or combination that may promise some temporary advantage, we are led upon that ground, then and there the great living principle upon which we have organized as a party is surrendered. The proposition now in our minds that this thing is wrong being once driven out and surrendered, then the institution of slavery necessarily becomes national.

One or two words more of what I did not think of when I arose. Suppose it is true that the Almighty has drawn a line across this continent, on the south side of which part of the people will hold the rest as slaves; that the Almighty ordered this; that it is right, unchangeably right, that men ought there to be held as slaves, and that their fellow men will always have the right to hold them as slaves. I ask you, this once admitted, how can you believe that it is not right for us, or for them coming here, to hold slaves on this other side of the line? Once we come to acknowledge that it is right, that it is the law of the Eternal Being, for slavery to exist on one side of that line, have we any sure ground to object to slaves being held on the other side? Once admit the position that a man rightfully holds another man as property on one side of the line, and you must, when it suits his convenience to come to the other side, admit that he has the same right to hold his property there. Once admit Judge Douglas's proposition and we must all finally give way. Although we may not bring ourselves to the idea that it is to our interest to have slaves in this Northern country, we shall soon bring ourselves to admit that, while we may not want them, if any one else does he has the moral right to have them. Step by step–south of the Judge's moral climate line in the States, then in the Territories everywhere, and then in all the States–it is thus that Judge Douglas would lead us inevitably to the nationalization of slavery. Whether by his doctrine of squatter sovereignty, or by the ground taken by him in his recent speeches in Memphis and through the South,–that wherever the climate makes it the interest of the inhabitants to encourage slave property, they will pass a slave code whether it is covertly nationalized, by Congressional legislation, or by the Dred Scott decision, or by the sophistical and misleading doctrine he has last advanced, the same goal is inevitably reached by the one or the other device. It is only travelling to the same place by different roads.

In this direction lies all the danger that now exists to the Republican cause. I take it that so far as concerns forcibly establishing slavery in the Territories by Congressional legislation, or by virtue of the Dred Scott decision, that day has passed. Our only serious danger is that we shall be led upon this ground of Judge Douglas, on the delusive assumption that it is a good way of whipping our opponents, when in fact, it is a way that leads straight to final surrender. The Republican party should not dally with Judge Douglas when it knows where his proposition and his leadership would take us, nor be disposed to listen to it because it was best somewhere else to support somebody occupying his ground. That is no just reason why we ought to go over to Judge Douglas, as we were called upon to do last year. Never forget that we have before us this whole matter of the right or wrong of slavery in this Union, though the immediate question is as to its spreading out into new Territories and States.

I do not wish to be misunderstood upon this subject of slavery in this country. I suppose it may long exist, and perhaps the best way for it to come to an end peaceably is for it to exist for a length of time. But I say that the spread and strengthening and perpetuation of it is an entirely different proposition. There we should in every way resist it as a wrong, treating it as a wrong, with the fixed idea that it must and will come to an end. If we do not allow ourselves to be allured from the strict path of our duty by such a device as shifting our ground and throwing ourselves into the rear of a leader who denies our first principle, denies that there is an absolute wrong in the institution of slavery, then the future of the Republican cause is safe and victory is assured. You Republicans of Illinois have deliberately taken your ground; you have heard the whole subject discussed again and again; you have stated your faith, in platforms laid down in a State Convention, and in a National Convention; you have heard and talked over and considered it until you are now all of opinion that you are on a ground of unquestionable right. All you have to do is to keep the faith, to remain steadfast to the right, to stand by your banner. Nothing should lead you to leave your guns. Stand together, ready, with match in hand. Allow nothing to turn you to the right or to the left. Remember how long you have been in setting out on the true course; how long you have been in getting your neighbors to understand and believe as you now do. Stand by your principles; stand by your guns; and victory complete and permanent is sure at the last.

[DOCUMENT 3-2]
SPEECH AT CINCINNATI, OHIO, SEPTEMBER 17, 1859 (EXCERPTS)

In 1859 Ohio Republicans invited Lincoln to campaign in their state for Republican candidates to counter a speech-making tour by Douglas on behalf of fellow Democrats. The invitation itself testified to Lincoln's growing reputation; the speeches added to his political stature. Lincoln also accepted invitations to speak in several other states during the fall contests.

I understand that you have had recently with you, my very distinguished friend, Judge Douglas, of Illinois, (laughter) and I understand, without having had an opportunity, (not greatly sought to be sure,) of seeing a report of the speech, that he made here, that he did me the honor to mention my humble name. I suppose that he did so for the purpose of making some objection to some sentiment at some time expressed by me. I should expect, it is true, that Judge Douglas had reminded you, or informed you, if you had never before heard it, that I had once in my life declared it as my opinion that this government cannot "endure permanently half slave and half free; that a house divided against itself cannot stand," and, as I had expressed it, I did not expect the house to fall; that I did not expect the Union to be dissolved; but, that I did expect that it would cease to be divided; that it would become all one thing or all the other, that either the opponents of Slavery would arrest the further spread of it, and place it where the public mind would rest in the belief that it was in the course of ultimate extinction; or the friends of Slavery will push it forward until it becomes alike lawful in all the States, old or new, Free as well as Slave. I did, fifteen months ago, express that opinion, and upon many occasions Judge Douglas has denounced it, and has greatly, intentionally or unintentionally, misrepresented my purpose in the expression of that opinion.

I presume, without having seen a report of his speech, that he did so here. I presume that he alluded also to that opinion in different language, having been expressed at a subsequent time by Governor Seward of New York, and that he took the two in a lump and denounced them; that he tried to point out that there was something couched in this opinion which led to the making of an entire uniformity of the local institutions of the various States of the Union, in utter disregard of the different States, which in their nature would seem to require a variety of institutions, and a variety of laws, conforming to the differences in the nature of the different States.

Not only so; I presume he insisted that this was a declaration of war between the Free and Slave States—that it was the sounding to the onset of continual war between the different States, the Slave and Free States.

This charge, in this form, was made by Judge Douglas on, I believe, the 9th of July, 1858, in Chicago, in my hearing. On the next evening, I made some reply to it. I informed him that many of the inferences he drew from that expression of mine were altogether foreign to any purpose entertained by me, and in so far as he should ascribe those inferences to me, as my purpose, he was entirely mistaken; and in so far as he might argue that whatever might be my purpose, actions, conforming to my views, would lead to these results, he might argue and establish if he could; but, so far as purposes were concerned, he was totally mistaken as to me.

When I made that reply to him—when I told him, on the question of declaring war between the different States of the Union, that I had not said I did not expect any peace upon this question until Slavery was exterminated; that I had only said I expected peace when that institution was put where the public mind should rest in the belief that it was in course of ultimate extinction; that I believed from the organization of our government, until a very recent period of time, the institution had been placed and continued upon such a basis; that we had had comparative peace upon that question through a portion of that period of time, only because the public mind rested in that belief in regard to it, and that when we returned to that position in relation to that matter, I supposed we should again have peace as we previously had. I assured him, as I now assure you, that I neither then had, nor have, or ever had, any purpose in any way of interfering with the institution of Slavery, where it exists. [Long continued applause.] I believe we have no power, under the Constitution of the United States; or rather under the form of government under which we live, to interfere with the institution of Slavery, or any other of the institutions of our sister States, be they Free or Slave States. [Cries of "Good," and applause.] I declared then and I now re-declare, that I have as little inclination to so interfere with the institution of Slavery where it now exists, through the instrumentality of the general Government, or any other instrumentality, as I believe we have no power to do so.

***

I will tell you, so far as I am authorized to speak for the Opposition, what we mean to do with you. We mean to treat you as near as we possibly can, like Washington, Jefferson and Madison treated you. [Cheers] We mean to leave you alone, and in no way to interfere with your institution; to abide by all and every compromise of the constitution, and, in a word, coming back to the original proposition, to treat you, so far as degenerated men (if we have degenerated) may, according to the examples of those noble fathers–Washington, Jefferson and Madison. [Applause] We mean to remember that you are as good as we; that there is no difference between us other than the difference of circumstances. We mean to recognise and bear in mind always that you have as good hearts in your bosoms as other people, or as we claim to have, and treat you accordingly. We mean to marry your girls when we have a chance–the white ones I mean–[laughter] and I have the honor to inform you that I once did have a chance in that way. [A voice, "Good for you," and applause]

I have told you what we mean to do. I want to know, now, when that thing takes place, what you mean to do. I often hear it intimated that you mean to divide the Union whenever a Republican, or anything like it, is elected President of the United States. [A voice, "That is so."] "That is so," one of them says. I wonder if he is a Kentuckian? [A voice, "He is a Douglas man."] Well, then, I want to know what you are going to do with your half of it? [Applause and laughter] Are you going to split the Ohio down through, and push your half off a piece? Or are you going to keep it right alongside of us outrageous fellows? Or are you going to build up a wall some way between your country and ours, by which that moveable property of yours can't come over here any more, to the danger of your losing it? Do you think you can better yourselves on that subject, by leaving us here under no obligation whatever to return those specimens of your moveable property that come hither? You have divided the Union because we would not do right with you as you think, upon that subject; when we cease to be under obligations to do anything for you, how much better off do you think you will be? Will you make war upon us and kill us all? Why, gentlemen, I think you are as gallant and as brave men as live; that you can fight as bravely in a good cause, man for man, as any other people living; that you have shown yourselves capable of this upon various occasions; but, man for man, you are not better than we are, and there are not so many of you as there are of us. [Loud cheering.] You will never make much of a hand at whipping us. If we were fewer in numbers than you, I think that you could whip us; if we were equal it would likely be a drawn battle; but being inferior in numbers, you will make nothing by attempting to master us.

I have taken upon myself in the name of some of you to say, that we expect upon these principles to ultimately beat them. In order to do so, I think we want and must have a national policy in regard to the institution of slavery, that acknowledges and deals with that institution as being wrong. (Loud cheering) Whoever desires the prevention of the spread of slavery and the nationalization of that institution, yields all, when he yields to any policy that either recognizes slavery as being right, or as being an indifferent thing. Nothing will make you successful but setting up a policy which shall treat the thing as being wrong. When I say this, I do not mean to say that this general government is charged with the duty of redressing or preventing all the wrongs in the world; but I do think that it is charged with the duty of preventing and redressing all wrongs which are wrongs to itself. This government is expressly charged with the duty of providing for the general welfare. We believe that the spreading out and perpetuity of the institution of slavery impairs the general welfare. We believe—nay, we know, that that is the only thing that has ever threatened the perpetuity of the Union itself. The only thing which has ever menaced the destruction of the government under which we live, is this very thing. To repress this thing, we think is providing for the general welfare. Our friends in Kentucky differ from us. We need not make our argument for them, but we who think it is wrong in all its relations, or in some of them at least, must decide as to our own actions, and our own course, upon our own judgment.

I say that we must not interfere with the institution of slavery in the states where it exists, because the constitution forbids it, and the general welfare does not require us to do so. We must not withhold an efficient fugitive slave law because the constitution requires us, as I understand it, not to withhold such a law. But we must prevent the outspreading of the institution, because neither the constitution nor general welfare requires us to extend it. We must prevent the revival of the African slave trade and the enacting by Congress of a territorial slave code. We must prevent each of these things being done by either Congresses or courts. The people of these United States are the rightful masters of both Congresses and courts (Applause) not to overthrow the constitution, but to overthrow the men who pervert that constitution.

[DOCUMENT 3-3]
ADDRESS AT COOPER INSTITUTE, NEW YORK CITY,
FEBRUARY 27, 1860

Lincoln accepted an invitation to speak at the Reverend Henry Ward Beecher's Plymouth Church in Brooklyn, New York, in February 1860; he would take advantage of the trip east to make other speeches as he made his way to New Hampshire to visit his eldest son, Robert, then a student at Phillips Exeter Academy. A group of New York Republicans, anxious to head off the presidential candidacy of Senator William H. Seward of New York, assumed control of the event and transferred its location to Manhattan's Cooper Union. Lincoln used the opportunity to offer his most detailed analysis of what the framers of the Constitution and members of the First Congress intended to do about slavery, to place the Republican party in that tradition, and to counter critics of the party.

On October 17, 1859, abolitionist John Brown led an attempt to instigate a slave uprising by seizing the federal arsenal at Harpers Ferry, Virginia. The raid failed, and Brown was executed on December 2.

MR. PRESIDENT AND FELLOW-CITIZENS OF NEW-YORK:–
The facts with which I shall deal this evening are mainly old and familiar; nor is there anything new in the general use I shall make of them. If there shall be any novelty, it will be in the mode of presenting the facts, and the inferences and observations following that presentation.

In his speech last autumn, at Columbus, Ohio, as reported in "The New-York Times," Senator Douglas said:

"Our fathers, when they framed the Government under which we live, understood this question just as well, end even better, than we do now."

I fully indorse this, and I adopt it as a text for this discourse. I so adopt it because it furnishes a precise and an agreed starting point for a discussion between Republicans and that wing of the Democracy headed by Senator Douglas. It simply leaves the inquiry: *"What was the understanding those fathers had of the question mentioned?"*

What is the frame of Government under which we live?

The answer must be: "The Constitution of the United States." That Constitution consists of the original, framed in 1787, (and under which the present government first went into operation,) and twelve subsequently framed amendments, the first ten of which were framed in 1789.

Who were our fathers that framed the Constitution? I suppose the "thirty-nine" who signed the original instrument may be fairly called our fathers who framed that part of the present Government. It is almost exactly true to say they framed it, and it is altogether true to say they fairly represented the opinion and sentiment of the whole nation at that time. Their names, being familiar to nearly all, and accessible to quite all, need not now be repeated.

I take these "thirty-nine" for the present, as being "our fathers who framed the Government under which we live."

What is the question which, according to the text, those fathers understood "just as well, and even better than we do now?"

It is this: Does the proper division of local from federal authority, or anything in the Constitution, forbid *our Federal Government* to control as to slavery in *our Federal Territories?*

Upon this, Senator Douglas holds the affirmative, and Republicans the negative. This affirmation and denial form an issue; and this issue—this question—is precisely what the text declares our fathers understood "better than we."

Let us now inquire whether the "thirty-nine," or any of them, ever acted upon this question; and if they did, how they acted upon it—how they expressed that better understanding?

In 1784, three years before the Constitution—the United States then owning the Northwestern Territory, and no other, the Congress of the Confederation had before them the question of prohibiting slavery in that Territory; and four of the "thirty-nine," who afterward framed the Constitution, were in that Congress, and voted on that question. Of these, Roger Sherman, Thomas Mifflin, and Hugh Williamson voted for the prohibition, thus showing that, in their understanding, no line dividing local from federal authority, nor anything else, properly forbade the Federal Government to control as to slavery in federal territory. The other of the four—James M'Henry—voted against the prohibition, showing that, for some cause, he thought it improper to vote for it.

In 1787, still before the Constitution, but while the Convention was in session framing it, and while the Northwestern Territory still was the only territory owned by the United States, the same question of prohibiting slavery in the territory again came before the Congress of the Confederation; and two more of the "thirty-nine" who afterward signed the Constitution, were in that Congress, and voted on the question. They were William Blount and William Few; and they both voted for the prohibition—thus showing that, in their understanding, no line dividing local from federal authority, nor anything else, properly forbade the Federal Government to control as to slavery in federal territory. This time the prohibition became a law, being part of what is now well known as the Ordinance of '87.

The question of federal control of slavery in the territories, seems not to have been directly before the Convention which framed the original Constitution; and hence it is not recorded that the "thirty-nine," or any of them, while engaged on that instrument, expressed any opinion of that precise question.

In 1789, by the first Congress which sat under the Constitution, an act was passed to enforce the Ordinance of '87, including the prohibition of slavery in the Northwestern Territory. The bill for this act was reported by one of the "thirty-nine," Thomas Fitzsimmons, then a member of the House of Representatives from Pennsylvania. It went through all its stages without a word of opposition, and finally passed both branches without yeas and nays, which is equivalent to an unanimous passage. In this Congress there were sixteen of the thirty-nine fathers who framed the original Constitution. They were John Langdon, Nicholas Gilman, Wm. S. Johnson, Roger Sherman, Robert Morris, Thos. Fitzsimmons, William Few, Abraham Baldwin, Rufus King, William Paterson, George Clymer, Richard Bassett, George Read, Pierce Butler, Daniel Carroll, James Madison.

This shows that, in their understanding, no line dividing local from federal authority, nor anything in the Constitution, properly forbade Congress to prohibit slavery in the federal territory; else both their fidelity to correct principle, and their oath to support the Constitution, would have constrained them to oppose the prohibition.

Again, George Washington, another of the "thirty-nine," was then President of the United States, and, as such, approved and signed the bill; thus completing its validity as a law, and thus showing that, in his understanding, no line dividing local from federal authority, nor anything in the Constitution, forbade the Federal Government to control as to slavery in federal territory.

No great while after the adoption of the original Constitution, North Carolina ceded to the Federal Government the country now constituting the State of Tennessee; and a few years later Georgia ceded that which now constitutes the States of Mississippi and Alabama. In both deeds of cession it was made a condition by the ceding States that the Federal Government should not prohibit slavery in the ceded country. Besides this, slavery was then actually in the ceded country. Under these circumstances, Congress, on taking charge of these countries, did not absolutely prohibit slavery within them. But they did interfere with it–take control of it–even there, to a certain extent. In 1798, Congress organized the Territory of Mississippi. In the act of organization, they prohibited the bringing of slaves into the Territory, from any place without the United States, by fine, and giving freedom to slaves so brought. This act passed both branches of Congress without yeas and nays. In that Congress were three of the "thirty-nine" who framed the original Constitution. They were John Langdon, George Read and Abraham Baldwin. They all, probably, voted for it. Certainly they would have placed their opposition to it upon record, if, in their understanding, any line dividing local from federal authority, or anything in the Constitution, properly forbade the Federal Government to control as to slavery in federal territory.

In 1803, the Federal Government purchased the Louisiana country. Our former territorial acquisitions came from certain of our own States; but this Louisiana country was acquired from a foreign nation. In 1804, Congress gave a territorial organization to that part of it which now constitutes the State of Louisiana. New Orleans, lying within that part, was an old and comparatively large city. There were other considerable towns and settlements, and slavery was extensively and thoroughly intermingled with the people. Congress did not, in the Territorial Act, prohibit slavery; but they did interfere with it—take control of it—in a more marked and extensive way than they did in the case of Mississippi. The substance of the provision therein made, in relation to slaves, was:

First. That no slave should be imported into the territory from foreign parts.

Second. That no slave should be carried into it who had been imported into the United States since the first day of May, 1798.

Third. That no slave should be carried into it, except by the owner, and for his own use as a settler; the penalty in all the cases being a fine upon the violator of the law, and freedom to the slave.

This act also was passed without yeas and nays. In the Congress which passed it, there were two of the "thirty-nine." They were Abraham Baldwin and Jonathan Dayton. As stated in the case of Mississippi, it is probable they both voted for it. They would not have allowed it to pass without recording their opposition to it, if, in their understanding, it violated either the line properly dividing local from federal authority, or any provision of the Constitution.

In 1819–20, came and passed the Missouri question. Many votes were taken, by yeas and nays, in both branches of Congress, upon the various phases of the general question. Two of the "thirty-nine"—Rufus King and Charles Pinckney—were members of that Congress. Mr. King steadily voted for slavery prohibition and against all compromises, while Mr. Pinckney as steadily voted against slavery prohibition and against all compromises. By this, Mr. King showed that, in his understanding, no line dividing local from federal authority, nor anything in the Constitution, was violated by Congress prohibiting slavery in federal territory; while Mr. Pinckney, by his votes, showed that, in his understanding, there was some sufficient reason for opposing such prohibition in that case.

The cases I have mentioned are the only acts of the "thirty-nine," or of any of them, upon the direct issue, which I have been able to discover.

To enumerate the persons who thus acted, as being four in 1784, two in 1787, seventeen in 1789, three in 1798, two in 1804, and two in 1819–20—there would be thirty of them. But this would be counting John Langdon, Roger Sherman, William Few, Rufus King, and George Read, each twice, and Abraham Baldwin, three times. The true number of those of the "thirty-nine" whom I have shown to have acted upon the question, which, by the text, they understood better than we, is twenty-three, leaving sixteen not shown to have acted upon it in any way.

Here, then, we have twenty-three out of our thirty-nine fathers "who framed the Government under which we live," who have, upon their official responsibility and their corporal oaths, acted upon the very question which the text affirms they "understood just as well, and even better than we do now;" and twenty-one of them—a clear majority of the whole "thirty-nine"—so acting upon it as to make them guilty of gross political impropriety and wilful perjury, if, in their understanding, any proper division between local and federal authority, or anything in the Constitution they had made themselves, and sworn to support, forbade the Federal Government to control as to slavery in the federal territories. Thus the twenty-one acted; and, as actions speak louder than words, so actions, under such responsibility, speak still louder.

Two of the twenty-three voted against Congressional prohibition of slavery in the federal territories, in the instances in which they acted upon the question. But for what reasons they so voted is not known. They may have done so because they thought a proper division of local from federal authority, or some provision or principle of the Constitution, stood in the way; or they may, without any such question, have voted against the prohibition, on what appeared to them to be sufficient grounds of expediency. No one who has sworn to support the Constitution, can conscientiously vote for what he understands to be an unconstitutional measure, however expedient he may think it; but one may and ought to vote against a measure which he deems constitutional, if, at the same time, he deems it inexpedient. It, therefore, would be unsafe to set down even the two who voted against the prohibition, as having done so because, in their understanding, any proper division of local from federal authority, or anything in the Constitution, forbade the Federal Government to control as to slavery in federal territory.

The remaining sixteen of the "thirty-nine," so far as I have discovered, have left no record of their understanding upon the direct question of federal control of slavery in the federal territories. But there is much reason to believe that their understanding upon that question would not have appeared different from that of their twenty-three compeers, had it been manifested at all.

For the purpose of adhering rigidly to the text, I have purposely omitted whatever understanding may have been manifested by any person, however distinguished, other than the thirty-nine fathers who framed the original Constitution; and, for the same reason, I have also omitted whatever understanding may have been manifested by any of the "thirty-nine" even, on any other phase of the general question of slavery. If we should look into their acts and declarations on those other phases, as the foreign slave trade, and the morality and policy of slavery generally, it would appear to us that on the direct question of federal control of slavery in federal territories, the sixteen, if they had acted at all, would probably have acted just as the twenty-three did. Among that sixteen were several of the most noted anti-slavery men of those times—as Dr. Franklin, Alexander Hamilton and Gouverneur Morris—while there was not one now known to have been otherwise, unless it may be John Rutledge, of South Carolina.

The sum of the whole is, that of our thirty-nine fathers who framed the original Constitution, twenty-one—a clear majority of the whole—certainly understood that no proper division of local from federal authority, nor any part of the Constitution, forbade the Federal Government to control slavery in the federal territories; while all the rest probably had the same understanding. Such, unquestionably, was the understanding of our fathers who framed the original Constitution; and the text affirms that they understood the question "better than we."

But, so far, I have been considering the understanding of the question manifested by the framers of the original Constitution. In and by the original instrument, a mode was provided for amending it; and, as I have already stated, the present frame of "the Government under which we live" consists of that original, and twelve amendatory articles framed and adopted since. Those who now insist that federal control of slavery in federal territories violates the Constitution, point us to the provisions which they suppose it thus violates; and, as I understand, they all fix upon provisions in these amendatory articles, and not in the original instrument. The Supreme Court, in the Dred Scott case, plant themselves upon the fifth amendment, which provides that no person shall be deprived of "life, liberty or property without due process of law;" while Senator Douglas and his peculiar adherents plant themselves upon the tenth amendment, providing that "the powers not delegated to the United States by the Constitution," "are reserved to the States respectively, or to the people."

Now, it so happens that these amendments were framed by the first Congress which sat under the Constitution–the identical Congress which passed the act already mentioned, enforcing the prohibition of slavery in the Northwestern Territory. Not only was it the same Congress, but they were the identical, same individual men who, at the same session, and at the same time within the session, had under consideration, and in progress toward maturity, these Constitutional amendments, and this act prohibiting slavery in all the territory the nation then owned. The Constitutional amendments were introduced before, and passed after the act enforcing the Ordinance of '87; so that, during the whole pendency of the act to enforce the Ordinance, the Constitutional amendments were also pending.

The seventy-six members of that Congress, including sixteen of the framers of the original Constitution, as before stated, were preeminently our fathers who framed that part of "the Government under which we live," which is now claimed as forbidding the Federal Government to control slavery in the federal territories.

Is it not a little presumptuous in any one at this day to affirm that the two things which that Congress deliberately framed, and carried to maturity at the same time, are absolutely inconsistent with each other? And does not such affirmation become impudently absurd when coupled with the other affirmation from the same mouth, that those who did the two things, alleged to be inconsistent, understood whether they really were inconsistent better than we–better than he who affirms that they are inconsistent?

It is surely safe to assume that the thirty-nine framers of the original Constitution, and the seventy-six members of the Congress which framed the amendments thereto, taken together, do certainly include those who may be fairly called "our fathers who framed the Government under which we live." And so assuming, I defy any man to show that any one of them ever, in his whole life, declared that, in his understanding, any proper division of local from federal authority, or any part of the Constitution, forbade the Federal Government to control as to slavery in the federal territories. I go a step further. I defy any one to show that any living man in the whole world ever did, prior to the beginning of the present century, (and I might almost say prior to the beginning of the last half of the present century,) declare that, in his understanding, any proper division of local from federal authority, or any part of the Constitution, forbade the Federal Government to control as to slavery in the federal territories. To those who now so declare, I give, not only "our fathers who framed the Government under which we live," but with them all other living men within the century in which it was framed, among whom to search, and they shall not be able to find the evidence of a single man agreeing with them.

Now, and here, let me guard a little against being misunderstood. I do not mean to say we are bound to follow implicitly in whatever our fathers did. To do so, would be to discard all the lights of current experience—to reject all progress—all improvement. What I do say is, that if we would supplant the opinions and policy of our fathers in any case, we should do so upon evidence so conclusive, and argument so clear, that even their great authority, fairly considered and weighed, cannot stand; and most surely not in a case whereof we ourselves declare they understood the question better than we.

If any man at this day sincerely believes that a proper division of local from federal authority, or any part of the Constitution, forbids the Federal Government to control as to slavery in the federal territories, he is right to say so, and to enforce his position by all truthful evidence and fair argument which he can. But he has no right to mislead others, who have less access to history, and less leisure to study it, into the false belief that "our fathers, who framed the Government under which we live," were of the same opinion—thus substituting falsehood and deception for truthful evidence and fair argument. If any man at this day sincerely believes "our fathers who framed the Government under which we live," used and applied principles, in other cases, which ought to have led them to understand that a proper division of local from federal authority or some part of the Constitution, forbids the Federal Government to control as to slavery in the federal territories, he is right to say so. But he should, at the same time, brave the responsibility of declaring that, in his opinion, he understands their principles better than they did themselves; and especially should he not shirk that responsibility by asserting that they "understood the question just as well, and even better, than we do now."

But enough! *Let all who believe that "our fathers, who framed the Government under which we live, understood this question just as well, end even better, than we do now," speak as they spoke, and act as they acted upon it. This is all Republicans ask—all Republicans desire—in relation to slavery. As those fathers marked it, so let it be again marked, as an evil not to be extended, but to be tolerated and protected only because of and so far as its actual presence among us makes that toleration and protection a necessity. Let all the guaranties those fathers gave it, be, not grudgingly, but fully and fairly maintained.* For this Republicans contend, and with this, so far as I know or believe, they will be content.

And now, if they would listen—as I suppose they will not—I would address a few words to the Southern people.

I would say to them:—You consider yourselves a reasonable and a just people; and I consider that in the general qualities of reason and justice you are not inferior to any other people. Still, when you speak of us Republicans, you do so only to denounce us as reptiles, or, at the best, as no better than outlaws. You will grant a hearing to pirates or murderers, but nothing like it to "Black Republicans." In all your contentions with one another, each of you deems an unconditional condemnation of "Black Republicanism" as the first thing to be attended to. Indeed, such condemnation of us seems to be an indispensable prerequisite—license, so to speak—among you to be admitted or permitted to speak at all. Now, can you, or not, be prevailed upon to pause and to consider whether this is quite just to us, or even to yourselves? Bring forward your charges and specifications, and then be patient long enough to hear us deny or justify.

You say we are sectional. We deny it. That makes an issue; and the burden of proof is upon you. You produce your proof; and what is it? Why, that our party has no existence in your section—gets no votes in your section. The fact is substantially true; but does it prove the issue? If it does, then in case we should, without change of principle, begin to get votes in your section, we should thereby cease to be sectional. You cannot escape this conclusion; and yet, are you willing to abide by it? If you are, you will probably soon find that we have ceased to be sectional, for we shall get votes in your section this very year. You will then begin to discover, as the truth plainly is, that your proof does not touch the issue. The fact that we get no votes in your section, is a fact of your making, and not of ours. And if there be fault in that fact, that fault is primarily yours, and remains so until you show that we repel you by some wrong principle or practice. If we do repel you by any wrong principle or practice, the fault is ours; but this brings you to where you ought to have started—to a discussion of the right or wrong of our principle. If our principle, put in practice, would wrong your section for the benefit of ours, or for any other object, then our principle, and we with it, are sectional, and are justly opposed and denounced as such. Meet us, then, on the question of whether our principle, put in practice, would wrong your section; and so meet us as if it were possible that something may be said on our side. Do you accept the challenge? No! Then you really believe that the principle which "our fathers who framed the Government under which we live" thought so clearly right as to adopt it, and indorse it again and again, upon their official oaths, is in fact so clearly wrong as to demand your condemnation without a moment's consideration.

Some of you delight to flaunt in our faces the warning against sectional parties given by Washington in his Farewell Address. Less than eight years before Washington gave that warning, he had, as President of the United States, approved and signed an act of Congress, enforcing the prohibition of slavery in the Northwestern Territory, which act embodied the policy of the Government upon that subject up to and at the very moment he penned that warning; and about one year after he penned it, he wrote La Fayette that he considered that prohibition a wise measure, expressing in the same connection his hope that we should at some time have a confederacy of free States.

Bearing this in mind, and seeing that sectionalism has since arisen upon this same subject, is that warning a weapon in your hands against us, or in our hands against you? Could Washington himself speak, would he cast the blame of that sectionalism upon us, who sustain his policy, or upon you who repudiate it? We respect that warning of Washington, and we commend it to you, together with his example pointing to the right application of it.

But you say you are conservative—eminently conservative—while we are revolutionary, destructive, or something of the sort. What is conservatism? Is it not adherence to the old and tried, against the new and untried? We stick to, contend for, the identical old policy on the point in controversy which was adopted by "our fathers who framed the Government under which we live;" while you with one accord reject, and scout, and spit upon that old policy, and insist upon substituting something new. True, you disagree among yourselves as to what that substitute shall be. You are divided on new propositions and plans, but you are unanimous in rejecting and denouncing the old policy of the fathers. Some of you are for reviving the foreign slave trade; some for a Congressional Slave-Code for the Territories; some for Congress forbidding the Territories to prohibit Slavery within their limits; some for maintaining Slavery in the Territories through the judiciary; some for the "gur-reat pur-rinciple" that "if one man would enslave another, no third man should object," fantastically called "Popular Sovereignty;" but never a man among you in favor of federal prohibition of slavery in federal territories, according to the practice of "our fathers who framed the Government under which we live." Not one of all your various plans can show a precedent or an advocate in the century within which our Government originated. Consider, then, whether your claim of conservatism for yourselves, and your charge of destructiveness against us, are based on the most clear and stable foundations.

Again, you say we have made the slavery question more prominent than it formerly was. We deny it. We admit that it is more prominent, but we deny that we made it so. It was not we, but you, who discarded the old policy of the fathers. We resisted, and still resist, your innovation; and thence comes the greater prominence of the question. Would you have that question reduced to its former proportions? Go back to that old policy. What has been will be again, under the same conditions. If you would have the peace of the old times, readopt the precepts and policy of the old times.

You charge that we stir up insurrections among your slaves. We deny it; and what is your proof? Harper's Ferry! John Brown!! John Brown was no Republican; and you have failed to implicate a single Republican in his Harper's Ferry enterprise. If any member of our party is guilty in that matter, you know it or you do not know it. If you do know it, you are inexcusable for not designating the man and proving the fact. If you do not know it, you are inexcusable for asserting it, and especially for persisting in the assertion after you have tried and failed to make the proof. You need not be told that persisting in a charge which one does not know to be true, is simply malicious slander.

Some of you admit that no Republican designedly aided or encouraged the Harper's Ferry affair; but still insist that our doctrines and declarations necessarily lead to such results. We do not believe it. We know we hold to no doctrine, and make no declaration, which were not held to and made by "our fathers who framed the Government under which we live." You never dealt fairly by us in relation to this affair. When it occurred, some important State elections were near at hand, and you were in evident glee with the belief that, by charging the blame upon us, you could get an advantage of us in those elections. The elections came, and your expectations were not quite fulfilled. Every Republican man knew that, as to himself at least, your charge was a slander, and he was not much inclined by it to cast his vote in your favor. Republican doctrines and declarations are accompanied with a continual protest against any interference whatever with your slaves, or with you about your slaves. Surely, this does not encourage them to revolt. True, we do, in common with "our fathers, who framed the Government under which we live," declare our belief that slavery is wrong; but the slaves do not hear us declare even this. For anything we say or do, the slaves would scarcely know there is a Republican party. I believe they would not, in fact, generally know it but for your misrepresentations of us, in their hearing. In your political contests among yourselves, each faction charges the other with sympathy with Black Republicanism; and then, to give point to the charge, defines Black Republicanism to simply be insurrection, blood and thunder among the slaves.

Slave insurrections are no more common now than they were before the Republican party was organized. What induced the Southampton insurrection, twenty-eight years ago, in which, at least, three times as many lives were lost as at Harper's Ferry? You can scarcely stretch your very elastic fancy to the conclusion that Southampton was "got up by Black Republicanism." In the present state of things in the United States, I do not think a general, or even a very extensive slave insurrection, is possible. The indispensable concert of action cannot be attained. The slaves have no means of rapid communication; nor can incendiary freemen, black or white, supply it. The explosive materials are everywhere in parcels; but there neither are, nor can be supplied, the indispensable connecting trains.

Much is said by Southern people about the affection of slaves for their masters and mistresses; and a part of it, at least, is true. A plot for an uprising could scarcely be devised and communicated to twenty individuals before some one of them, to save the life of a favorite master or mistress, would divulge it. This is the rule; and the slave revolution in Hayti was not an exception to it, but a case occurring under peculiar circumstances. The gunpowder plot of British history, though not connected with slaves, was more in point. In that case, only about twenty were admitted to the secret; and yet one of them, in his anxiety to save a friend, betrayed the plot to that friend, and, by consequence, averted the calamity. Occasional poisonings from the kitchen, and open or stealthy assassinations in the field, and local revolts extending to a score or so, will continue to occur as the natural results of slavery; but no general insurrection of slaves, as I think, can happen in this country for a long time. Whoever much fears, or much hopes for such an event, will be alike disappointed.

In the language of Mr. Jefferson, uttered many years ago, "It is still in our power to direct the process of emancipation, and deportation, peaceably, and in such slow degrees, as that the evil will wear off insensibly; and their places be, *pari passu,* filled up by free white laborers. If, on the contrary, it is left to force itself on, human nature must shudder at the prospect held up.

Mr. Jefferson did not mean to say, nor do I, that the power of emancipation is in the Federal Government. He spoke of Virginia; and, as to the power of emancipation, I speak of the slaveholding States only. The Federal Government, however, as we insist, has the power of restraining the extension of the institution–the power to insure that a slave insurrection shall never occur on any American soil which is now free from slavery.

John Brown's effort was peculiar. It was not a slave insurrection. It was an attempt by white men to get up a revolt among slaves, in which the slaves refused to participate. In fact, it was so absurd that the slaves, with all their ignorance, saw plainly enough it could not succeed. That affair, in its philosophy, corresponds with the many attempts, related in history, at the assassination of kings and emperors. An enthusiast broods over the oppression of a people till he fancies himself commissioned by Heaven to liberate them. He ventures the attempt, which ends in little else than his own execution. Orsini's attempt on Louis Napoleon, and John Brown's attempt at Harper's Ferry were, in their philosophy, precisely the same. The eagerness to cast blame on old England in the one case, and on New England in the other, does not disprove the sameness of the two things.

And how much would it avail you, if you could, by the use of John Brown, Helper's Book, and the like, break up the Republican organization? Human action can be modified to some extent, but human nature cannot be changed. There is a judgment and a feeling against slavery in this nation, which cast at least a million and a half of votes. You cannot destroy that judgment and feeling–that sentiment–by breaking up the political organization which rallies around it. You can scarcely scatter and disperse an army which has been formed into order in the face of your heaviest fire; but if you could, how much would you gain by forcing the sentiment which created it out of the peaceful channel of the ballot-box, into some other channel? What would that other channel probably be? Would the number of John Browns be lessened or enlarged by the operation?

But you will break up the Union rather than submit to a denial of your Constitutional rights.

That has a somewhat reckless sound; but it would be palliated, if not fully justified, were we proposing, by the mere force of numbers, to deprive you of some right, plainly written down in the Constitution. But we are proposing no such thing.

When you make these declarations, you have a specific and well-understood allusion to an assumed Constitutional right of yours, to take slaves into the federal territories, and to hold them there as property. But no such right is specifically written in the Constitution. That instrument is literally silent about any such right. We, on the contrary, deny that such a right has any existence in the Constitution, even by implication.

Your purpose, then, plainly stated, is, that you will destroy the Government, unless you be allowed to construe and enforce the Constitution as you please, on all points in dispute between you and us. You will rule or ruin in all events.

This, plainly stated, is your language. Perhaps you will say the Supreme Court has decided the disputed Constitutional question in your favor. Not quite so. But waiving the lawyer's distinction between dictum and decision, the Court have decided the question for you in a sort of way. The Court have substantially said, it is your Constitutional right to take slaves into the federal territories, and to hold them there as property. When I say the decision was made in a sort of way, I mean it was made in a divided Court, by a bare majority of the Judges, and they not quite agreeing with one another in the reasons for making it; that it is so made as that its avowed supporters disagree with one another about its meaning, and that it was mainly based upon a mistaken statement of fact– the statement in the opinion that "the right of property in a slave is distinctly and expressly affirmed in the Constitution."

An inspection of the Constitution will show that the right of property in a slave is not "*distinctly* and *expressly* affirmed" in it. Bear in mind, the Judges do not pledge their judicial opinion that such right is *impliedly* affirmed in the Constitution; but they pledge their veracity that it is "*distinctly* and *expressly*" affirmed there–"distinctly," that is, not mingled with anything else–"expressly," that is, in words meaning just that, without the aid of any inference, and susceptible of no other meaning.

If they had only pledged their judicial opinion that such right is affirmed in the instrument by implication, it would be open to others to show that neither the word "slave" nor "slavery" is to be found in the Constitution, nor the word "property" even, in any connection with language alluding to the things slave, or slavery, and that wherever in that instrument the slave is alluded to, he is called a "person;"–and wherever his master's legal right in relation to him is alluded to, it is spoken of as "service or labor which may be due,"–as a debt payable in service or labor. Also, it would be open to show, by contemporaneous history, that this mode of alluding to slaves and slavery, instead of speaking of them, was employed on purpose to exclude from the Constitution the idea that there could be property in man.

To show all this, is easy and certain.

When this obvious mistake of the Judges shall be brought to their notice, is it not reasonable to expect that they will withdraw the mistaken statement, and reconsider the conclusion based upon it?

And then it is to be remembered that "our fathers, who framed the Government under which we live"–the men who made the Constitution–decided this same Constitutional question in our favor, long ago–decided it without division among themselves, when making the decision; without division among themselves about the meaning of it after it was made, and, so far as any evidence is left, without basing it upon any mistaken statement of facts.

Under all these circumstances, do you really feel yourselves justified to break up this Government, unless such a court decision as yours is, shall be at once submitted to as a conclusive and final rule of political action? But you will not abide the election of a Republican President! In that supposed event, you say, you will destroy the Union; and then, you say, the great crime of having destroyed it will be upon us! That is cool. A highwayman holds a pistol to my ear, and mutters through his teeth, "Stand and deliver, or I shall kill you, and then you will be a murderer!"

To be sure, what the robber demanded of me–my money–was my own; and I had a clear right to keep it; but it was no more my own than my vote is my own; and the threat of death to me, to extort my money, and the threat of destruction to the Union, to extort my vote, can scarcely be distinguished in principle.

A few words now to Republicans. *It is exceedingly desirable that all parts of this great Confederacy shall be at peace, and in harmony, one with another. Let us Republicans do our part to have it so. Even though much provoked, let us do nothing through passion and ill temper. Even though the southern people will not so much as listen to us, let us calmly consider their demands, and yield to them if, in our deliberate view of our duty, we possibly can.* Judging by all they say and do, and by the subject and nature of their controversy with us, let us determine, if we can, what will satisfy them.

Will they be satisfied if the Territories be unconditionally surrendered to them? We know they will not. In all their present complaints against us, the Territories are scarcely mentioned. Invasions and insurrections are the rage now. Will it satisfy them, if, in the future, we have nothing to do with invasions and insurrections? We know it will not. We so know, because we know we never had anything to do with invasions and insurrections; and yet this total abstaining does not exempt us from the charge and the denunciation.

The question recurs, what will satisfy them? Simply this: We must not only let them alone, but we must, somehow, convince them that we do let them alone. This, we know by experience, is no easy task. We have been so trying to convince them from the very beginning of our organization, but with no success. In all our platforms and speeches we have constantly protested our purpose to let them alone; but this has had no tendency to convince them. Alike unavailing to convince them, is the fact that they have never detected a man of us in any attempt to disturb them.

These natural, and apparently adequate means all failing, what will convince them? This, and this only: cease to call slavery *wrong*, and join them in calling it *right*. And this must be done thoroughly—done in *acts* as well as in *words*. Silence will not be tolerated—we must place ourselves avowedly with them. Senator Douglas's new sedition law must be enacted and enforced, suppressing all declarations that slavery is wrong, whether made in politics, in presses, in pulpits, or in private. We must arrest and return their fugitive slaves with greedy pleasure. We must pull down our Free State constitutions. The whole atmosphere must be disinfected from all taint of opposition to slavery, before they will cease to believe that all their troubles proceed from us.

I am quite aware they do not state their case precisely in this way. Most of them would probably say to us, "Let us alone, *do* nothing to us, and *say* what you please about slavery." But we do let them alone—have never disturbed them—so that, after all, it is what we say, which dissatisfies them. They will continue to accuse us of doing, until we cease saying.

I am also aware they have not, as yet, in terms, demanded the overthrow of our Free-State Constitutions. Yet those Constitutions declare the wrong of slavery, with more solemn emphasis, than do all other sayings against it; and when all these other sayings shall have been silenced, the overthrow of these Constitutions will be demanded, and nothing be left to resist the demand. It is nothing to the contrary, that they do not demand the whole of this just now. Demanding what they do, and for the reason they do, they can voluntarily stop nowhere short of this consummation. Holding, as they do, that slavery is morally right, and socially elevating, they cannot cease to demand a full national recognition of it, as a legal right, and a social blessing.

Nor can we justifiably withhold this, on any ground save our conviction that slavery is wrong. If slavery is right, all words, acts, laws, and constitutions against it, are themselves wrong, and should be silenced, and swept away. If it is right, we cannot justly object to its nationality—its universality; if it is wrong, they cannot justly insist upon its extension—its enlargement. All they ask, we could readily grant, if we thought slavery right; all we ask, they could as readily grant, if they thought it wrong. Their thinking it right, and our thinking it wrong, is the precise fact upon which depends the whole controversy. Thinking it right, as they do, they are not to blame for desiring its full recognition, as being right; but, thinking it wrong, as we do, can we yield to them? Can we cast our votes with their view, and against our own? In view of our moral, social, and political responsibilities, can we do this?

Wrong as we think slavery is, we can yet afford to let it alone where it is, because that much is due to the necessity arising from its actual presence in the nation; but can we, while our votes will prevent it, allow it to spread into the National Territories, and to overrun us here in these Free States? If our sense of duty forbids this, then let us stand by our duty, fearlessly and effectively. Let us be diverted by none of those sophistical contrivances wherewith we are so industriously plied and belabored—contrivances such as groping for some middle ground between the right and the wrong, vain as the search for a man who should be neither a living man nor a dead man—such as a policy of "don't care" on a question about which all true men do care—such as Union appeals beseeching true Union men to yield to Disunionists, reversing the divine rule, and calling, not the sinners, but the righteous to repentance—such as invocations to Washington, imploring men to unsay what Washington said, and undo what Washington did.

Neither let us be slandered from our duty by false accusations against us, nor frightened from it by menaces of destruction to the Government nor of dungeons to ourselves. LET US HAVE FAITH THAT RIGHT MAKES MIGHT, AND IN THAT FAITH, LET US, TO THE END, DARE TO DO OUR DUTY AS WE UNDERSTAND IT.

Preserving the Union, 1860–1862

CHAPTER FOUR

ON THE NIGHT OF NOVEMBER 6, 1860, election returns established that Abraham Lincoln would become the sixteenth president of the United States. Not everyone was willing to abide by that result. During the fall campaign, many white Southerners revived the call for secession raised during the election of 1856, claiming that the South and slavery would not be safe under a Republican president. Disregarding Lincoln's promise not to touch slavery where it already existed because it was protected by the Constitution, advocates of secession portrayed him as an abolitionist bent on destroying the peculiar institution one way or another.

As talk of secession heated up, Congress met. Immediately several leaders offered compromise plans, many of which included provisions preserving the right of slavery to expand into at least some territories. In letters to Republican congressman William Kellogg of Illinois [Document 4-1] and Republican party leader Thurlow Weed [Document 4-3], Lincoln made clear his opposition to any agreement that provided for the expansion of slavery into the territories, while reaffirming his willingness to accept legislation to enforce existing constitutional protections for slavery. Only once did he bend at all from this position, when he told William H. Seward, the senator from New York who had been the front-runner for the 1860 Republican nomination (and who Lincoln had already tapped as his secretary of state), that he was willing to abide a proposal to admit the territory of New Mexico as a state without reference to slavery.[1] To North Carolina's John A. Gilmer, he reiterated his position on slavery and related questions [Document 4-2]; he expressed wonderment about Southern fears as to his intentions to an old fellow Whig, Alexander Stephens, who had served with Lincoln in Congress [Document 4-4]. Nevertheless, as he told Republican congressman James T. Hale of Pennsylvania, he saw secession as little more than blackmail [Document 4-5].

Lincoln left Springfield bound for Washington on February 11, 1861, a day before his fifty-second birthday. By that time seven states already had seceded and other slaveholding states had discussed the possibility of doing so. Moreover, representatives of the seceded states were meeting in Montgomery, Alabama, to establish a new slaveholding republic, headed by Jefferson Davis and none other than Alexander Stephens as provisional president and vice president, respectively. While the news must have suggested to Lincoln the seriousness of the crisis, he was not sure how to respond. As he made his way to Washington, he offered a series of speeches in which he fumbled in discussing the secession crisis, managing to intensify concerns while making light of the possibility of war—demonstrating the wisdom of his earlier commitment to make no public statements and his well-founded uneasiness about making extemporaneous remarks. He thus took the opportunity of his first inaugural address [Document 4-6] to offer his well-considered views on the present crisis in a document designed to reassure Southern whites that they had nothing to fear from him while reminding them and everyone else that he would not accept secession.

For nearly six weeks the new president explored various ways to avert war without accepting disunion, but eventually he accepted the risk of war in deciding to resupply the United States garrison holding Fort Sumter, located in the harbor of Charleston, South Carolina. In response, Confederate forces opened fire on the fort early on the morning of April 12, 1861. Upon hearing the news of the fort's capitulation, Lincoln called for the formation of a 75,000-man volunteer militia to put down the "insurrection"; this in turn helped advocates of secession carry the day in Virginia, North Carolina, Tennessee, and Arkansas, although in each case the news of Fort Sumter alone tipped the scales in favor of that course of action. In four other states, secession failed to carry the day, although not without a struggle in Missouri, Maryland, and Kentucky. By the time Congress convened in special session on July 4, 1861, preparations for war were well underway, spurred by a series of minor engagements. Lincoln greeted Congress with a special message [Document 4-7], which in emphasis, tone, and function bears comparison with his inaugural remarks made exactly four months previous.

During the first year of the war Lincoln was careful to avoid doing anything to justify charges that he was waging a war of abolition. His restraint was explained by a combination of his understanding of the constitutional powers of the presidency in particular and the federal government in general concerning slavery, the need to pacify the border states in order to retain their allegiance, and a desire to revive and cultivate unionist sentiment in the seceded states by refraining from an attack on slavery. These notions gained clear expression in his decision to revoke General John C. Frémont's orders providing for the emancipation of secessionist slaveholders' slaves in Missouri under the auspices of martial law. Lincoln explained his reasoning in a letter to fellow Illinois politician Orville H. Browning [Document 4-8]. However, he was willing to set forth a plan of gradual and compensated emancipation followed by the voluntary colonization of freed blacks in his first annual message to Congress in December [Document 4-9], noting that Congress had already provided for the confiscation of slaves who had been employed in support of the Confederacy. In March 1862, he built on that proposal with a special message calling for the adoption of a plan of gradual and compensated emancipation [Document 4-10], reminding critics that the sum thus allocated to reimburse former slaveholders in the loyal border states and the District of Columbia would be less than the cost of three months of war. It was thus with some delight in April 1862 that he approved legislation abolishing slavery in the District of Columbia because it embraced the principles of compensation and colonization. That he was not willing to move any faster toward emancipation became evident the following month, when he revoked another general's attempt to declare emancipation as part of the imposition of martial law [Document 4-11]; however, a careful reading of the entire document reveals that he was already contemplating the prospects of doing so.

---

1. Lincoln to William H. Seward, February 1, 1861, in Fehrenbacher, *Lincoln: Speeches and Writings,* 2:197–198. The territory of New Mexico was much larger than the boundaries of the present-day state, including what is now Arizona and parts of Nevada and Colorado; the proposal to admit it as a state came from Republicans who correctly anticipated that white Southerners would oppose it. However, Lincoln also claimed that on "the question of extending slavery under the national auspices," he was "inflexible" in his opposition: "I am for no compromise which *assists* or *permits* the extension of the institution on soil owned by the nation."

[DOCUMENT 4-1]
TO WILLIAM KELLOGG, DECEMBER 11, 1860

Learning that proposals providing for a compromise on the issue of slavery in the territories were circulating throughout Congress in December 1860, Lincoln made his wishes known to one Illinois Republican representative. While he was unhappy with the present Fugitive Slave Law, passed in 1850, Lincoln believed that a revised law would be consistent with constitutional provisions for the recovery of fugitive slaves.

Private & confidential.
Hon. William Kellogg.   Springfield, Ills.
My dear Sir—   Dec. 11. 1860
    Entertain no proposition for a compromise in regard to the *extension* of slavery. The instant you do, they have us under again; all our labor is lost, and sooner or later must be done over. Douglas is sure to be again trying to bring in his "Pop. Sov." Have none of it. The tug has to come & better now than later.
    You know I think the fugitive slave clause of the constitution ought to be enforced—to put it on the mildest form, ought not to be resisted.
In haste Yours as ever   A. Lincoln

[DOCUMENT 4-2]
TO JOHN A. GILMER, DECEMBER 15, 1860

John A. Gilmer of North Carolina had been a prominent Whig politician; Lincoln considered including him in his initial cabinet. However, Gilmer pressed for federal protection of slavery in the territories, a position unacceptable to the president-elect.

Strictly confidential.
Hon. John A. Gilmer: Springfield, Ill. Dec 15, 1860.
    My dear Sir—Yours of the 10th is received. I am greatly disinclined to write a letter on the subject embraced in yours; and I would not do so, even privately as I do, were it not that I fear you might misconstrue my silence. Is it desired that I shall shift the ground upon which I have been elected? I can not do it. You need only to acquaint yourself with that ground, and press it on the attention of the South. It is all in print and easy of access. May I be pardoned if I ask whether even you have

ever attempted to procure the reading of the Republican platform, or my speeches, by the Southern people? If not, what reason have I to expect that any additional production of mine would meet a better fate? It would make me appear as if I repented for the crime of having been elected, and was anxious to apologize and beg forgiveness. To so represent me, would be the principal use made of any letter I might now thrust upon the public. My old record cannot be so used; and that is precisely the reason that some new declaration is so much sought.

Now, my dear sir, be assured, that I am not questioning *your* candor; I am only pointing out, that, while a new letter would hurt the cause which I think a just one, you can quite as well effect every patriotic object with the old record. Carefully read pages 18, 19, 74, 75, 88, 89, & 267 of the volume of Joint Debates between Senator Douglas and myself, with the Republican Platform adopted at Chicago, and all your questions will be substantially answered. I have no thought of recommending the abolition of slavery in the District of Columbia, nor the slave trade among the slave states, even on the conditions indicated; and if I were to make such recommendation, it is quite clear Congress would not follow it.

As to employing slaves in Arsenals and Dockyards, it is a thing I never thought of in my life, to my recollection, till I saw your letter; and I may say of it, precisely as I have said of the two points above.

As to the use of patronage in the slave states, where there are few or no Republicans, I do not expect to inquire for the politics of the appointee, or whether he does or not own slaves. I intend in that matter to accommodate the people in the several localities, if they themselves will allow me to accommodate them. In one word, I never have been, am not now, and probably never shall be, in a mood of harassing the people, either North or South.

On the territorial question, I am inflexible, as you see my position in the book. On that, there is a difference between you and us; and it is the only substantial difference. You think slavery is right and ought to be extended; we think it is wrong and ought to be restricted. For this, neither has any just occasion to be angry with the other.

As to the state laws, mentioned in your sixth question, I really know very little of them. I never have read one. If any of them are in conflict with the fugitive slave clause, or any other part of the constitution, I certainly should be glad of their repeal; but I could hardly be justified, as a citizen of Illinois, or as President of the United States, to recommend the repeal of a statute of Vermont, or South Carolina.

With the assurance of my highest regards I subscribe myself
Your obt. Servt.,

A. Lincoln

P.S. The documents referred to, I suppose you will readily find in Washington.   A. L.

[DOCUMENT 4-3]
TO THURLOW WEED, DECEMBER 17, 1860

Thurlow Weed of New York had been the campaign manager for Lincoln's main rival of the 1860 Republican presidential nomination; at present he was contemplating calling for a meeting of state governors to discuss the present crisis and perhaps frame a compromise proposal. (The meeting never materialized).

Private & confidential.
Hon. Thurlow Weed   Springfield, Ills–Dec. 17–1860
My dear Sir   Yours of the 11th. was received two days ago. Should the convocation of Governors, of which you speak, seem desirous to know my views on the present aspect of things, tell them you judge from my speeches that I will be inflexible on the territorial question; that I probably think either the Missouri line extended, or Douglas' and Eli Thayer's Pop. Sov. would lose us every thing we gained by the election; that filibustering for all South of us, and making slave states of it, would follow in spite of us, under either plan.

Also, that I probably think all opposition, real and apparent, to the fugitive slave [clause] of the constitution ought to be withdrawn.

I believe you can pretend to find but little, if any thing, in my speeches, about secession; but my opinion is that no state can, in any way lawfully, get out of the Union, without the consent of the others; and that it is the duty of the President, and other government functionaries to run the machine as it is. Yours very truly

A. Lincoln

[DOCUMENT 4-4]
TO ALEXANDER H. STEPHENS, DECEMBER 22, 1860

Lincoln had first met Alexander H. Stephens of Georgia when the two served together as fellow Whigs in Congress; at this time Stephens was leading the opposition to immediate secession in Georgia. Eventually he became vice president of the new Confederate States of America.

For your own eye only.

Hon. A. H. Stephens–   Springfield, Ills.

My dear Sir   Dec. 22, 1860

Your obliging answer to my short note is just received, and for which please accept my thanks. I fully appreciate the present peril the country is in, and the weight of responsibility on me.

Do the people of the South really entertain fears that a Republican administration would, *directly,* or *indirectly,* interfere with their slaves, or with them, about their slaves? If they do, I wish to assure you, as once a friend, and still, I hope, not an enemy, that there is no cause for such fears.

The South would be in no more danger in this respect, than it was in the days of Washington. I suppose, however, this does not meet the case. You think slavery is *right* and ought to be extended; while we think it is *wrong* and ought to be restricted. That I suppose is the rub. It certainly is the only substantial difference between us.

Yours very truly   A. Lincoln

[DOCUMENT 4-5]
TO JAMES T. HALE, JANUARY 11, 1861

Republican Congressman James T. Hale of Pennsylvania was serving on a committee charged with drawing up a compromise that featured a proposed constitutional amendment prohibiting Congress from abolishing slavery, the revision of the Fugitive Slave Act of 1850, and the revival of the Missouri Compromise line and its extension westward.

Confidential.

Hon. J. T. Hale   Springfield, Ill. Jan'y. 11th 1861.

My dear Sir–Yours of the 6th is received. I answer it only because I fear you would misconstrue my silence. What is our present condition? We have just carried an election on principles fairly stated to the people. Now we are told in advance, the government shall be broken up, unless we surrender to those we have beaten, before we take the offices. In this they are either attempting to play upon us, or they are in dead earnest. Either way, if we surrender, it is the end of us, and of the government. They will repeat the experiment upon us *ad libitum.* A year will not pass, till we shall have to take Cuba as a condition upon which they will stay in the Union. They now have the Constitution, under which we have lived over seventy years, and acts of Congress of their own framing, with no prospect of their being changed; and they can never have a more shallow pretext for breaking up the government, or extorting a compromise, than now. There is, in my judgment, but one compromise which would really settle the slavery question, and that would be a prohibition against acquiring any more territory.

Yours very truly,   A. Lincoln

[DOCUMENT 4-6]
FIRST INAUGURAL ADDRESS, MARCH 4, 1861

Leaving Springfield on February 11, 1861, Lincoln made his way to the nation's capital via train. Along the way he participated in several ceremonies and offered some impromptu remarks, several of which demonstrated the wisdom of his earlier determination to say nothing lest he confuse and alarm Americans. This made what he had to say about the present crisis in his inaugural address all the more important; he had shared drafts of the document with his secretary of state-designate, Seward, and other advisers.

                                                          March 4, 1861

Fellow citizens of the United States:

In compliance with a custom as old as the government itself, I appear before you to address you briefly, and to take, in your presence, the oath prescribed by the Constitution of the United States, to be taken by the President "before he enters on the execution of his office."

I do not consider it necessary, at present, for me to discuss those matters of administration about which there is no special anxiety, or excitement.

Apprehension seems to exist among the people of the Southern States, that by the accession of a Republican Administration, their property, and their peace, and personal security, are to be endangered. There has never been any reasonable cause for such apprehension. Indeed, the most ample evidence to the contrary has all the while existed, and been open to their inspection. It is found in nearly all the published speeches of him who now addresses you. I do but quote from one of those speeches when I declare that "I have no purpose, directly or indirectly, to interfere with the institution of slavery in the States where it exists. I believe I have no lawful right to do so, and I have no inclination to do so." Those who nominated and elected me did so with full knowledge that I had made this, and many similar declarations, and had never recanted them. And more than this, they placed in the platform, for my acceptance, and as a law to themselves, and to me, the clear and emphatic resolution which I now read:

"*Resolved,* That the maintenance inviolate of the rights of the States, and especially the right of each State to order and control its own domestic institutions according to its own judgment exclusively, is essential to that balance of power on which the perfection and endurance of our political fabric depend; and we denounce the lawless invasion by armed force of the soil of any State or Territory, no matter under what pretext, as among the gravest of crimes."

I now reiterate these sentiments: and in doing so, I only press upon the public attention the most conclusive evidence of which the case is susceptible, that the property, peace and security of no section are to be in anywise endangered by the now incoming Administration. I add too, that all the protection which, consistently with the Constitution and the laws, can be given, will be cheerfully given to all the States when lawfully demanded, for whatever cause—as cheerfully to one section, as to another.

There is much controversy about the delivering up of fugitives from service or labor. The clause I now read is as plainly written in the Constitution as any other of its provisions:

"No person held to service or labor in one State, under the laws thereof, escaping into another, shall, in consequence of any law or regulation therein, be discharged from such service or labor, but shall be delivered up on claim of the party to whom such service or labor may be due."

It is scarcely questioned that this provision was intended by those who made it, for the reclaiming of what we call fugitive slaves; and the intention of the law-giver is the law. All members of Congress swear their support to the whole Constitution—to this provision as much as to any other. To the proposition, then, that slaves whose cases come within the terms of this clause, "shall be delivered up," their oaths are unanimous. Now, if they would make the effort in good temper, could they not, with nearly equal unanimity, frame and pass a law, by means of which to keep good that unanimous oath?

There is some difference of opinion whether this clause should be enforced by national or by state authority; but surely that difference is not a very material one. If the slave is to be surrendered, it can be of but little consequence to him, or to others, by which authority it is done. And should any one, in any case, be content that his oath shall go unkept, on a merely unsubstantial controversy as to *how* it shall be kept?

Again, in any law upon this subject, ought not all the safeguards of liberty known in civilized and humane jurisprudence to be introduced, so that a free man be not, in any case, surrendered as a slave? And might it not be well, at the same time, to provide by law for the enforcement of that clause in the Constitution which guarranties that "The citizens of each State shall be entitled to all previleges and immunities of citizens in the several States?"

I take the official oath to-day, with no mental reservations, and with no purpose to construe the Constitution or laws, by any hypercritical rules. And while I do not choose now to specify particular acts of Congress as proper to be enforced, I do suggest, that it will be much safer for all, both in official and private stations, to conform to, and abide by, all those acts which stand unrepealed, than to violate any of them, trusting to find impunity in having them held to be unconstitutional.

It is seventy-two years since the first inauguration of a President under our national Constitution. During that period fifteen different and greatly distinguished citizens, have, in succession, administered the executive branch of the government. They have conducted it through many perils; and, generally, with great success. Yet, with all this scope for precedent, I now enter upon the same task for the brief constitutional term of four years, under great and peculiar difficulty. A disruption of the Federal Union heretofore only menaced, is now formidably attempted.

I hold, that in contemplation of universal law, and of the Constitution, the Union of these States is perpetual. Perpetuity is implied, if not expressed, in the fundamental law of all national governments. It is safe to assert that no government proper, ever had a provision in its organic law for its own termination. Continue to execute all the express provisions of our national Constitution, and the Union will endure forever—it being impossible to destroy it, except by some action not provided for in the instrument itself.

Again, if the United States be not a government proper, but an association of States in the nature of contract merely, can it, as a contract, be peaceably unmade, by less than all the parties who made it? One party to a contract may violate it—break it, so to speak; but does it not require all to lawfully rescind it?

Descending from these general principles, we find the proposition that, in legal contemplation, the Union is perpetual, confirmed by the history of the Union itself. The Union is much older than the Constitution. It was formed in fact, by the Articles of Association in 1774. It was matured and continued by the Declaration of Independence in 1776. It was further matured and the faith of all the then thirteen States expressly plighted and engaged that it should be perpetual, by the Articles of Confederation in 1778. And finally, in 1787, one of the declared objects for ordaining and establishing the Constitution, was *"to form a more perfect union."*

But if destruction of the Union, by one, or by a part only, of the States, be lawfully possible, the Union is *less* perfect than before the Constitution, having lost the vital element of perpetuity.

It follows from these views that no State, upon its own mere motion, can lawfully get out of the Union,–that *resolves* and *ordinances* to that effect are legally void; and that acts of violence, within any State or States, against the authority of the United States, are insurrectionary or revolutionary, according to circumstances.

I therefore consider that, in view of the Constitution and the laws, the Union is unbroken; and, to the extent of my ability, I shall take care, as the Constitution itself expressly enjoins upon me, that the laws of the Union be faithfully executed in all the States. Doing this I deem to be only a simple duty on my part; and I shall perform it, so far as practicable, unless my rightful masters, the American people, shall withhold the requisite means, or, in some authoritative manner, direct the contrary. I trust this will not be regarded as a menace, but only as the declared purpose of the Union that it *will* constitutionally defend, and maintain itself.

In doing this there needs to be no bloodshed or violence; and there shall be none, unless it be forced upon the national authority. The power confided to me, will be used to hold, occupy, and possess the property, and places belonging to the government, and to collect the duties and imposts; but beyond what may be necessary for these objects, there will be no invasion–no using of force against, or among the people anywhere. Where hostility to the United States, in any interior locality, shall be so great and so universal, as to prevent competent resident citizens from holding the Federal offices, there will be no attempt to force obnoxious strangers among the people for that object. While the strict legal right may exist in the government to enforce the exercise of these offices, the attempt to do so would be so irritating, and so nearly impracticable with all, that I deem it better to forego, for the time, the uses of such offices.

The mails, unless repelled, will continue to be furnished in all parts of the Union. So far as possible, the people everywhere shall have that sense of perfect security which is most favorable to calm thought and reflection. The course here indicated will be followed, unless current events, and experience, shall show a modification, or change, to be proper; and in every case and exigency, my best discretion will be exercised, according to circumstances actually existing, and with a view and a hope of a peaceful solution of the national troubles, and the restoration of fraternal sympathies and affections.

That there are persons in one section, or another who seek to destroy the Union at all events, and are glad of any pretext to do it, I will neither affirm or deny; but if there be such, I need address no word to them. To those, however, who really love the Union, may I not speak?

Before entering upon so grave a matter as the destruction of our national fabric, with all its benefits, its memories, and its hopes, would it not be wise to ascertain precisely why we do it? Will you hazard so desperate a step, while there is any possibility that any portion of the ills you fly from, have no real existence? Will you, while the certain ills you fly to, are greater than all the real ones you fly from? Will you risk the commission of so fearful a mistake?

All profess to be content in the Union, if all constitutional rights can be maintained. Is it true, then, that any right, plainly written in the Constitution, has been denied? I think not. Happily the human mind is so constituted, that no party can reach to the audacity of doing this. Think, if you can, of a single instance in which a plainly written provision of the Constitution has ever been denied. If, by the mere force of numbers, a majority should deprive a minority of any clearly written constitutional right, it might, in a moral point of view, justify revolution—certainly would, if such right were a vital one. But such is not our case. All the vital rights of minorities, and of individuals, are so plainly assured to them, by affirmations and negations, guarranties and prohibitions, in the Constitution, that controversies never arise concerning them. But no organic law can ever be framed with a provision specifically applicable to every question which may occur in practical administration. No foresight can anticipate, nor any document of reasonable length contain express provisions for all possible questions. Shall fugitives from labor be surrendered by national or by State authority? The Constitution does not expressly say. *May* Congress prohibit slavery in the territories? The Constitution does not expressly say. *Must* Congress protect slavery in the territories? The Constitution does not expressly say.

From questions of this class spring all our constitutional controversies, and we divide upon them into majorities and minorities. If the minority will not acquiesce, the majority must, or the government must cease. There is no other alternative; for continuing the government, is acquiescence on one side or the other. If a minority, in such case, will secede rather than acquiesce, they make a precedent which, in turn, will divide and ruin them; for a minority of their own will secede from them, whenever a majority refuses to be controlled by such minority. For instance, why may not any portion of a new confederacy, a year or two hence, arbitrarily secede again, precisely as portions of the present Union now claim to secede from it. All who cherish disunion sentiments, are now being educated to the exact temper of doing this. Is there such perfect identity of interests among the States to compose a new Union, as to produce harmony only, and prevent renewed secession?

Plainly, the central idea of secession, is the essence of anarchy. A majority, held in restraint by constitutional checks, and limitations, and always changing easily, with deliberate changes of popular opinions and sentiments, is the only true sovereign of a free people. Whoever rejects it, does, of necessity, fly to anarchy or to despotism. Unanimity is impossible; the rule of a minority, as a permanent arrangement, is wholly inadmissable; so that, rejecting the majority principle, anarchy, or despotism in some form, is all that is left.

I do not forget the position assumed by some, that constitutional questions are to be decided by the Supreme Court; nor do I deny that such decisions must be binding in any case, upon the parties to a suit, as to the object of that suit, while they are also entitled to very high respect and consideration, in all parallel cases, by all other departments of the government. And while it is obviously possible that such decision may be erroneous in any given case, still the evil effect following it, being limited to that particular case, with the chance that it may be over-ruled, and never become a precedent for other cases, can better be borne than could the evils of a different practice. At the same time the candid citizen must confess that if the policy of the government, upon vital questions, affecting the whole people, is to be irrevocably fixed by decisions of the Supreme Court, the instant they are made, in ordinary litigation between parties, in personal actions, the people will have ceased, to be their own rulers, having, to that extent, practically resigned their government, into the hands of that eminent tribunal. Nor is there, in this view, any assault upon the court, or the judges. It is a duty, from which they may not shrink, to decide cases properly brought before them; and it is no fault of theirs, if others seek to turn their decisions to political purposes.

One section of our country believes slavery is *right,* and ought to be extended, while the other believes it is *wrong,* and ought not to be extended. This is the only substantial dispute. The fugitive slave clause of the Constitution, and the law for the suppression of the foreign slave trade, are each as well enforced, perhaps, as any law can ever be in a community where the moral sense of the people imperfectly supports the law itself. The great body of the people abide by the dry legal obligation in both cases, and a few break over in each. This, I think, cannot be perfectly cured; and it would be worse in both cases *after* the separation of the sections, than before. The foreign slave trade, now imperfectly suppressed, would be ultimately revived without restriction, in one section; while fugitive slaves, now only partially surrendered, would not be surrendered at all, by the other.

Physically speaking, we cannot separate. We cannot remove our respective sections from each other, nor build an impassable wall between them. A husband and wife may be divorced, and go out of the presence, and beyond the reach of each other; but the different parts of our country cannot do this. They cannot but remain face to face; and intercourse, either amicable or hostile, must continue between them. Is it possible then to make that intercourse more advantageous, or more satisfactory, *after* separation than *before?* Can aliens make treaties easier than friends can make laws? Can treaties be more faithfully enforced between aliens, than laws can among friends? Suppose you go to war, you cannot fight always; and when, after much loss on both sides, and no gain on either, you cease fighting, the identical old questions, as to terms of intercourse, are again upon you.

This country, with its institutions, belongs to the people who inhabit it. Whenever they shall grow weary of the existing government, they can exercise their *constitutional* right of amending it, or their *revolutionary* right to dismember, or overthrow it. I can not be ignorant of the fact that many worthy, and patriotic citizens are desirous of having the national constitution amended. While I make no recommendation of amendments, I fully recognize the rightful authority of the people over the whole subject, to be exercised in either of the modes prescribed in the instrument itself; and I should, under existing circumstances, favor, rather than oppose, a fair oppertunity being afforded the people to act upon it.

I will venture to add that, to me, the convention mode seems preferable, in that it allows amendments to originate with the people themselves, instead of only permitting them to take, or reject, propositions, originated by others, not especially chosen for the purpose, and which might not be precisely such, as they would wish to either accept or refuse. I understand a proposed amendment to the Constitution–which amendment, however, I have not seen, has passed Congress, to the effect that the federal government, shall never interfere with the domestic institutions of the States, including that of persons held to service. To avoid misconstruction of what I have said, I depart from my purpose not to speak of particular amendments, so far as to say that, holding such a provision to now be implied constitutional law, I have no objection to its being made express, and irrevocable.

The Chief Magistrate derives all his authority from the people, and they have conferred none upon him to fix terms for the separation of the States. The people themselves can do this also if they choose; but the executive, as such, has nothing to do with it. His duty is to administer the present government, as it came to his hands, and to transmit it, unimpaired by him, to his successor.

Why should there not be a patient confidence in the ultimate justice of the people? Is there any better, or equal hope, in the world? In our present differences, is either party without faith of being in the right? If the Almighty Ruler of nations, with his eternal truth and justice, be on your side of the North, or on yours of the South, that truth, and that justice, will surely prevail, by the judgment of this great tribunal, the American people.

By the frame of the government under which we live, this same people have wisely given their public servants but little power for mischief; and have, with equal wisdom, provided for the return of that little to their own hands at very short intervals.

While the people retain their virtue, and vigilance, no administration, by any extreme of wickedness or folly, can very seriously injure the government, in the short space of four years.

My countrymen, one and all, think calmly and *well,* upon this whole subject. Nothing valuable can be lost by taking time. If there be an object to *hurry* any of you, in hot haste, to a step which you would never take *deliberately,* that object will be frustrated by taking time; but no good object can be frustrated by it. Such of you as are now dissatisfied, still have the old Constitution unimpaired, and, on the sensitive point, the laws of your own framing under it; while the new administration will have no immediate power, if it would, to change either. If it were admitted that you who are dissatisfied, hold the right side in the dispute, there still is no single good reason for precipitate action. Intelligence, patriotism, Christianity, and a firm reliance on Him, who has never yet forsaken this favored land, are still competent to adjust, in the best way, all our present difficulty.

In *your* hands, my dissatisfied fellow countrymen, and not in *mine,* is the momentous issue of civil war. The government will not assail *you.* You can have no conflict, without being yourselves the aggressors. *You* have no oath registered in Heaven to destroy the government, while *I* shall have the most solemn one to "preserve, protect and defend" it.

I am loth to close. We are not enemies, but friends. We must not be enemies. Though passion may have strained, it must not break our bonds of affection. The mystic chords of memory, streching from every battle-field, and patriot grave, to every living heart and hearthstone, all over this broad land, will yet swell the chorus of the Union, when again touched, as surely they will be, by the better angels of our nature.

[DOCUMENT 4-7]
MESSAGE TO CONGRESS, JULY 4, 1861

On April 12, 1861, Confederate forces opened fire on Fort Sumter, a fortification in Charleston Harbor, South Carolina, occupied by a small garrison of United States soldiers. Two days later the fort formally surrendered; the following day Lincoln called for 75,000 volunteers, organized as militia by the states, to put down what he termed an insurrection. However, he decided not to call Congress into special session until July 4, 1861, allowing himself nearly three months to respond to the crisis. Although four more states joined the Confederacy, Lincoln was able to head off secession movements in Maryland and Missouri, while he tolerated Kentucky's declaration of neutrality. By the time Congress met, Lincoln was prepared to offer his explanation of the crisis as he sought sanction for his acts.

Fellow-citizens of the Senate and House of Representatives:

Having been convened on an extraordinary occasion, as authorized by the Constitution, your attention is not called to any ordinary subject of legislation.

At the beginning of the present Presidential term four months ago, the functions of the Federal Government were found to be generally suspended within the several States of South Carolina, Georgia, Alabama, Mississippi, Louisiana, and Florida, excepting only those of the Post Office Department.

Within these States, all the Forts, Arsenals, Dock-yards, Custom-houses, and the like, including the movable and stationary property in, and about them, had been seized, and were held in open hostility to this Government, excepting only Forts Pickens, Taylor, and Jefferson, on, and near the Florida coast, and Fort Sumter, in Charleston harbor, South Carolina. The Forts thus seized had been put in improved condition; new ones had been built; and armed forces had been organized, and were organizing, all avowedly with the same hostile purpose.

The Forts remaining in the possession of the Federal government, in, and near, these States, were either besieged or menaced by warlike preparations; and especially Fort Sumter was nearly surrounded by well-protected hostile batteries, with guns equal in quality to the best of its own, and outnumbering the latter as perhaps ten to one. A disproportionate share, of the Federal muskets and rifles, had somehow found their way into these States, and had been seized, to be used against the government. Accumulations of the public revenue, lying within them, had been seized for the same object. The Navy was scattered in distant seas; leaving but a very small part of it within the immediate reach of the government. Officers of the Federal Army and Navy, had resigned in great numbers; and, of those resigning, a large proportion had taken up arms against the government. Simultaneously, and in connection, with all this, the purpose to sever the Federal Union, was openly avowed. In accordance with this purpose, an ordinance had been adopted in each of these States, declaring the States, respectively, to be separated from the National Union. A formula for instituting a combined government of these states had been promulgated; and this illegal organization, in the character of confederate States was already invoking recognition, aid, and intervention, from Foreign Powers.

Finding this condition of things, and believing it to be an imperative duty upon the incoming Executive, to prevent, if possible, the consummation of such attempt to destroy the Federal Union, a choice of means to that end became indispensable. This choice was made; and was declared in the Inaugural address. The policy chosen looked to the exhaustion of all peaceful measures, before a resort to any stronger ones. It sought only to hold the public places and property, not already wrested from the Government, and to collect the revenue; relying for the rest, on time, discussion, and the ballot-box. It promised a continuance of the mails, at government expense, to the very people who were resisting the government; and it gave repeated pledges against any disturbance to any of the people, or any of their rights. Of all that which a president might constitutionally, and justifiably, do in such a case, everything was foreborne, without which, it was believed possible to keep the government on foot.

On the 5th of March, (the present incumbent's first full day in office) a letter of Major Anderson, commanding at Fort Sumter, written on the 28th of February, and received at the War Department on the 4th of March, was, by that Department, placed in his hands. This letter expressed the professional opinion of the writer, that re-inforcements could not be thrown into that Fort within the time for his relief, rendered necessary by the limited supply of provisions, and with a view of holding possession of the same, with a force of less than twenty thousand good, and well-disciplined men. This opinion was concurred in by all the officers of his command; and their *memoranda* on the subject, were made enclosures of Major Anderson's letter. The whole was immediately laid before Lieutenant General Scott, who at once concurred with Major Anderson in opinion. On reflection, however, he took full time, consulting with other officers, both of the Army and the Navy; and, at the end of four days, came reluctantly, but decidedly, to the same conclusion as before. He also stated at the same time that no such sufficient force was then at the control of the Government, or could be raised, and brought to the ground, within the time when the provisions in the Fort would be exhausted. In a purely military point of view, this reduced the duty of the administration, in the case, to the mere matter of getting the garrison safely out of the Fort.

It was believed, however, that to so abandon that position, under the circumstances, would be utterly ruinous; that the *necessity* under which it was to be done, would not be fully understood—that, by many, it would be construed as a part of a *voluntary* policy—that, at home, it would discourage the friends of the Union, embolden its adversaries, and go far to insure to the latter, a recognition abroad—that, in fact, it would be our national destruction consummated. This could not be allowed. Starvation was not yet upon the garrison; and ere it would be reached, *Fort Pickens* might be reinforced. This last, would be a clear indication of *policy,* and would better enable the country to accept the evacuation of Fort Sumter, as a military *necessity.* An order was at once directed to be sent for the landing of the troops from the Steamship Brooklyn, into Fort Pickens. This order could not go by land, but must take the longer, and slower route by sea. The first return news from the order was received just one week before the fall of Fort Sumter. The news itself was, that the officer commanding the Sabine, to which vessel the troops had been transferred from the Brooklyn, acting upon some *quasi* armistice of the late administration, (and of the existence of which, the present administration, up to the time the order was despatched, had only too vague and uncertain rumors, to fix attention) had refused to land the troops. To now re-inforce Fort Pickens, before a crisis would be reached at Fort Sumter was impossible—rendered so by the near exhaustion of provisions in the latter-named Fort. In precaution against such a conjuncture, the government had, a few days before, commenced preparing an expedition, as well adapted as might be, to relieve Fort Sumter, which expedition was intended to be ultimately used, or not, according to circumstances. The strongest anticipated case, for using it, was now presented; and it was resolved to send it forward. As had been intended, in this contingency, it was also re-solved to notify the Governor of South Carolina, that he might expect an attempt would be made to provision the Fort; and that, if the at-tempt should not be resisted, there would be no effort to throw in men, arms, or ammunition, without further notice, or in case of an attack upon the Fort. This notice was accordingly given; whereupon the Fort was attacked, and bombarded to its fall, without even awaiting the ar-rival of the provisioning expedition.

It is thus seen that the assault upon, and reduction of, Fort Sumter, was, in no sense, a matter of self defence on the part of the assailants. They well knew that the garrison in the Fort could, by no possibility, commit aggression upon them. They knew–they were expressly noti-fied–that the giving of bread to the few brave and hungry men of the garrison, was all which would on that occasion be attempted, unless themselves, by resisting so much, should provoke more. They knew that this Government desired to keep the garrison in the Fort, not to assail them, but merely to maintain visible possession, and thus to pre-serve the Union from actual, and immediate dissolution–trusting, as herein-before stated, to time, discussion, and the ballot-box, for final adjustment; and they assailed, and reduced the Fort, for precisely the reverse object–to drive out the visible authority of the Federal Union, and thus force it to immediate dissolution.

That this was their object, the Executive well understood; and hav-ing said to them in the inaugural address, "You can have no conflict without being yourselves the aggressors," he took pains, not only to keep this declaration good, but also to keep the case so free from the power of ingenious sophistry, as that the world should not be able to misunderstand it. By the affair at Fort Sumter, with its surrounding cir-cumstances, that point was reached. Then, and thereby, the assailants of the Government, began the conflict of arms, without a gun in sight, or in expectancy, to return their fire, save only the few in the Fort, sent to that harbor, years before, for their own protection, and still ready to give that protection, in whatever was lawful. In this act, discarding all else, they have forced upon the country, the distinct issue: "Immediate dissolution, or blood."

And this issue embraces more than the fate of these United States. It presents to the whole family of man, the question, whether a constitu-tional republic, or a democracy–a government of the people, by the same people–can, or cannot, maintain its territorial integrity, against its own domestic foes. It presents the question, whether discontented individuals, too few in numbers to control administration, according to organic law, in any case, can always, upon the pretences made in this case, or on any other pretences, or arbitrarily, without any pretence, break up their Government, and thus practically put an end to free government upon the earth. It forces us to ask: "Is there, in all republics, this inherent, and fatal weakness?" "Must a government, of necessity, be too *strong* for the liberties of its own people, or too *weak* to maintain its own existence?"

So viewing the issue, no choice was left but to call out the war power of the Government; and so to resist force, employed for its destruction, by force, for its preservation.

The call was made; and the response of the country was most gratifying; surpassing, in unanimity and spirit, the most sanguine expectation. Yet none of the States commonly called Slave-states, except Delaware, gave a Regiment through regular State organization. A few regiments have been organized within some others of those states, by individual enterprise, and received into the government service. Of course the seceded States, so called, (and to which Texas had been joined about the time of the inauguration,) gave no troops to the cause of the Union. The border States, so called, were not uniform in their actions; some of them being almost *for* the Union, while in others—as Virginia, North Carolina, Tennessee, and Arkansas—the Union sentiment was nearly repressed, and silenced. The course taken in Virginia was the most remarkable—perhaps the most important. A convention, elected by the people of that State, to consider this very question of disrupting the Federal Union, was in session at the capital of Virginia when Fort Sumter fell. To this body the people had chosen a large majority of *professed* Union men. Almost immediately after the fall of Sumter, many members of that majority went over to the original disunion minority, and, with them, adopted an ordinance for withdrawing the State from the Union. Whether this change was wrought by their great approval of the assault upon Sumter, or their great resentment at the government's resistance to that assault, is not definitely known. Although they submitted the ordinance, for ratification, to a vote of the people, to be taken on a day then somewhat more than a month distant, the convention, and the Legislature, (which was also in session at the same time and place) with leading men of the State, not members of either, immediately commenced acting, as if the State were already out of the Union. They pushed military preparations vigorously forward all over the state. They seized the United States Armory at Harper's Ferry, and the Navy-yard at Gosport, near Norfolk. They received—perhaps invited—into their state, large bodies of troops, with their warlike appointments, from the so-called seceded States. They formally entered into a treaty of temporary alliance, and co-operation with the so-called "Confederate States," and sent members to their Congress at Montgomery. And, finally, they permitted the insurrectionary government to be transferred to their capital at Richmond.

The people of Virginia have thus allowed this giant insurrection to make its nest within her borders; and this government has no choice left but to deal with it, *where* it finds it. And it has the less regret, as the loyal citizens have, in due form, claimed its protection. Those loyal citizens, this government is bound to recognize, and protect, as being Virginia.

In the border States, so called—in fact, the middle states—there are those who favor a policy which they call "armed neutrality"—that is, an arming of those states to prevent the Union forces passing one way, or the disunion, the other, over their soil. This would be disunion completed. Figuratively speaking, it would be the building of an impassable wall along the line of separation. And yet, not quite an impassable one; for, under the guise of neutrality, it would tie the hands of the Union men, and freely pass supplies from among them, to the insurrectionists, which it could not do as an open enemy. At a stroke, it would take all the trouble off the hands of secession, except only what proceeds from the external blockade. It would do for the disunionists that which, of all things, they most desire feed them well, and give them disunion without a struggle of their own. It recognizes no fidelity to the Constitution, no obligation to maintain the Union; and while very many who have favored it are, doubtless, loyal citizens, it is, nevertheless, treason in effect.

Recurring to the action of the government, it may be stated that, at first, a call was made for seventy-five thousand militia; and rapidly following this, a proclamation was issued for closing the ports of the insurrectionary districts by proceedings in the nature of Blockade. So far all was believed to be strictly legal. At this point the insurrectionists announced their purpose to enter upon the practice of privateering.

Other calls were made for volunteers, to serve three years, unless sooner discharged; and also for large additions to the regular Army and Navy. These measures, whether strictly legal or not, were ventured upon, under what appeared to be a popular demand, and a public necessity; trusting, then as now, that Congress would readily ratify them. It is believed that nothing has been done beyond the constitutional competency of Congress.

Soon after the first call for militia, it was considered a duty to authorize the Commanding General, in proper cases, according to his discretion, to suspend the privilege of the writ of habeas corpus; or, in

other words, to arrest, and detain, without resort to the ordinary processes and forms of law, such individuals as he might deem dangerous
to the public safety. This authority has purposely been exercised but
very sparingly. Nevertheless, the legality and propriety of what has been
done under it, are questioned; and the attention of the country has
been called to the proposition that one who is sworn to "take care that
the laws be faithfully executed," should not himself violate them. Of
course some consideration was given to the questions of power, and
propriety, before this matter was acted upon. The whole of the laws
which were required to be faithfully executed, were being resisted, and
failing of execution, in nearly one-third of the States. Must they be
allowed to finally fail of execution, even had it been perfectly clear,
that by the use of the means necessary to their execution, some single
law, made in such extreme tenderness of the citizen's liberty, that practically, it relieves more of the guilty, than of the innocent, should, to a
very limited extent, be violated? To state the question more directly,
are all the laws, *but one,* to go unexecuted, and the government itself go
to pieces, lest that one be violated? Even in such a case, would not the
official oath be broken, if the government should be overthrown, when
it was believed that disregarding the single law, would tend to preserve
it? But it was not believed that this question was presented. It was not
believed that any law was violated. The provision of the Constitution
that "The privilege of the writ of habeas corpus, shall not be suspended
unless when, in cases of rebellion or invasion, the public safety may
require it," is equivalent to a provision—is a provision—that such privilege may be suspended when, in cases of rebellion, or invasion, the
public safety *does* require it. It was decided that we have a case of rebellion, and that the public safety does require the qualified suspension of
the privilege of the writ which was authorized to be made. Now it is
insisted that Congress, and not the Executive, is vested with this power.
But the Constitution itself, is silent as to which, or who, is to exercise
the power; and as the provision was plainly made for a dangerous emer-
gency, it cannot be believed the framers of the instrument intended,
that in every case, the danger should run its course, until Congress
could be called together; the very assembling of which might be prevented, as was intended in this case, by the rebellion.

No more extended argument is now offered; as an opinion, at some
length, will probably be presented by the Attorney General. Whether
there shall be any legislation upon the subject, and if any, what, is submitted entirely to the better judgment of Congress.

The forbearance of this government had been so extraordinary, and
so long continued, as to lead some foreign nations to shape their action

as if they supposed the early destruction of our national Union was probable. While this, on discovery, gave the Executive some concern, he is now happy to say that the sovereignty, and rights of the United States, are now everywhere practically respected by foreign powers; and a general sympathy with the country is manifested throughout the world.

The reports of the Secretaries of the Treasury, War, and the Navy, will give the information in detail deemed necessary, and convenient for your deliberation, and action; while the Executive, and all the Departments, will stand ready to supply omissions, or to communicate new facts, considered important for you to know.

It is now recommended that you give the legal means for making this contest a short, and a decisive one; that you place at the control of the government, for the work, at least four hundred thousand men, and four hundred millions of dollars. That number of men is about one tenth of those of proper ages within the regions where, apparently, *all* are willing to engage; and the sum is less than a twentythird part of the money value owned by the men who seem ready to devote the whole. A debt of six hundred millions of dollars *now,* is a less sum per head, than was the debt of our revolution, when we came out of that struggle; and the money value in the country now, bears even a greater proportion to what it was *then,* than does the population. Surely each man has as strong a motive *now,* to *preserve* our liberties, as each had *then,* to *establish* them.

A right result, at this time, will be worth more to the world, than ten times the men, and ten times the money. The evidence reaching us from the country, leaves no doubt, that the material for the work is abundant; and that it needs only the hand of legislation to give it legal sanction, and the hand of the Executive to give it practical shape and efficiency. One of the greatest perplexities of the government, is to avoid receiving troops faster than it can provide for them. In a word, the people will save their government, if the government itself, will do its part, only indifferently well.

It might seem, at first thought, to be of little difference whether the present movement at the South be called "secession" or "rebellion." The movers, however, well understand the difference. At the beginning, they knew they could never raise their treason to any respectable magnitude, by any name which implies *violation* of law. They knew their people possessed as much of moral sense, as much of devotion to law and order, and as much pride in, and reverence for, the history, and government, of their common country, as any other civilized, and patriotic people. They knew they could make no advancement directly in the teeth of these strong and noble sentiments. Accordingly they commenced by an insidious debauching of the public mind. They invented an ingenious sophism, which, if conceded, was followed by perfectly logical steps, through all the incidents, to the complete destruction of the Union. The sophism itself is, that any state of the Union may, *consistently* with the national Constitution, and therefore *lawfully,* and *peacefully,* withdraw from the Union, without the consent of the Union, or of any other state. The little disguise that the supposed right is to be exercised only for just cause, themselves to be the sole judge of its justice, is too thin to merit any notice.

With rebellion thus sugar-coated, they have been drugging the public mind of their section for more than thirty years, and, until at length, they have brought many good men to a willingness to take up arms against the government the day *after* some assemblage of men have enacted the farcical presence of taking their State out of the Union, who could have been brought to no such thing the day *before.*

This sophism derives much—perhaps the whole—of its currency, from the assumption, that there is some omnipotent, and sacred supremacy, pertaining to a *State*–to each State of our Federal Union. Our States have neither more, nor less power, than that reserved to them, in the Union, by the Constitution—no one of them ever having been a State *out* of the Union. The original ones passed into the Union even *before* they cast off their British colonial dependence; and the new ones each came into the Union directly from a condition of dependence, excepting Texas. And even Texas, in its temporary independence, was never designated a State. The new ones only took the designation of States, on coming into the Union, while that name was first adopted for the old ones, in, and by, the Declaration of Independence. Therein the "United Colonies" were declared to be "Free and Independent States"; but, even then, the object plainly was not to declare their independence of *one another,* or of the *Union;* but directly the contrary, as their mutual pledge, and their mutual action, before, at the time, and afterwards, abundantly show. The express plighting of faith, by each and all of the original thirteen, in the Articles of Confederation, two years later, that the Union shall be perpetual, is most conclusive. Having never been States, either in substance, or in name, *outside* of the Union, whence this magical omnipotence of "State rights," asserting a claim of power to lawfully destroy the Union itself? Much is said about the "sovereignty" of the States; but the word, even, is not in the national Constitution; nor, as is believed, in any of the State constitutions. What is a "sovereignty," in the political sense of the term? Would it be far wrong to define it "A political community, without a political superior"? Tested by this, no one of our States, except Texas, ever was a sovereignty. And even Texas gave up the character on coming into the Union; by which act, she acknowledged the Constitution of the United States, and the laws and treaties of the United States made in pursuance of the Constitution, to be, for her, the supreme law of the land. The States have their *status* IN the Union, and they have no other *legal status*. If they break from this, they can only do so against law, and by revolution. The Union, and not themselves separately, procured their independence, and their liberty. By conquest, or purchase, the Union gave each of them, whatever of independence, and liberty, it has. The Union is older than any of the States; and, in fact, it created them as States. Originally, some dependent colonies made the Union; and, in turn, the Union threw off their old dependence, for them, and made them States, such as they are. Not one of them ever had a State constitution, independent of the Union. Of course, it is not forgotten that all the new States framed their constitutions, before they entered the Union; nevertheless, dependent upon, and preparatory to, coming into the Union.

Unquestionably the States have the powers, and rights, reserved to them in, and by the National Constitution; but among these, surely, are not included all conceivable powers, however mischievous, or destructive; but, at most, such only, as were known in the world, at the time, as governmental powers; and certainly, a power to destroy the government itself, had never been known as a governmental—as a merely administrative power. This relative matter of National power, and State rights, as a principle, is no other than the principle of *generality,* and *locality.* Whatever concerns the whole, should be confided to the whole—to the general government; while, whatever concerns *only* the State, should be left exclusively, to the State. This is all there is of original principle about it. Whether the National Constitution, in defining boundaries between the two, has applied the principle with exact accuracy, is not to be questioned. We are all bound by that defining, without question.

What is now combatted, is the position that secession is *consistent* with the Constitution—is *lawful,* and *peaceful.* It is not contended that there is any express law for it; and nothing should ever be implied as law, which leads to unjust, or absurd consequences. The nation purchased, with money, the countries out of which several of these States were formed. Is it just that they shall go off without leave, and without refunding? The nation paid very large sums, (in the aggregate, I believe, nearly a hundred millions) to relieve Florida of the aboriginal tribes. Is it just that she shall now be off without consent, or without making any return? The nation is now in debt for money applied to the benefit of these so-called seceding States, in common with the rest. Is it just, either that creditors shall go unpaid, or the remaining States pay the whole? A part of the present national debt was contracted to pay the old debts of Texas. Is it just that she shall leave, and pay no part of this herself?

Again, if one State may secede, so may another; and when all shall have seceded, none is left to pay the debts. Is this quite just to creditors? Did we notify them of this sage view of ours, when we borrowed their money? If we now recognize this doctrine, by allowing the seceders to go in peace, it is difficult to see what we can do, if others choose to go, or to extort terms upon which they will promise to remain.

The seceders insist that our Constitution admits of secession. They have assumed to make a National Constitution of their own, in which, of necessity, they have either *discarded,* or *retained,* the right of secession, as they insist, it exists in ours. If they have discarded it, they thereby admit that, on principle, it ought not to be in ours. If they have retained it, by their own construction of ours they show that to be consistent they must secede from one another, whenever they shall find it the easiest way of settling their debts, or effecting any other selfish, or unjust object. The principle itself is one of disintegration, and upon which no government can possibly endure.

If all the States, save one, should assert the power to *drive* that one out of the Union, it is presumed the whole class of seceder politicians would at once deny the power, and denounce the act as the greatest outrage upon State rights. But suppose that precisely the same act, instead of being called "driving the one out," should be called "the seceding of the others from that one," it would be exactly what the seceders claim to do; unless, indeed, they make the point, that the one, because it is a minority, may rightfully do, what the others, because they are a majority, may not rightfully do. These politicians are subtle, and profound, on the rights of minorities. They are not partial to that power which made the Constitution, and speaks from the preamble, calling itself "We, the People."

It may well be questioned whether there is, to-day, a majority of the legally qualified voters of any State, except perhaps South Carolina, in favor of disunion. There is much reason to believe that the Union men are the majority in many, if not in every other one, of the so-called seceded States. The contrary has not been demonstrated in any one of them. It is ventured to affirm this, even of Virginia and Tennessee; for the result of an election, held in military camps, where the bayonets are all on one side of the question voted upon, can scarcely be considered as demonstrating popular sentiment. At such an election, all that large class who are, at once, *for* the Union, and *against* coercion, would be coerced to vote against the Union.

It may be affirmed, without extravagance, that the free institutions we enjoy, have developed the powers, and improved the condition, of our whole people, beyond any example in the world. Of this we now have a striking, and an impressive illustration. So large an army as the government has now on foot, was never before known, without a soldier in it, but who had taken his place there, of his own free choice. But more than this: there are many single Regiments whose members, one and another, possess full practical knowledge of all the arts, sciences, professions, and whatever else, whether useful or elegant, is known in the world; and there is scarcely one, from which there could not be selected, a President, a Cabinet, a Congress, and perhaps a Court, abundantly competent to administer the government itself. Nor do I say this is not true, also, in the army of our late friends, now adversaries, in this contest; but if it is, so much better the reason why the government, which has conferred such benefits on both them and us, should not be broken up. Whoever, in any section, proposes to abandon such a government, would do well to consider, in deference to what principle it is, that he does it—what better he is likely to get in its stead—whether the substitute will give, or be intended to give, so much of good to the people. There are some foreshadowings on this subject. Our adversaries have adopted some Declarations of Independence; in which, unlike the good old one, penned by Jefferson, they omit the words "all men are created equal." Why? They have adopted a temporary national constitution, in the preamble of which, unlike our good old one, signed by Washington, they omit "We, the People," and substitute "We, the deputies of the sovereign and independent States." Why? Why this deliberate pressing out of view, the rights of men, and the authority of the people?

This is essentially a People's contest. On the side of the Union, it is a struggle for maintaining in the world, that form, and substance of government, whose leading object is, to elevate the condition of men— to lift artificial weights from all shoulders—to clear the paths of laudable pursuit for all—to afford all, an unfettered start, and a fair chance, in the race of life. Yielding to partial, and temporary departures, from necessity, this is the leading object of the government for whose existence we contend.

I am most happy to believe that the plain people understand, and appreciate this. It is worthy of note, that while in this, the government's hour of trial, large numbers of those in the Army and Navy, who have been favored with the offices, have resigned, and proved false to the hand which had pampered them, not one common soldier, or common sailor is known to have deserted his flag.

Great honor is due to those officers who remain true, despite the example of their treacherous associates; but the greatest honor, and most important fact of all, is the unanimous firmness of the common soldiers, and common sailors. To the last man, so far as known, they have successfully resisted the traitorous efforts of those, whose commands, but an hour before, they obeyed as absolute law. This is the patriotic instinct of the plain people. They understand, without an argument, that destroying the government, which was made by Washington, means no good to them.

Our popular government has often been called an experiment. Two points in it, our people have already settled—the successful *establishing,* and the successful *administering* of it. One still remains—its successful *maintenance* against a formidable internal attempt to overthrow it. It is now for them to demonstrate to the world, that those who can fairly carry an election, can also suppress a rebellion—that ballots are the rightful, and peaceful, successors of bullets; and that when ballots have fairly, and constitutionally, decided, there can be no successful appeal, back to bullets; that there can be no successful appeal, except to ballots themselves, at succeeding elections. Such will be a great lesson of peace; teaching men that what they cannot take by an election, neither can they take it by a war—teaching all, the folly of being the beginners of a war.

Lest there be some uneasiness in the minds of candid men, as to what is to be the course of the government, towards the Southern States, *after* the rebellion shall have been suppressed, the Executive deems it proper to say, it will be his purpose then, as ever, to be guided by the Constitution, and the laws; and that he probably will have no different understanding of the powers, and duties of the Federal government, relatively to the rights of the States, and the people, under the Constitution, than that expressed in the inaugural address.

He desires to preserve the government, that it may be administered for all, as it was administered by the men who made it. Loyal citizens everywhere, have the right to claim this of their government; and the government has no right to withhold, or neglect it. It is not perceived that, in giving it, there is any coercion, any conquest, or any subjugation, in any just sense of those terms.

The Constitution provides, and all the States have accepted the provision, that "The United States shall guarantee to every State in this

Union a republican form of government." But, if a State may lawfully go out of the Union, having done so, it may also discard the republican form of government; so that to prevent its going out, is an indispensable *means,* to the *end,* of maintaining the guaranty mentioned; and when an end is lawful and obligatory, the indispensable means to it, are also lawful, and obligatory.

It was with the deepest regret that the Executive found the duty of employing the war-power, in defence of the government, forced upon him. He could but perform this duty, or surrender the existence of the government. No compromise, by public servants, could, in this case, be a cure; not that compromises are not often proper, but that no popular government can long survive a marked precedent, that those who carry an election, can only save the government from immediate destruction, by giving up the main point, upon which the people gave the election. The people themselves, and not their servants, can safely reverse their own deliberate decisions. As a private citizen, the Executive could not have consented that these institutions shall perish; much less could he, in betrayal of so vast, and so sacred a trust, as these free people had confided to him. He felt that he had no moral right to shrink; nor even to count the chances of his own life, in what might follow. In full view of his great responsibility, he has, so far, done what he has deemed his duty. You will now, according to your own judgment, perform yours. He sincerely hopes that your views, and your action, may so accord with his, as to assure all faithful citizens, who have been disturbed in their rights, of a certain, and speedy restoration to them, under the Constitution, and the laws.

And having thus chosen our course, without guile, and with pure purpose, let us renew our trust in God, and go forward without fear, and with manly hearts.   Abraham Lincoln
July 4, 1861.

[DOCUMENT 4-8]
TO ORVILLE H. BROWNING, SEPTEMBER 22, 1861

On August 30, 1861, General John C. Frémont, as part of imposing martial law in Missouri, declared free the slaves owned by secessionist sympathizers. The declaration came at an inopportune time, for Kentuckians were involved in a heated debate about whether the state should secede, stay in the Union, or remain neutral, and Lincoln feared that a vigorous blow against slavery would push that state into the Confederate camp. After Frémont refused Lincoln's re-

quest to revise the proclamation in line with present congressional legislation concerning the confiscation of slaves employed in the Confederate war effort, the president revoked it; he explained why to Republican senator Orville H. Browning of Illinois, a long-time political associate.

Private & confidential.

Hon. O. H. Browning   Executive Mansion

My dear Sir   Washington Sept 22d 1861.

Yours of the 17th is just received; and coming from you, I confess it astonishes me. That you should object to my adhering to a law, which you had assisted in making, and presenting to me, less than a month before, is odd enough. But this is a very small part. Genl. Fremont's proclamation, as to confiscation of property, and the liberation of slaves, is *purely political,* and not within the range of *military* law, or necessity. If a commanding General finds a necessity to seize the farm of a private owner, for a pasture, an encampment, or a fortification, he has the right to do so, and to so hold it, as long as the necessity lasts; and this is within military law, because within military necessity. But to say the farm shall no longer belong to the owner, or his heirs forever; and this as well when the farm is not needed for military purposes as when it is, is purely political, without the savor of military law about it. And the same is true of slaves. If the General needs them, he can seize them, and use them; but when the need is past, it is not for him to fix their permanent future condition. That must be settled according to laws made by law-makers, and not by military proclamations. The proclamation in the point in question, is simply "dictatorship." It assumes that the general may do *anything* he pleases—confiscate the lands and free the slaves of *loyal* people, as well as of disloyal ones. And going the whole figure I have no doubt would be more popular with some thoughtless people, than that which has been done! But I cannot assume this reckless position; nor allow others to assume it on my responsibility. You speak of it as being the only means of *saving* the government. On the contrary it is itself the surrender of the government. Can it be pretended that it is any longer the government of the U.S.–any government of Constitution and laws,–wherein a General or a President, may make permanent rules of property by proclamation?

I do not say Congress might not with propriety pass a law, on the point, just such as General Fremont proclaimed. I do not say I might not, as a member of Congress, vote for it. What I object to, is, that I as President, shall expressly or impliedly seize and exercise the permanent legislative functions of the government.

So much as to principle. Now as to policy. No doubt the thing was popular in some quarters, and would have been more so if it had been a general declaration of emancipation. The Kentucky Legislature would not budge till that proclamation was modified; and Gen. Anderson telegraphed me that on the news of Gen. Fremont having actually issued deeds of manumission, a whole company of our Volunteers threw down their arms and disbanded. I was so assured, as to think it probable, that the very arms we had furnished Kentucky would be turned against us. I think to lose Kentucky is nearly the same as to lose the whole game. Kentucky gone, we can not hold Missouri, nor, as I think, Maryland. These all against us, and the job on our hands is too large for us. We would as well consent to separation at once, including the surrender of this capitol. On the contrary, if you will give up your restlessness for new positions, and back me manfully on the grounds upon which you and other kind friends gave me the election, and have approved in my public documents, we shall go through triumphantly.

You must not understand I took my course on the proclamation *because* of Kentucky. I took the same ground in a private letter to General Fremont before I heard from Kentucky.

You think I am inconsistent because I did not also forbid Gen. Fremont to shoot men under the proclamation. I understand that part to be within military law; but I also think, and so privately wrote Gen. Fremont, that it is impolitic in this, that our adversaries have the power, and will certainly exercise it, to shoot as many of our men as we shoot of theirs. I did not say this in the public letter, because it is a subject I prefer not to discuss in the hearing of our enemies.

There has been no thought of removing Gen. Fremont on any ground connected with his proclamation; and if there has been any wish for his removal on any ground, our mutual friend Sam. Glover can probably tell you what it was. I hope no real necessity for it exists on any ground.

Suppose you write to Hurlbut and get him to resign. Your friend as ever   A. Lincoln

[DOCUMENT 4-9]
FIRST ANNUAL MESSAGE, DECEMBER 3, 1861 (EXCERPT)

In his first annual message, Lincoln for the first time openly advocated legislation to carry out a policy of compensated emancipation followed by the colonization of free and freed blacks.

Under and by virtue of the act of Congress entitled "An act to confiscate property used for insurrectionary purposes," approved August, 6, 1861, the legal claims of certain persons to the labor and service of certain other persons have become forfeited; and numbers of the latter, thus liberated, are already dependent on the United States, and must be provided for in some way. Besides this, it is not impossible that some of the States will pass similar enactments for their own benefit respectively, and by operation of which persons of the same class will be thrown upon them for disposal. In such case I recommend that Congress provide for accepting such persons from such States, according to some mode of valuation, in lieu, *pro tanto,* of direct taxes, or upon some other plan to be agreed on with such States respectively; that such persons, on such acceptance by the general government, be at once deemed free; and that, in any event, steps be taken for colonizing both classes, (or the one first mentioned, if the other shall not be brought into existence,) at some place, or places, in a climate congenial to them. It might be well to consider, too,–whether the free colored people already in the United States could not, so far as individuals may desire, be included in such colonization.

To carry out the plan of colonization may involve the acquiring of territory, and also the appropriation of money beyond that to be expended in the territorial acquisition. Having practiced the acquisition of territory for nearly sixty years, the question of constitutional power to do so is no longer an open one with us. The power was questioned at first by Mr. Jefferson, who, however, in the purchase of Louisiana, yielded his scruples on the plea of great expediency. If it be said that the only legitimate object of acquiring territory is to furnish homes for white men, this measure effects that object; for the emigration of colored men leaves additional room for white men remaining or coming here. Mr. Jefferson, however, placed the importance of procuring Louisiana more on political and commercial grounds than on providing room for population.

On this whole proposition,–including the appropriation of money with the acquisition of territory, does not the expediency amount to absolute necessity–that, without which the government itself cannot be perpetuated? The war continues. In considering the policy to be adopted for suppressing the insurrection, I have been anxious and careful that the inevitable conflict for this purpose shall not degenerate into a violent and remorseless revolutionary struggle. I have, therefore, in every case, thought it proper to keep the integrity of the Union prominent as the primary object of the contest on our part, leaving all questions which are not of vital military importance to the more deliberate action of the legislature.

[DOCUMENT 4-10]
MESSAGE TO CONGRESS, MARCH 6, 1862

In March 1862 Lincoln pushed again for a policy of gradual and compensated emancipation, this time by proposing a specific resolution. The next month Congress passed the resolution.

Fellow-citizens of the Senate, and House of Representatives,

I recommend the adoption of a Joint Resolution by your honorable bodies which shall be substantially as follows:

"Resolved that the United States ought to co-operate with any state which may adopt gradual abolishment of slavery, giving to such state pecuniary aid, to be used by such state in it's discretion, to compensate for the inconveniences public and private, produced by such change of system"

If the proposition contained in the resolution does not meet the approval of Congress and the country, there is the end; but if it does command such approval, I deem it of importance that the states and people immediately interested, should be at once distinctly notified of the fact, so that they may begin to consider whether to accept or reject it. The federal government would find it's highest interest in such a measure, as one of the most efficient means of self-preservation. The leaders of the existing insurrection entertain the hope that this government will ultimately be forced to acknowledge the independence of some part of the disaffected region, and that all the slave states North of such part will then say "the Union, for which we have struggled, being already gone, we now choose to go with the Southern section." To deprive them of this hope, substantially ends the rebellion; and the initiation of emancipation completely deprives them of it, as to all the states initiating it. The point is not that *all* the states tolerating slavery would very soon, if at all, initiate emancipation; but that, while the offer is equally made to all, the more Northern shall, by such initiation, make it certain to the more Southern, that in no event, will the former ever join the latter, in their proposed confederacy. I say "initiation" because, in my judgment, gradual, and not sudden emancipation, is better for all. In the mere financial, or pecuniary view, any member of Congress, with the census-tables and Treasury-reports before him, can readily see for himself how very soon the current expenditures of this war would purchase, at fair valuation, all the slaves in any named State. Such a proposition, on the part of the general government, sets up no claim of a right, by federal authority, to interfere with slavery within state limits, referring, as it does, the absolute control of the subject, in each case, to the state and it's people, immediately interested. It is proposed as a matter of perfectly free choice with them.

In the annual message last December, I thought fit to say "The Union must be preserved; and hence all indispensable means must be employed." I said this, not hastily, but deliberately. War has been made, and continues to be, an indispensable means to this end. A practical re-acknowledgement of the national authority would render the war unnecessary, and it would at once cease. If, however, resistance continues, the war must also continue; and it is impossible to foresee all the incidents, which may attend and all the ruin which may follow it. Such as may seem indispensable, or may obviously promise great efficiency towards ending the struggle, must and will come.

The proposition now made, though an offer only, I hope it may be esteemed no offence to ask whether the pecuniary consideration tendered would not be of more value to the States and private persons concerned, than are the institution, and property in it, in the present aspect of affairs.

While it is true that the adoption of the proposed resolution would be merely initiatory, and not within itself a practical measure, it is recommended in the hope that it would soon lead to important practical results. In full view of my great responsibility to my God, and to my country, I earnestly beg the attention of Congress and the people to the subject.   Abraham Lincoln
                                                                        March 6. 1862.

[DOCUMENT 4-11]
PROCLAMATION REVOKING DAVID HUNTER'S EMANCIPATION ORDER, MAY 19, 1862

On May 9, 1862, General David Hunter, commanding the Department of the South (including Georgia, Florida, and South Carolina), having already imposed martial law on the area under his jurisdiction, declared free all slaves who resided therein. Unlike Frémont, whose August 1861 proclamation concerned a state still considered in the Union (Missouri), Hunter struck at slavery within the borders of the Confederacy, and failed to distinguish between loyal and disloyal masters. Lincoln revoked the general's order, and explained why in the following proclamation.

By the President of The United States of America.
A Proclamation.

Whereas there appears in the public prints, what purports to be a proclamation, of Major General Hunter, in the words and figures following, towit:

Headquarters Department of the South,
Hilton Head, S.C., May 9, 1862

General Orders No. 11.–The three States of Georgia, Florida and South Carolina, comprising the military department of the south, having deliberately declared themselves no longer under the protection of the United States of America, and having taken up arms against the said United States, it becomes a military necessity to declare them under martial law. This was accordingly done on the 25th day of April, 1862. Slavery and martial law in a free country are altogether incompatible; the persons in these three States–Georgia, Florida and South Carolina–heretofore held as slaves, are therefore declared forever free.

David Hunter,
(Official)   Major General Commanding.
Ed. W. Smith, Acting Assistant Adjutant General.

And whereas the same is producing some excitement, and misunderstanding: therefore

I, Abraham Lincoln, president of the United States, proclaim and declare, that the government of the United States, had no knowledge, information, or belief, of an intention on the part of General Hunter to issue such a proclamation; nor has it yet, any authentic information that the document is genuine. And further, that neither General Hunter, nor any other commander, or person, has been authorized by the Government of the United States, to make proclamations declaring the slaves of any State free; and that the supposed proclamation, now in question, whether genuine or false, is altogether void, so far as respects such declaration.

I further make known that whether it be competent for me, as Commander-in-Chief of the Army and Navy, to declare the Slaves of any state or states, free, and whether at any time, in any case, it shall have become a necessity indispensable to the maintainance of the government, to exercise such supposed power, are questions which, under my responsibility, I reserve to myself, and which I can not feel justified in leaving to the decision of commanders in the field. These are totally different questions from those of police regulations in armies and camps.

On the sixth day of March last, by a special message, I recommended to Congress the adoption of a joint resolution to be substantially as follows:

Resolved, That the United States ought to co-operate with any State which may adopt a gradual abolishment of slavery, giving to such State pecuniary aid, to be used by such State in its discretion to com pensate for the inconveniences, public and private, produced by such change of system.

The resolution, in the language above quoted, was adopted by large majorities in both branches of Congress, and now stands an authentic, definite, and solemn proposal of the nation to the States and people most immediately interested in the subject matter. To the people of those states I now earnestly appeal. I do not argue. I beseech you to make the arguments for yourselves. You can not if you would, be blind to the signs of the times. I beg of you a calm and enlarged consideration of them, ranging, if it may be, far above personal and partizan politics. This proposal makes common cause for a common object, casting no reproaches upon any. It acts not the pharisee. The change it contemplates would come gently as the dews of heaven, not rending or wrecking anything. Will you not embrace it? So much good has not been done, by one effort, in all past time, as, in the providence of God, it is now your high previlege to do. May the vast future not have to lament that you have neglected it.

In witness whereof, I have hereunto set my hand, and caused the seal of the United States to be affixed.

Done at the City of Washington this nineteenth day of May, in the year of our Lord one thousand eight hundred and sixty-two, and of the Independence of the United States the eighty-sixth.

Abraham Lincoln

By the President:
William H. Seward, Secretary of State.

The Winding Road to Emancipation, 1862–1863

CHAPTER FIVE

MILITARY REVERSES AT THE END OF JUNE 1862 and the public response to them pressed Lincoln to revisit the question of emancipation. Although Union forces captured Corinth, Mississippi, at the end of May, the triumph proved anticlimactic; all eyes were focused on the progress of George B. McClellan's Army of the Potomac as it crept toward the Confederate capital at Richmond, Virginia. At the end of June, Robert E. Lee drove McClellan away in a series of battles; McClellan's own melodramatic descriptions of his situation added to the resulting sense of crisis in the North. "I expect to maintain this contest until successful, or till I die, or am conquered, or my term expires, or Congress or the country forsakes me," Lincoln told his secretary of state, William H. Seward, but he was loathe to take new steps lest they add to a growing sense of desperation.[1]

Both advocates and opponents of emancipation realized that the setback in front of Richmond would fuel debate over whether the Union should adopt abolition as a war aim. For months Congress had wrangled over additional confiscation legislation that would strike new blows at slavery; abolitionists and some Republicans continued to pressure the administration to act more vigorously against slavery, while more conservative Republicans and other political leaders warned that the escalation of the conflict would smother Southern unionism, energize Democratic opposition, and fracture the coalition formed in support of a war avowedly waged to save the Union and nothing more. Other circumstances also influenced Lincoln's thinking on the issue. In contrast to 1861, when the allegiance of the border states hung in the balance, by the summer of 1862 Union military successes had secured those states. On the other hand, Lincoln's hopes for a resurgence of Southern unionism were beginning to fade: in West Tennessee most civilians proved recalcitrant Confederates under Union occupation, while in Louisiana most unionists appeared timid and too concerned about slavery. The president concluded that he gained little and lost much by continuing to woo these reluctant unionists.

In July 1862 Lincoln began to share with others evidence that he was rethinking emancipation. Once more he pressed for compensated emancipation, reminding the congressional delegations from several border states that the friction of military conflict was eroding the peculiar institution and that he had to heed the demands of war supporters who pressured him to do more against slavery [Document 5-1]. When a large majority of those present rejected his proposal, the president realized that persuasion would accomplish little; the day after the meeting he told several members of the cabinet that he was approaching the conclusion "that we must free the slaves or be ourselves subdued."[2] Four days later Congress passed a second confiscation act, declaring free the slaves of secessionist masters; Lincoln questioned whether Congress could in fact exercise that right constitutionally. What Congress could not do, however, the president might well do, using the war powers of his office as constitutional justification. On July 22, he shared with his cabinet the idea of a proclamation of emancipation [Document 5-2]; after much discussion, he decided not to press for it in the wake of the Union's recent military defeats.

While for the moment Lincoln had stayed his hand, he was not dissuaded of the necessity of some commitment to emancipation as a war measure. In a series of letters he revealed that he was abandoning old assumptions and embracing new measures. To Maryland Democrat Reverdy Johnson, who reported that Louisiana unionists were angry with military measures against slavery, Lincoln explained that the best way for white Southerners to save slavery was to return to the Union [Document 5-3]. Dismay with the passivity of Southern unionists also appeared in letters to Cuthbert Bullitt, who had shared with Lincoln the grumblings of his fellow Louisiana unionist Thomas J. Durant [Document 5-4], and to August Belmont, a prominent financier and New York Democrat, who had passed on yet another letter from a Louisiana slaveholder [Document 5-5].

Even as he moved away from his earlier concerns about emancipation, Lincoln still moved cautiously, aware that he had to prepare public opinion for so dramatic and far-reaching a measure. In explaining his thoughts on colonization to a delegation of black leaders [Document 5-6], he revealed his continuing doubts about whether blacks and whites could live together in harmony in post-emancipation America;

at the same time he hoped that by drawing attention once more to colonization he might assuage white fears about the consequences of abolition. However, the overwhelming negative response offered by blacks and white abolitionists served to remind him that such a solution was less likely than ever. Eight days later he offered Americans yet another glimpse of his thinking in replying to an antislavery pronunciamento harshly critical of Lincoln prepared by the Republican editor of the *New York Tribune,* Horace Greeley. Artfully sidestepping the editor's attacks (while managing to misspell his name), Lincoln clearly set forth how emancipation fit into his larger aim to save the Union, distinguishing between what he could do as president and what he personally preferred [Document 5-7]–a distinction often lost on modern critics. Moreover, as David Donald has pointed out, in choosing to use the word "paramount," Lincoln meant that while his principal aim was to save the Union, it was not his sole aim.[3]

Lincoln pursued this course of setting forth the grounds upon which he would press for emancipation even as he fended off criticism from critics impatient for him to act now. One such opportunity was his response to a series of resolutions passed by a convention of Christians who had met at Chicago [Document 5-8]. In remarks foreshadowing his second inaugural address, the president shared his impression that God's will might not coincide with the wishes of either side; he also raised questions about the impact of an emancipation proclamation. Four days later, on September 17, McClellan attacked Lee at Antietam Creek, Maryland. Lee's subsequent withdrawal, ending two weeks of operations north of the Potomac River, gave Lincoln the victory he was looking for, and on September 22 he issued a preliminary Emancipation Proclamation [Document 5-9].

The September proclamation bears comparison, not only with the July draft [Document 5-2] and the final proclamation [Document 5-12], but with other measures pointing in the same direction. Some of Lincoln's critics argue quite erroneously that the "final Emancipation Proclamation freed not a single slave who was not already entitled to freedom by act of Congress"; in fact, Lincoln's proclamation encompassed all slaves in areas designated as in rebellion–those owned by secessionists and unionists alike–while the Second Confiscation Act aimed to free only those slaves who belonged to secessionists.[4] He had decided to create a concrete incentive for Southern unionists to act now if they wanted to preserve slavery, demonstrating that the September proclamation was as much a document of reconstruction as it was one of promised emancipation, for in it Lincoln made his final pre-emancipation offer of reunion on the old terms (already somewhat altered by war) to white Southerners.

Lincoln expressed skepticism that the proclamation would actually help him much in the short run in his efforts to solidify support for the war effort; rather, he focused his energy on pushing for the reestablishment of loyal sentiment through the holding of congressional elections in occupied areas of the Confederacy [Document 5-10]. At the same time, he pressed once more for compensation and colonization in his second annual message [Document 5-11]. It is well worth noting that in his first annual message [Document 4-9] he had advocated colonization as a way to make sure that the war "shall not degenerate into a violent and remorseless revolutionary struggle"; now he pushed for it, at the conclusion of his second message, in language often quoted with admiration by Lincoln scholars as an example of his faith in the American nation and its political values. Establishing the context of those remarks sets them in a different light.

On January 1, 1863, Lincoln signed the Emancipation Proclamation [Document 5-12]. In its final form it reflected both political deals (such as the successful effort of Tennessee's military governor, Andrew Johnson, to exclude all of Tennessee from the proclamation) and Lincoln's readiness to enlist blacks in the Union army. Just over a week later, in response to the critical queries of an Illinois Democrat-turned-general, John A. McClernand, Lincoln explained why he acted as he did, while leaving the door open to future solutions [Document 5-13].

1. Lincoln to William H. Seward, June 28, 1862, in Fehrenbacher, *Lincoln: Speeches and Writings*, 2:335.

2. Donald, *Lincoln*, 362.

3. Ibid., 368–69.

4. For an example of the error, see Barbara J. Fields, "Who Freed the Slaves?", in Geoffrey Ward et al., *The Civil War*, New York, 1994 [1990], 153.

[DOCUMENT 5-1]
REMARKS TO BORDER STATE REPRESENTATIVES, JULY 12, 1862

As the second session of the Thirty-seventh Congress drew to a close, Lincoln, still anxious for Congress to pass legislation to implement his plan of gradual, compensated emancipation, met with senators and representatives from the slave states still in the Union (including representatives from western Virginia and Tennessee). A majority of those present resisted his plea for action; a smaller number endorsed his policy. Congress took no additional action on Lincoln's plan before adjourning.

Gentlemen. After the adjournment of Congress, now very near, I shall have no opportunity of seeing you for several months. Believing that you of the border-states hold more power for good than any other equal number of members, I feel it a duty which I can not justifiably waive, to make this appeal to you. I intend no reproach or complaint when I assure you that in my opinion, if you all had voted for the resolution in the gradual emancipation message of last March, the war would now be substantially ended. And the plan therein proposed is yet one of the most potent, and swift means of ending it. Let the states which are in rebellion see, definitely and certainly, that, in no event, will the states you represent ever join their proposed Confederacy, and they can not, much longer maintain the contest. But you can not divest them of their hope to ultimately have you with them so long as you show a determination to perpetuate the institution within your own states. Beat them at elections, as you have overwhelmingly done, and, nothing daunted, they still claim you as their own. You and I know what the lever of their power is. Break that lever before their faces, and they can shake you no more forever.

Most of you have treated me with kindness and consideration; and I trust you will not now think I improperly touch what is exclusively your own, when, for the sake of the whole country I ask "Can you, for your states, do better than to take the course I urge?" Discarding *punctillio*, and maxims adapted to more manageable times, and looking only to the unprecedentedly stern facts of our case, can you do better in any possible event? You prefer that the constitutional relation of the states to the nation shall be practically restored, without disturbance of the institution; and if this were done, my whole duty, in this respect, under the constitution, and my oath of office, would be performed. But it is not done, and we are trying to accomplish it by war. The incidents of the war can not be avoided. If the war continue long, as it must, if the object be not sooner attained, the institution in your states will be extinguished by mere friction and abrasion–by the mere incidents of the war. It will be gone, and you will have nothing valuable in lieu of it. Much of it's value is gone already. How much better for you, and for your people, to take the step which, at once, shortens the war, and secures substantial compensation for that which is sure to be wholly lost in any other event. How much better to thus save the money which else we sink forever in the war. How much better to do it while we can, lest the war ere long render us pecuniarily unable to do it. How much better for you, as seller, and the nation as buyer, to sell out, and buy out, that without which the war could never have been, than to sink both the thing to be sold, and the price of it, in cutting one another's throats.

I do not speak of emancipation *at once,* but of a *decision* at once to emancipate *gradually.* Room in South America for colonization, can be obtained cheaply, and in abundance; and when numbers shall be large enough to be company and encouragement for one another, the freed people will not be so reluctant to go.

I am pressed with a difficulty not yet mentioned–one which threatens division among those who, united are none too strong. An instance of it is known to you. Gen. Hunter is an honest man. He was, and I hope, still is, my friend. I valued him none the less for his agreeing with me in the general wish that all men everywhere, could be free. He proclaimed all men free within certain states, and I repudiated the proclamation. He expected more good, and less harm from the measure, than I could believe would follow. Yet in repudiating it, I gave dissatisfaction, if not offence, to many whose support the country can not afford to lose. And this is not the end of it. The pressure, in this direction, is still upon me, and is increasing. By conceding what I now ask, you can relieve me, and much more, can relieve the country, in this important point. Upon these considerations I have again begged your attention to the message of March last. Before leaving the Capital, consider and discuss it among yourselves. You are patriots and statesmen; and, as such, I pray you, consider this proposition; and, at the least, commend it to the consideration of your states and people. As you would perpetuate popular government for the best people in the world, I beseech you that you do in no wise omit this. Our common country is in great peril, demanding the loftiest views, and boldest action to bring it speedy relief. Once relieved, it's form of government is saved to the world; it's beloved history, and cherished memories, are vindicated; and it's happy future fully assured, and rendered inconceivably grand. To you, more than to any others, the previlege is given, to assure that happiness, and swell that grandeur, and to link your own names therewith forever.

[DOCUMENT 5-2]
DRAFT OF EMANCIPATION PROCLAMATION, JULY 22, 1862

Lincoln shared this draft of the Emancipation Proclamation with his cabinet on July 22. After some discussion he decided not to issue it until Union armies scored a victory in the field.

In pursuance of the sixth section of the act of congress entitled "An act to suppress insurrection and to punish treason and rebellion, to seize and confiscate property of rebels, and for other purposes" Approved July 17. 1862, and which act, and the Joint Resolution explanatory thereof, are herewith published, I, Abraham Lincoln, President of the United States, do hereby proclaim to, and warn all persons within the contemplation of said sixth section to cease participating in, aiding, countenancing, or abetting the existing rebellion, or any rebellion against the government of the United States, and to return to their proper allegiance to the United States, on pain of the forfeitures and seizures, as within and by said sixth section provided.

And I hereby make known that it is my purpose, upon the next meeting of congress, to again recommend the adoption of a practical measure for tendering pecuniary aid to the free choice or rejection, of any and all States which may then be recognizing and practically sustaining the authority of the United States, and which may then have voluntarily adopted, or thereafter may voluntarily adopt, gradual abolishment of slavery within such State or States—that the object is to practically restore, thenceforward to be maintain[ed], the constitutional relation between the general government, and each, and all the states, wherein that relation is now suspended, or disturbed; and that, for this object, the war, as it has been, will be, prossecuted. And, as a fit and necessary military measure for effecting this object, I, as Commander-in-Chief of the Army and Navy of the United States, do order and declare that on the first day of January in the year of Our Lord one thousand, eight hundred and sixtythree, all persons held as slaves within any state or states, wherein the constitutional authority of the United

States shall not then be practically recognized, submitted to, and maintained, shall then, thenceforward, and forever, be free.

Emancipation Proclamation
as first sketched and
shown to the Cabinet in
July 1862.

[DOCUMENT 5-3]
TO REVERDY JOHNSON, JULY 26, 1862

Democrat Reverdy Johnson of Maryland had been sent by the Lincoln administration to investigate charges of misconduct by Major General Benjamin F. Butler in Louisiana. Johnson concluded that Union military activities in freeing slaves promised to hamper attempts at reconstruction by alienating whites; he was particularly outraged at the protection given refugee blacks by Brigadier General John W. Phelps, who had clashed with Butler over the proper policy to pursue toward blacks. Johnson asked the state's military governor, George F. Shepley, to deliver his letter to Lincoln personally. In turn, Lincoln directed Secretary of the Treasury Salmon P. Chase, an advocate of emancipation and the enlistment of blacks, to forward this letter to Johnson through Butler—thus informing Butler that the administration was not in favor of coddling slaveholders who did not labor for reunion.

PRIVATE   Executive Mansion,
Hon Reverdy Johnson   Washington, July 26, 1862.
My Dear Sir. Yours of the 16th. by the hand of Governor Shepley is received. It seems the Union feeling in Louisiana is being crushed out by the course of General Phelps. Please pardon me for believing that is a false pretense. The people of Louisiana—all intelligent people every where— know full well, that I never had a wish to touch the foundations of their society, or any right of theirs. With perfect knowledge of this, they forced a necessity upon me to send armies among them, and it is their own fault, not mine, that they are annoyed by the presence of General Phelps. They also know the remedy—know how to be cured of General Phelps. Remove the necessity of his presence. And might it not be well for them to consider whether they have not already had *time* enough to do this? If they can conceive of anything worse than General Phelps, within my power, would they not better be looking out for it? They very well know the way to avert all this is simply to take their place in the Union upon the old terms. If they will not do this, should they not receive harder blows rather than lighter ones?

You are ready to say I apply to *friends* what is due only to *enemies*. I distrust the *wisdom* if not the *sincerity* of friends, who would hold my hands while my enemies stab me. This appeal of professed friends has paralyzed me more in this struggle than any other one thing. You remember telling me the day after the Baltimore mob in April 1861, that it would crush all Union feeling in Maryland for me to attempt bringing troops over Maryland soil to Washington. I brought the troops notwithstanding, and yet there was Union feeling enough left to elect a Legislature the next autumn which in turn elected a very excellent Union U.S. Senator!

I am a patient man—always willing to forgive on the Christian terms of repentance; and also to give ample *time* for repentance. Still I must save this government if possible. What I *cannot* do, of course I *will* not do; but it may as well be understood, once for all, that I shall not surrender this game leaving any available card unplayed.

Yours truly   A Lincoln

[DOCUMENT 5-4]
TO CUTHBERT BULLITT, JULY 28, 1862

Thomas J. Durant, a New Orleans lawyer, slaveowner, and unionist, shared his opposition to Phelps's activities in a letter to Cuthbert Bullitt, a merchant; Bullitt passed the letter on to Secretary of State William H. Seward, who showed it to Lincoln.

PRIVATE

Cuthbert Bullitt Esq   Washington D.C.
New Orleans La.   July 28. 1862

Sir: The copy of a letter addressed to yourself by Mr. Thomas J. Durant, has been shown to me. The writer appears to be an able, a dispassionate, and an entirely sincere man. The first part of the letter is devoted to an effort to show that the Secession Ordinance of Louisiana was adopted against the will of a majority of the people. This is probably true; and in that fact may be found some instruction. Why did they allow the Ordinance to go into effect? Why did they not assert themselves? Why stand passive and allow themselves to be trodden down by a minority? Why did they not hold popular meetings, and have a convention of their own, to express and enforce the true sentiment of the state? If preorganization was against them *then,* why not do this *now,* that the United States Army is present to protect them? The paralysis—the dead palsy—of the government in this whole struggle is, that this class of men will do nothing for the government, nothing for themselves, except demanding that the government shall not strike its open enemies, lest they be struck by accident!

Mr. Durant complains that in various ways the relation of master and slave is disturbed by the presence of our Army; and he considers it particularly vexatious that this, in part, is done under cover of an act of Congress, while constitutional guaranties are suspended on the plea of military necessity. The truth is, that what is done, and omitted, about slaves, is done and omitted on the same military necessity. It is a military necessity to have men and money; and we can get neither, in sufficient numbers, or amounts, if we keep from, or drive from, our lines, slaves coming to them. Mr. Durant cannot be ignorant of the pressure in this direction; nor of my efforts to hold it within bounds till he, and such as he shall have time to help themselves.

I am not posted to speak understandingly on all the police regulations of which Mr. Durant complains. If experience shows any one of them to be wrong, let them be set right. I think I can perceive, in the freedom of trade, which Mr. Durant urges, that he would relieve both friends and enemies from the pressure of the blockade. By this he would serve the enemy more effectively than the enemy is able to serve himself. I do not say or believe that to serve the enemy is the purpose of Mr. Durant; or that he is conscious of any purpose, other than national and patriotic ones. Still, if there were a class of men who, having no choice of sides in the contest, were anxious only to have quiet and comfort for themselves while it rages, and to fall in with the victorious side at the end of it, without loss to themselves, their advice as to the mode of conducting the contest would be precisely such as his is. He speaks of no duty—apparently thinks of none—resting upon Union men. He even thinks it injurious to the Union cause that they should be restrained in trade and passage without taking sides. They are to touch neither a sail nor a pump, but to be merely passengers,—dead-heads at that—to be carried snug and dry, throughout the storm, and safely landed right side up. Nay, more; even a mutineer is to go untouched lest these sacred passengers receive an accidental wound.

Of course the rebellion will never be suppressed in Louisiana, if the professed Union men there will neither help to do it, nor permit the government to do it without their help.

Now, I think the true remedy is very different from what is suggested by Mr. Durant. It does not lie in rounding the rough angles of the war, but in removing the necessity for the war. The people of Louisiana who wish protection to person and property, have but to reach forth their hands and take it. Let them, in good faith, reinaugurate the national authority, and set up a State Government conforming thereto under the constitution. They know how to do it, and can have the protection of the Army while doing it. The Army will be withdrawn so soon as such State government can dispense with its presence; and the people of the State can then upon the old Constitutional terms, govern themselves to their own liking. This is very simple and easy.

If they will not do this, if they prefer to hazard all for the sake of destroying the government, it is for them to consider whether it is probable I will surrender the government to save them from losing all. If they decline what I suggest, you scarcely need to ask what I will do. What would you do in my position? Would you drop the war where it is? Or, would you prosecute it in future, with elder-stalk squirts, charged with rose water? Would you deal lighter blows rather than heavier ones? Would you give up the contest, leaving any available means unapplied.

I am in no boastful mood. I shall not do *more* than I can, and I shall do *all* I can to save the government, which is my sworn duty as well as my personal inclination. I shall do nothing in malice. What I deal with is too vast for malicious dealing. Yours truly

A. Lincoln

[DOCUMENT 5-5]
TO AUGUST BELMONT, JULY 31, 1862

August Belmont of New York was a prominent Democratic adviser and financier; among his correspondents was the commander of the Army of the Potomac, George B. McClellan. Belmont had passed on an excerpt from another letter about conditions in Louisiana to Thurlow Weed, Seward's political confidant; the excerpt quoted a prominent plantation owner who had once supported the Confederacy as saying that Lincoln could end the rebellion simply by supporting a settlement based upon the simple restoration of the Union; Belmont urged Weed to transmit the letter to Lincoln.

July 31, 1862.

Dear Sir: You send to Mr. Weed an extract from a letter written at New Orleans the 9th instant, which is shown to me. You do not give the writer's name; but plainly he is a man of ability, and probably of some note. He says: "The time has arrived when Mr. Lincoln must take a decisive course. Trying to please everybody, he will satisfy nobody. A vacillating policy in matters of importance is the very worst. Now is the time, if ever, for honest men who love their country to rally to its support. Why will not the North say officially that it wishes for the restoration of the Union as it was?"

And so, it seems, this is the point on which the writer thinks I have no policy. Why will he not read and understand what I have said?

The substance of the very declaration he desires is in the inaugural, in each of the two regular messages to Congress, and in many, if not all, the minor documents issued by the Executive since the inauguration.

Broken eggs cannot be mended; but Louisiana has nothing to do now but to take her place in the Union as it was, barring the already broken eggs. The sooner she does so, the smaller will be the amount of that which will be past mending. This government cannot much longer play a game in which it stakes all, and its enemies stake nothing. Those enemies must understand that they cannot experiment for ten years trying to destroy the government, and if they fail still come back into the Union unhurt. If they expect in any contingency to ever have the Union as it was, I join with the writer in saying, "Now is the time."

How much better it would have been for the writer to have gone at this, under the protection of the army at New Orleans, than to have sat down in a closet writing complaining letters northward!

Yours truly,   A. Lincoln

[DOCUMENT 5-6]
REMARKS ON COLONIZATION TO BLACK MINISTERS, AUGUST 14, 1862

On August 14, Lincoln spoke to a delegation of black leaders at the White House. What follows is a newspaper transcript of their meeting. Although Congress had failed to implement Lincoln's plan for emancipation and colonization, both the legislation ending slavery in the District of Columbia (signed into law by Lincoln on April 16, 1862) and the Second Confiscation Act (signed into law by Lincoln on July 17, 1862) contained provisions for colonization. Members of the delegation responded that they were willing to investigate colonization; most other blacks rejected the notion and criticized the delegation.

Joseph Jenkins Roberts became the first president of Liberia in 1848; he was president of Liberia College when he visited Lincoln in August 1862.

August 14, 1862

This afternoon the President of the United States gave audience to a Committee of colored men at the White House. They were introduced by the Rev. J. Mitchell, Commissioner of Emigration. E. M. Thomas, the Chairman, remarked that they were there by invitation to hear what the Executive had to say to them. Having all been seated, the President, after a few preliminary observations, informed them that a sum of money had been appropriated by Congress, and placed at his disposition for the purpose of aiding the colonization in some country of the people, or a portion of them, of African descent, thereby making it his duty, as it had for a long time been his inclination, to favor that cause; and why, he asked, should the people of your race be colonized, and where? Why should they leave this country? This is, perhaps, the first question for proper consideration. You and we are different races. We have between us a broader difference than exists between almost any other two races. Whether it is right or wrong I need not discuss, but this physical difference is a great disadvantage to us both, as I think your race suffer very greatly, many of them by living among us, while ours suffer from your presence. In a word we suffer on each side. If this is admitted, it affords a reason at least why we should be separated. You here are freemen I suppose.

A VOICE: Yes, sir.

The President–Perhaps you have long been free, or all your lives. Your race are suffering, in my judgment, the greatest wrong inflicted on any people. But even when you cease to be slaves, you are yet far removed from being placed on an equality with the white race. You are cut off from many of the advantages which the other race enjoy. The aspiration of men is to enjoy equality with the best when free, but on this broad continent, not a single man of your race is made the equal of a single man of ours. Go where you are treated the best, and the ban is still upon you.

I do not propose to discuss this, but to present it as a fact with which we have to deal. I cannot alter it if I would. It is a fact, about which we all think and feel alike, I and you. We look to our condition, owing to the existence of the two races on this continent. I need not recount to you the effects upon white men, growing out of the institution of Slavery. I believe in its general evil effects on the white race. See our present condition–the country engaged in war!–our white men cutting one another's throats, none knowing how far it will extend; and then consider what we know to be the truth. But for your race among us there could not be war, although many men engaged on either side do not care for you one way or the other. Nevertheless, I repeat, without the institution of Slavery and the colored race as a basis, the war could not have an existence.

It is better for us both, therefore, to be separated. I know that there are free men among you, who even if they could better their condition are not as much inclined to go out of the country as those, who being slaves could obtain their freedom on this condition. I suppose one of the principal difficulties in the way of colonization is that the free colored man cannot see that his comfort would be advanced by it. You may believe you can live in Washington or elsewhere in the United States the remainder of your life, perhaps more so than you can in any foreign country, and hence you may come to the conclusion that you have nothing to do with the idea of going to a foreign country. This is (I speak in no unkind sense) an extremely selfish view of the case.

But you ought to do something to help those who are not so fortunate as yourselves. There is an unwillingness on the part of our people, harsh as it may be, for you free colored people to remain with us. Now, if you could give a start to white people, you would open a wide door for many to be made free. If we deal with those who are not free at the beginning, and whose intellects are clouded by Slavery, we have very poor materials to start with. If intelligent colored men, such as are before me, would move in this matter, much might be accomplished. It is exceedingly important that we have men at the beginning capable of thinking as white men, and not those who have been systematically oppressed.

There is much to encourage you. For the sake of your race you should sacrifice something of your present comfort for the purpose of being as grand in that respect as the white people. It is a cheering thought throughout life that something can be done to ameliorate the condition of those who have been subject to the hard usage of the world. It is difficult to make a man miserable while he feels he is worthy of himself, and claims kindred to the great God who made him. In the American Revolutionary war sacrifices were made by men engaged in it; but they were cheered by the future. Gen. Washington himself endured greater physical hardships than if he had remained a British subject. Yet he was a happy man, because he was engaged in benefiting his race—something for the children of his neighbors, having none of his own.

The colony of Liberia has been in existence a long time. In a certain sense it is a success. The old President of Liberia, Roberts, has just been with me—the first time I ever saw him. He says they have within the bounds of that colony between 300,000 and 400,000 people, or more than in some of our old States, such as Rhode Island or Delaware, or in some of our newer States, and less than in some of our larger ones. They are not all American colonists, or their descendants. Something less than 12,000 have been sent thither from this country. Many of the original settlers have died, yet, like people elsewhere, their offspring outnumber those deceased.

The question is if the colored people are persuaded to go anywhere, why not there? One reason for an unwillingness to do so is that some of you would rather remain within reach of the country of your nativity. I do not know how much attachment you may have toward our race. It does not strike me that you have the greatest reason to love them. But still you are attached to them at all events.

The place I am thinking about having for a colony is in Central America. It is nearer to us than Liberia—not much more than one-fourth as far as Liberia, and within seven days' run by steamers. Unlike Liberia it is on a great line of travel—it is a highway. The country is a very excellent one for any people, and with great natural resources and advantages, and especially because of the similarity of climate with your native land—thus being suited to your physical condition.

The particular place I have in view is to be a great highway from the Atlantic or Caribbean Sea to the Pacific Ocean, and this particular place has all the advantages for a colony. On both sides there are harbors among the finest in the world. Again, there is evidence of very rich coal mines. A certain amount of coal is valuable in any country, and there may be more than enough for the wants of the country. Why I attach so much importance to coal is, it will afford an opportunity to the inhabitants for immediate employment till they get ready to settle permanently in their homes.

If you take colonists where there is no good landing, there is a bad show; and so where there is nothing to cultivate, and of which to make a farm. But if something is started so that you can get your daily bread as soon as you reach there, it is a great advantage. Coal land is the best thing I know of with which to commence an enterprise.

To return, you have been talked to upon this subject, and told that a speculation is intended by gentlemen, who have an interest in the country, including the coal mines. We have been mistaken all our lives if we do not know whites as well as blacks look to their self-interest. Unless among those deficient of intellect everybody you trade with makes something. You meet with these things here as elsewhere.

If such persons have what will be an advantage to them, the question is whether it cannot be made of advantage to you. You are intelligent, and know that success does not as much depend on external help as on self-reliance. Much, therefore, depends upon yourselves. As to the coal mines, I think I see the means available for your self-reliance.

I shall, if I get a sufficient number of you engaged, have provisions made that you shall not be wronged. If you will engage in the enterprise I will spend some of the money intrusted to me. I am not sure you will succeed. The Government may lose the money, but we cannot succeed unless we try; but we think, with care, we can succeed.

The political affairs in Central America are not in quite as satisfactory condition as I wish. There are contending factions in that quarter; but it is true all the factions are agreed alike on the subject of colonization, and want it, and are more generous than we are here. To your colored race they have no objection. Besides, I would endeavor to have you made equals, and have the best assurance that you should be the equals of the best.

The practical thing I want to ascertain is whether I can get a number of able-bodied men, with their wives and children, who are willing to go, when I present evidence of encouragement and protection. Could I get a hundred tolerably intelligent men, with their wives and children, to "cut their own fodder," so to speak? Can I have fifty? If I could find twenty-five able-bodied men, with a mixture of women and children, good things in the family relation, I think I could make a successful commencement.

I want you to let me know whether this can be done or not. This is the practical part of my wish to see you. These are subjects of very great importance, worthy of a month's study, [instead] of a speech delivered in an hour. I ask you then to consider seriously not pertaining to yourselves merely, nor for your race, and ours, for the present time, but as one of the things, if successfully managed, for the good of mankind—not confined to the present generation, but as

> "From age to age descends the lay,
> To millions yet to be,
> Till far its echoes roll away,
> Into eternity."

The above is merely given as the substance of the President's remarks.

The Chairman of the delegation briefly replied that "they would hold a consultation and in a short time give an answer." The President said: "Take your full time—no hurry at all."

The delegation then withdrew.

[DOCUMENT 5-7]
TO HORACE GREELEY, AUGUST 22, 1862

On August 19, 1862, the New York Tribune *published a public letter from Horace Greeley to the president. Titled "The Prayer of Twenty Millions," it called upon Lincoln to strike at slavery and act vigorously to enforce the Second Confiscation Act, which called for the emancipation of slaves belonging to secessionists.*

Hon. Horace Greely: Executive Mansion,
Dear Sir   Washington, August 22, 1862.
I have just read yours of the 19th. addressed to myself through the New-York Tribune. If there be in it any statements, or assumptions of fact, which I may know to be erroneous, I do not, now and here, controvert them. If there be in it any inferences which I may believe to be falsely drawn, I do not now and here, argue against them. If there be perceptable in it an impatient and dictatorial tone, I waive it in deference to an old friend, whose heart I have always supposed to be right.
As to the policy I "seem to be pursuing" as you say, I have not meant to leave any one in doubt.
I would save the Union. I would save it the shortest way under the Constitution. The sooner the national authority can be restored; the nearer the Union will be "the Union as it was." If there be those who would not save the Union, unless they could at the same time *save* slavery, I do not agree with them. If there be those who would not save the Union unless they could at the same time *destroy* slavery, I do not agree with them. My paramount object in this struggle *is* to save the Union, and is *not* either to save or to destroy slavery. If I could save the Union without freeing *any* slave I would do it, and if I could save it by freeing *all* the slaves I would do it; and if I could save it by freeing some and leaving others alone I would also do that. What I do about slavery, and the colored race, I do because I believe it helps to save the Union; and what I forbear, I forbear because I do *not* believe it would help to save the Union. I shall do *less* whenever I shall believe what I am doing hurts the cause, and I shall do *more* whenever I shall believe doing more will help the cause. I shall try to correct errors when shown to be errors; and I shall adopt new views so fast as they shall appear to be true views.
I have here stated my purpose according to my view of *official* duty; and I intend no modification of my oft-expressed *personal* wish that all men every where could be free. Yours,   A. Lincoln

[DOCUMENT 5-8]
REPLY TO CHICAGO EMANCIPATION MEMORIAL, SEPTEMBER 13, 1862 (EXCERPTS)

On September 7, 1862, a meeting of Christians in Chicago passed a memorial in support of emancipation; six days later a delegation presented the memorial to the president, who that very morning had sprained his wrist in struggling to control his horse on a morning ride. Perhaps the pain from the accident, as well as his anxiety over military operations in Maryland, contributed to the tone of his comments as reported in the Chicago Tribune.

September 13, 1862

"The subject presented in the memorial is one upon which I have thought much for weeks past, and I may even say for months. I am approached with the most opposite opinions and advice, and that by religious men, who are equally certain that they represent the Divine will. I am sure that either the one or the other class is mistaken in that belief, and perhaps in some respects both. I hope it will not be irreverent for me to say that if it is probable that God would reveal his will to others, on a point so connected with my duty, it might be supposed he would reveal it directly to me; for, unless I am more deceived in myself than I often am, it is my earnest desire to know the will of Providence in this matter. *And if I can learn what it is I will do it!* These are not, however, the days of miracles, and I suppose it will be granted that I am not to expect a direct revelation. I must study the plain physical facts of the case, ascertain what is possible and learn what appears to be wise and right. The subject is difficult, and good men do not agree. For instance, the other day four gentlemen of standing and intelligence (naming one or two of the number) from New York called, as a delegation, on business connected with the war; but, before leaving, two of them earnestly beset me to proclaim general emancipation, upon which the other two at once attacked them! You know, also, that the last session of Congress had a decided majority of antislavery men, yet they could not unite on this policy. And the same is true of the religious people. Why, the rebel soldiers are praying with a great deal more earnestness, I fear, than our own troops, and expecting God to favor their side; for one of our soldiers, who had been taken prisoner, told Senator Wilson, a few days since, that he met with nothing so discouraging as the evident sincerity of those he was among in their prayers. But we will talk over the merits of the case.

What *good* would a proclamation of emancipation from me do, especially as we are now situated? I do not want to issue a document that the whole world will see must necessarily be inoperative, like the Pope's bull against the comet! Would *my word* free the slaves, when I cannot even enforce the Constitution in the rebel States? Is there a single court, or magistrate, or individual that would be influenced by it there? And what reason is there to think it would have any greater effect upon the slaves than the late law of Congress, which I approved, and which offers protection and freedom to the slaves of rebel masters who come within our lines? Yet I cannot learn that that law has caused a single slave to come over to us. And suppose they could be induced by a proclamation of freedom from me to throw themselves upon us, *what should we do with them?* How can we feed and care for such a multitude? Gen. Butler wrote me a few days since that he was issuing more rations to the slaves who have rushed to him than to all the white troops under his command. They *eat,* and that is all, though it is true Gen. Butler is feeding the whites also by the thousand; for it nearly amounts to a famine there. If, now, the pressure of the war should call off our forces from New Orleans to defend some other point, what is to prevent the masters from reducing the blacks to slavery again; for I am told that whenever the rebels take any black prisoners, free or slave, they immediately auction them off! They did so with those they took from a boat that was aground in the Tennessee river a few days ago. *And then I am very ungenerously attacked for it!* For instance, when, after the late battles at and near Bull Run, an expedition went out from Washington under a flag of truce to bury the dead and bring in the wounded, and the rebels seized the blacks who went along to help and sent them into slavery, Horace Greeley said in his paper that the Government would probably do nothing about it. What *could* I do? [Here your delegation suggested that this was a gross outrage on a flag of truce, which covers and protects all over which it waves, and that whatever he could do if *white* men had been similarly detained he *could* do in this case.]

"Now, then, tell me, if you please, what possible result of good would follow the issuing of such a proclamation as you desire? Understand, I raise no objections against it on legal or constitutional grounds; for, as commander-in-chief of the army and navy, in time of war, I suppose I have a right to take any measure which may best subdue the enemy. Nor do I urge objections of a moral nature, in view of possible consequences of insurrection and massacre at the South. I view the matter as a practical war measure, to be decided upon according to the advantages or disadvantages it may offer to the suppression of the rebellion."

⁕

"I admit that slavery is the root of the rebellion, or at least its *sine qua non*. The ambition of politicians may have instigated them to act, but they would have been impotent without slavery as their instrument. I will also concede that emancipation would help us in Europe, and convince them that we are incited by something more than ambition. I grant further that it would help *somewhat* at the North, though not so much, I fear, as you and those you represent imagine. Still, some additional strength would be added in that way to the war. And then unquestionably it would weaken the rebels by drawing off their laborers, which is of great importance. But I am not so sure we could do much with the blacks. If we were to arm them, I fear that in a few weeks the arms would be in the hands of the rebels; and indeed thus far we have not had arms enough to equip our white troops. I will mention another thing, though it meet only your scorn and contempt: There are fifty thousand bayonets in the Union armies from the Border Slave States. It would be a serious matter if, in consequence of a proclamation such as you desire, they should go over to the rebels. I do not think they all would—not so many indeed as a year ago, or as six months ago—not so many to-day as yesterday. Every day increases their Union feeling. They are also getting their pride enlisted, and want to beat the rebels. Let me say one thing more: I think you should admit that we already have an important principle to rally and unite the people in the fact that constitutional government is at stake. This is a fundamental idea, going down about as deep as any thing."

⁕

"Do not misunderstand me, because I have mentioned these objections. They indicate the difficulties that have thus far prevented my action in some such way as you desire. I have not decided against a proclamation of liberty to the slaves, but hold the matter under advisement. And I can assure you that the subject is on my mind, by day and night, more than any other. Whatever shall appear to be God's will I will do. I trust that, in the freedom with which I have canvassed your views, I have not in any respect injured your feelings."

[DOCUMENT 5-9]
PRELIMINARY EMANCIPATION PROCLAMATION,
SEPTEMBER 22, 1862

On September 17, 1862, George B. McClellan's Army of the Potomac and Robert E. Lee's Army of Northern Virginia battled along Antietam Creek in Maryland, just outside the town of Sharpsburg. Two days later the Confederates withdrew uncontested across the Potomac River into Virginia. Deciding that the outcome bore sufficient resemblance to a victory, Lincoln decided to issue the following proclamation.

By the President of the
United States of America
A Proclamation.

I, Abraham Lincoln, President of the United States of America, and Commander-in-chief of the Army and Navy thereof, do hereby proclaim and declare that hereafter, as heretofore, the war will be prossecuted for the object of practically restoring the constitutional relation between the United States, and each of the states, and the people thereof, in which states that relation is, or may be suspended, or disturbed.

That it is my purpose, upon the next meeting of Congress to again recommend the adoption of a practical measure tendering pecuniary aid to the free acceptance or rejection of all slave-states, so called, the people whereof may not then be in rebellion against the United States, and which states, may then have voluntarily adopted, or thereafter may voluntarily adopt, immediate, or gradual abolishment of slavery within their respective limits; and that the effort to colonize persons of African descent, with their consent, upon this continent, or elsewhere, with the previously obtained consent of the Governments existing there, will be continued.

That on the first day of January in the year of our Lord, one thousand eight hundred and sixty-three, all persons held as slaves within any state, or designated part of a state, the people whereof shall then be in rebellion against the United States shall be then, thenceforward, and forever free; and the executive government of the United States, including the military and naval authority thereof, will recognize and maintain the freedom of such persons, and will do no act or acts to repress such persons, or any of them, in any efforts they may make for their actual freedom.

That the executive will, on the first day of January aforesaid, by proclamation, designate the States, and parts of states, if any, in which the people thereof respectively, shall then be in rebellion against the United States; and the fact that any state, or the people thereof shall, on that day be, in good faith represented in the Congress of the United States, by members chosen thereto, at elections wherein a majority of the qualified voters of such state shall have participated, shall, in the absence of strong countervailing testimony, be deemed conclusive evidence that such state and the people thereof, are not then in rebellion against the United States.

That attention is hereby called to an act of Congress entitled "An act to make an additional Article of War" approved March 13, 1862, and which act is in the words and figure following:

> *Be it enacted by the Senate and House of Representatives of the United States of America in Congress assembled,* That hereafter the following shall be promulgated as an additional article of war for the government of the army of the United States, and shall be obeyed and observed as such:
>
> Article–. All officers or persons in the military or naval service of the United States are prohibited from employing any of the forces under their respective commands for the purpose of returning fugitives from service or labor, who may have escaped from any persons to whom such service or labor is claimed to be due, and any officer who shall be found guilty by a court-martial of violating this article shall be dismissed from the service.
>
> SEC. 2. And be it further enacted, That this act shall take effect from and after its passage.

Also to the ninth and tenth sections of an act entitled "An Act to suppress Insurrection, to punish Treason and Rebellion, to seize and confiscate property of rebels, and for other purposes," approved July 17, 1862, and which sections are in the words and figures following:

> SEC. 9. *And be it further enacted,* That all slaves of persons who shall hereafter be engaged in rebellion against the government of the United States, or who shall in any way give aid or comfort thereto, escaping from such persons and taking refuge within the lines of the army; and all slaves captured from such persons or deserted by them and coming under the control of the government of the United States; and all slaves of such persons found on (or) being within any place occupied by rebel forces and afterwards occupied by the forces of the United States, shall

be deemed captives of war, and shall be forever free of their servitude and not again held as slaves.

SEC. 10. *And be it further enacted,* That no slave escaping into any State, Territory, or the District of Columbia, from any other State, shall be delivered up, or in any way impeded or hindered of his liberty, except for crime, or some offence against the laws, unless the person claiming said fugitive shall first make oath that the person to whom the labor or service of such fugitive is alleged to be due is his lawful owner, and has not borne arms against the United States in the present rebellion, nor in any way given aid and comfort thereto; and no person engaged in the military or naval service of the United States shall, under any presence whatever, assume to decide on the validity of the claim of any person to the service or labor of any other person, or surrender up any such person to the claimant, on pain of being dismissed from the service.

And I do hereby enjoin upon and order all persons engaged in the military and naval service of the United States to observe, obey, and enforce, within their respective spheres of service, the act, and sections above recited.

And the executive will in due time recommend that all citizens of the United States who shall have remained loyal thereto throughout the rebellion, shall (upon the restoration of the constitutional relation between the United States, and their respective states, and people, if that "elation shall have been suspended or disturbed) be compensated for all losses by acts of the United States, including the loss of slaves.

In witness whereof, I have hereunto set my hand, and caused the seal of the United States to be affixed. Done at the City of Washington, this twenty second day of September, in the year of our Lord, one thousand eight hundred and sixty two, and of the Independence of the United States, the eighty seventh.

By the President: Abraham Lincoln
   William H. Seward, Secretary of State.

[DOCUMENT 5-10]
To Benjamin F. Butler, et al., October 14, 1862

In the hundred days between the issuance of the preliminary Emancipation Proclamation and January 1, 1863, Lincoln worked hard to hold elections in those portions of the Confederacy under Union control, reminding white Southerners that this was their last chance to check the onset of emancipation. Elec-

tions were held in Louisiana, but military operations disrupted similar efforts in Tennessee and Arkansas.

Andrew Johnson was presently military governor of Tennessee; Ulysses S. Grant was formally put in charge of the Department of Tennessee on October 25, 1862. Frederick Steele commanded Union forces in Arkansas; John S. Phelps was that state's military governor.

(Copy).

Executive Mansion,
Washington, October 14. 1862

Major General Butler, Governor Shepley, & all having military and naval authority under the United States within the State of Louisiana.

The bearer of this, Hon. John E. Bouligny, a citizen of Louisiana, goes to that State seeking to have such of the people thereof as desire to avoid the unsatisfactory prospect before them, and to have peace again upon the old terms under the constitution of the United States, to manifest such desire by elections of members to the Congress of the United States particularly, and perhaps a legislature, State officers, and United States Senators friendly to their object. I shall be glad for you and each of you, to aid him and all others acting for this object, as much as possible. In all available ways give the people a chance to express their wishes at these elections. Follow forms of law as far as convenient, but at all events get the expression of the largest number of the people possible. All see how such action will connect with, and affect the proclamation of September 22nd. Of course the men elected should be gentlemen of character, willing to swear support to the constitution, as of old, and known to be above reasonable suspicion of duplicity. Yours very Respectfully   A. Lincoln

[Endorsement]

Similar letter to Gen. Grant, Gov. Johnson & others in Tenn. dated Oct. 21. 1862.
And to, Steele, Phelps & others in Arkansas.
Nov. 18. 1862

[DOCUMENT 5-11]
SECOND ANNUAL MESSAGE, DECEMBER 1, 1862 (EXCERPTS)

In this message, Lincoln once again pushed for his plan of gradual, compensated emancipation and colonization, this time in the form of specific constitutional amendments. Congress did not adopt his suggestions. The final two paragraphs of the message are often quoted out of context; they bear comparison with the final paragraph from the portion of the First Annual Message herein repro-

duced [Document 4-9], which is also often quoted without reference to the context in which it appears.

...On the twenty-second day of September last a proclamation was issued by the Executive, a copy of which is herewith submitted.

In accordance with the purpose expressed in the second paragraph of that paper, I now respectfully recall your attention to what may be called "compensated emancipation."

A nation may be said to consist of its territory, its people, and its laws. The territory is the only part which is of certain durability. "One generation passeth away, and another generation cometh, but the earth abideth forever." It is of the first importance to duly consider, and estimate, this ever-enduring part. That portion of the earth's surface which is owned and inhabited by the people of the United States, is well adapted to be the home of one national family; and it is not well adapted for two, or more. Its vast extent, and its variety of climate and productions, are of advantage, in this age, for one people, whatever they might have been in former ages. Steam, telegraphs, and intelligence, have brought these, to be an advantageous combination, for one united people.

In the inaugural address I briefly pointed out the total inadequacy of disunion, as a remedy for the differences between the people of the two sections. I did so in language which I cannot improve, and which, therefore, I beg to repeat:

"One section of our country believes slavery is *right,* and ought to be extended, while the other believes it is *wrong,* and ought not to be extended. This is the only substantial dispute. The fugitive slave clause of the Constitution, and the law for the suppression of the foreign slave trade, are each as well enforced, perhaps, as any law can ever be in a community where the moral sense of the people imperfectly supports the law itself. The great body of the people abide by the dry legal obligation in both cases, and a few break over in each. This, I think, cannot be perfectly cured; and it would be worse in both cases *after* the separation of the sections, than before. The foreign slave trade, now imperfectly suppressed, would be ultimately revived without restriction in one section; while fugitive slaves, now only partially surrendered, would not be surrendered at all by the other.

"Physically speaking, we cannot separate. We cannot remove our respective sections from each other, nor build an impassable wall between them. A husband and wife may be divorced, and go out of the presence, and beyond the reach of each other; but the different parts of our country cannot do this. They cannot but remain face to face; and intercourse, either amicable or hostile, must continue between them. Is it possible, then, to make that intercourse more advantageous, or more satisfactory, *after* separation than *before?* Can aliens make treaties, easier than friends can make laws? Can treaties be more faithfully enforced between aliens, than laws can among friends? Suppose you go to war, you cannot fight always; and when, after much loss on both sides, and no gain on either, you cease fighting, the identical old questions, as to terms of intercourse, are again upon you."

There is no line, straight or crooked, suitable for a national boundary, upon which to divide. Trace through, from east to west, upon the line between the free and slave country, and we shall find a little more than one-third of its length are rivers, easy to be crossed, and populated, or soon to be populated, thickly upon both sides; while nearly all its remaining length, are merely surveyor's lines, over which people may walk back and forth without any consciousness of their presence. No part of this line can be made any more difficult to pass, by writing it down on paper, or parchment, as a national boundary. The fact of separation, if it comes, gives up, on the part of the seceding section, the fugitive slave clause, along with all other constitutional obligations upon the section seceded from, while I should expect no treaty stipulation would ever be made to take its place.

But there is another difficulty. The great interior region, bounded east by the Alleghanies, north by the British dominions, west by the Rocky mountains, and south by the line along which the culture of corn and cotton meets, and which includes part of Virginia, part of Tennessee, all of Kentucky, Ohio, Indiana, Michigan, Wisconsin, Illinois, Missouri, Kansas, Iowa, Minnesota and the Territories of Dakota, Nebraska, and part of Colorado, already has above ten millions of people, and will have fifty millions within fifty years, if not prevented by any political folly or mistake. It contains more than one-third of the country owned by the United States–certainly more than one million of square miles. Once half as populous as Massachusetts already is, it would have more than seventy-five millions of people. A glance at the map shows that, territorially speaking, it is the great body of the republic. The other parts are but marginal borders to it, the magnificent region sloping west from the rocky mountains to the Pacific, being the deepest, and also the richest, in undeveloped resources. In the production of provisions, grains, grasses, and all which proceed from them, this great interior region is naturally one of the most important in the world. Ascertain from the statistics the small proportion of the region which has, as yet, been brought into cultivation, and also the large and rapidly increasing amount of its products, and we shall be overwhelmed with the magnitude of the prospect presented. And yet this region has no sea-coast, touches no ocean anywhere. As part of one nation, its people now find, and may forever find, their way to Europe by New York, to South America and Africa by New Orleans, and to Asia by San Francisco. But separate our common country into two nations, as designed by the present rebellion, and every man of this great interior region is thereby cut off from some one or more of these outlets, not, perhaps, by a physical barrier, but by embarrassing and onerous trade regulations.

And this is true, *wherever* a dividing, or boundary line, may be fixed. Place it between the now free and slave country, or place it south of Kentucky, or north of Ohio, and still the truth remains, that none south of it, can trade to any port or place north of it, and none north of it, can trade to any port or place south of it, except upon terms dictated by a government foreign to them. These outlets, east, west, and south, are indispensable to the well-being of the people inhabiting, and to inhabit, this vast interior region. *Which* of the three may be the best, is no proper question. All, are better than either, and all, of right, belong to that people, and to their successors forever. True to themselves, they will not ask *where* a line of separation shall be, but will vow, rather, that there shall be no such line. Nor are the marginal regions less interested in these communications to, and through them, to the great outside world. They too, and each of them, must have access to this Egypt of the West, without paying toll at the crossing of any national boundary.

Our national strife springs not from our permanent part; not from the land we inhabit; not from our national homestead. There is no possible severing of this, but would multiply, and not mitigate, evils among us. In all its adaptations and aptitudes, it demands union, and abhors separation. In fact, it would, ere long, force reunion, however much of blood and treasure the separation might have cost.

Our strife pertains to ourselves—to the passing generations of men; and it can, without convulsion, be hushed forever with the passing of one generation.

In this view, I recommend the adoption of the following resolution and articles amendatory to the Constitution of the United States:

"Resolved by the Senate and House of Representatives of the United States of America in Congress assembled, (two thirds of both houses concurring,) That the following articles be proposed to the legislatures (or conventions) of the several States as amendments to the Constitution of the

United States, all or any of which articles when ratified by three-fourths of the said legislatures (or conventions) to be valid as part or parts of the said Constitution, viz:

"Article ——.

"Every State, wherein slavery now exists, which shall abolish the same therein, at any time, or times, before the first day of January, in the year of our Lord one thousand and nine hundred, shall receive compensation from the United States as follows, to wit:

"The President of the United States shall deliver to every such State, bonds of the United States, bearing interest at the rate of —— per cent, per annum, to an amount equal to the aggregate sum of   for each slave shown to have been therein, by the eighth census of the United States, said bonds to be delivered to such State by instalments, or in one parcel, at the completion of the abolishment, accordingly as the same shall have been gradual, or at one time, within such State; and interest shall begin to run upon any such bond, only from the proper time of its delivery as aforesaid. Any State having received bonds as aforesaid, and afterwards reintroducing or tolerating slavery therein, shall refund to the United States the bonds so received, or the value thereof, and all interest paid thereon.

"Article ——.

"All slaves who shall have enjoyed actual freedom by the chances of the war, at any time before the end of the rebellion, shall be forever free; but all owners of such, who shall not have been disloyal, shall be compensated for them, at the same rates as is provided for States adopting abolishment of slavery, but in such way, that no slave shall be twice accounted for.

"Article ——.

"Congress may appropriate money, and otherwise provide, for colonizing free colored persons, with their own consent, at any place or places without the United States."

I beg indulgence to discuss these proposed articles at some length. Without slavery the rebellion could never have existed; without slavery it could not continue.

Among the friends of the Union there is great diversity, of sentiment, and of policy, in regard to slavery, and the African race amongst us. Some would perpetuate slavery; some would abolish it suddenly, and without compensation; some would abolish it gradually, and with compensation; some would remove the freed people from us, and some would retain them with us; and there are yet other minor diversities. Because of these diversities, we waste much strength in struggles among ourselves. By mutual concession we should harmonize, and act together. This would be compromise; but it would be compromise among the friends, and not with the enemies of the Union. These articles are intended to embody a plan of such mutual concessions. If the plan shall be adopted, it is assumed that emancipation will follow, at least, in several of the States.

As to the first article, the main points are: first, the emancipation; secondly, the length of time for consummating it—thirty-seven years; and thirdly, the compensation.

The emancipation will be unsatisfactory to the advocates of perpetual slavery; but the length of time should greatly mitigate their dissatisfaction. The time spares both races from the evils of sudden derangement—in fact, from the necessity of any derangement—while most of those whose habitual course of thought will be disturbed by the measure will have passed away before its consummation. They will never see it. Another class will hail the prospect of emancipation, but will deprecate the length of time. They will feel that it gives too little to the now living slaves. But it really gives them much. It saves them from the vagrant destitution which must largely attend immediate emancipation in localities where their numbers are very great; and it gives the inspiring assurance that their posterity shall be free forever. The plan leaves to each State, choosing to act under it, to abolish slavery now, or at the end of the century, or at any intermediate time, or by degrees, extending over the whole or any part of the period; and it obliges no two states to proceed alike. It also provides for compensation, and generally the mode of making it. This, it would seem, must further mitigate the dissatisfaction of those who favor perpetual slavery, and especially of those who are to receive the compensation. Doubtless some of those who are to pay, and not to receive will object. Yet the measure is both just and economical. In a certain sense the liberation of slaves is the destruction of property—property acquired by descent, or by purchase, the same as any other property. It is no less true for having been often said, that the people of the south are not more responsible for the original introduction of this property, than are the people of the north; and when it is remembered how unhesitatingly we all use cotton and sugar, and share the profits of dealing in them, it may not be quite safe to say, that the south has been more responsible than the north for its continuance. If then, for a common object, this property is to be sacrificed is it not just that it be done at a common charge?

And if, with less money, or money more easily paid, we can preserve the benefits of the Union by this means, than we can by the war alone, is it not also economical to do it? Let us consider it then. Let us ascertain the sum we have expended in the war since compensated emancipation was proposed last March, and consider whether, if that measure had been promptly accepted, by even some of the slave States, the same sum would not have done more to close the war, than has been otherwise done. If so the measure would save money, and, in that view, would be a prudent and economical measure. Certainly it is not so easy to pay *something* as it is to pay *nothing;* but it is easier to pay a large sum than it is to pay a larger one. And it is easier to pay any sum *when* we are able, than it is to pay it *before* we are able. The war requires large sums, and requires them at once. The aggregate sum necessary for compensated emancipation, of course, would be large. But it would require no ready cash; nor the bonds even, any faster than the emancipation progresses. This might not, and probably would not, close before the end of the thirty-seven years. At that time we shall probably have a hundred millions of people to share the burden, instead of thirty one millions, as now. And not only so, but the increase of our population may be expected to continue for a long time after that period, as rapidly as before; because our territory will not have become full. I do not state this inconsiderately. At the same ratio of increase which we have maintained, on an average, from our first national census, in 1790, until that of 1860, we should, in 1900, have a population of 103,208,415. And why may we not continue that ratio far beyond that period? Our abundant room—our broad national homestead—is our ample resource. Were our territory as limited as are the British Isles, very certainly our population could not expand as stated. Instead of receiving the foreign born, as now, we should be compelled to send part of the native born away. But such is not our condition. We have two millions nine hundred and sixty-three thousand square miles. Europe has three millions and eight hundred thousand, with a population averaging seventy-three and one-third persons to the square mile. Why may not our country, at some time, average as many? Is it less fertile? Has it more waste surface, by mountains, rivers, lakes, deserts, or other causes? Is it inferior to Europe in any natural advantage? If, then, we are, at some time, to be as populous as Europe, how soon? As to when this *may* be, we can judge by the past and the present; as to when it *will* be, if ever, depends much on whether we maintain the Union.

The proposed emancipation would shorten the war, perpetuate peace, insure this increase of population, and proportionately the wealth of the country. With these, we should pay all the emancipation would cost, together with our other debt, easier than we should pay our other debt, without it. If we had allowed our old national debt to run at six per cent. per annum, simple interest, from the end of our revolutionary struggle until to day, without paying anything on either principal or interest, each man of us would owe less upon that debt now, than each man owed upon it then; and this because our increase of men, through the whole period, has been greater than six per cent.; has run faster than the interest upon the debt. Thus, time alone relieves a debtor nation, so long as its population increases faster than unpaid interest accumulates on its debt.

This fact would be no excuse for delaying payment of what is justly due; but it shows the great importance of time in this connexion—the great advantage of a policy by which we shall not have to pay until we number a hundred millions, what, by a different policy, we would have to pay now, when we number but thirty one millions. In a word, it shows that a dollar will be much harder to pay for the war, than will be a dollar for emancipation on the proposed plan. And then the latter will cost no blood, no precious life. It will be a saving of both.

As to the second article, I think it would be impracticable to return to bondage the class of persons therein contemplated. Some of them, doubtless, in the property sense, belong to loyal owners; and hence, provision is made in this article for compensating such.

The third article relates to the future of the freed people. It does not oblige, but merely authorizes, Congress to aid in colonizing such as may consent. This ought not to be regarded as objectionable, on the one hand, or on the other, in so much as it comes to nothing, unless by the mutual consent of the people to be deported, and the American voters, through their representatives in Congress.

I cannot make it better known than it already is, that I strongly favor colonization. And yet I wish to say there is an objection urged against free colored persons remaining in the country, which is largely imaginary, if not sometimes malicious.

It is insisted that their presence would injure, and displace white labor and white laborers. If there ever could be a proper time for mere catch arguments, that time surely is not now. In times like the present, men should utter nothing for which they would not willingly be responsible through time and in eternity. Is it true, then, that colored people can displace any more white labor, by being free, than by remaining slaves? If they stay in their old places, they jostle no white laborers; if they leave their old places, they leave them open to white laborers. Logically, there is neither more nor less of it. Emancipation, even without deportation, would probably enhance the wages of white labor, and, very surely, would not reduce them. Thus, the customary amount of labor would still have to be performed; the freed people would surely not do more than their old proportion of it, and very probably, for a time, would do less, leaving an increased part to white laborers, bringing their labor into greater demand, and, consequently, enhancing the wages of it. With deportation, even to a limited extent, enhanced wages to white labor is mathematically certain. Labor is like any other commodity in the market—increase the demand for it, and you increase the price of it. Reduce the supply of black labor, by colonizing the black laborer out of the country, and, by precisely so much, you increase the demand for, and wages of, white labor.

But it is dreaded that the freed people will swarm forth, and cover the whole land? Are they not already in the land? Will liberation make them any more numerous? Equally distributed among the whites of the whole country, and there would be but one colored to seven whites. Could the one, in any way, greatly disturb the seven? There are many communities now, having more than one free colored person, to seven whites; and this, without any apparent consciousness of evil from it. The District of Columbia, and the States of Maryland and Delaware, are all in this condition. The District has more than one free colored to six whites; and yet, in its frequent petitions to Congress, I believe it has never presented the presence of free colored persons as one of its grievances. But why should emancipation south, send the free people north? People, of any color, seldom run, unless there be something to run from. *Heretofore* colored people, to some extent, have fled north from bondage; and *now,* perhaps, from both bondage and destitution. But if gradual emancipation and deportation be adopted, they will have neither to flee from. Their old masters will give them wages at least until new laborers can be procured; and the freed men, in turn, will gladly give their labor for the wages, till new homes can be found for them, in congenial climes, and with people of their own blood and race. This proposition can be trusted on the mutual interests involved. And, in any event, cannot the north decide for itself, whether to receive them?

Again, as practice proves more than theory, in any case, has there been any irruption of colored people northward, because of the abolishment of slavery in this District last spring?

What I have said of the proportion of free colored persons to the whites, in the District, is from the census of 1860, having no reference to persons called contrabands, nor to those made free by the act of Congress abolishing slavery here.

The plan consisting of these articles is recommended, not but that a restoration of the national authority would be accepted without its adoption.

Nor will the war, nor proceedings under the proclamation of September 22, 1862, be stayed because of the *recommendation* of this plan. Its timely *adoption,* I doubt not, would bring restoration and thereby stay both.

And, notwithstanding this plan, the recommendation that Congress provide by law for compensating any State which may adopt emancipation, before this plan shall have been acted upon, is hereby earnestly renewed. Such would be only an advance part of the plan, and the same arguments apply to both.

This plan is recommended as a means, not in exclusion of, but additional to, all others for restoring and preserving the national authority throughout the Union. The subject is presented exclusively in its economical aspect. The plan would, I am confident, secure peace more speedily, and maintain it more permanently, than can be done by force alone; while all it would cost, considering amounts, and manner of payment, and times of payment, would be easier paid than will be the additional cost of the war, if we rely solely upon force. It is much–very much–that it would cost no blood at all.

The plan is proposed as permanent constitutional law. It cannot become such without the concurrence of, first, two-thirds of Congress, and, afterwards, three-fourths of the States. The requisite three-fourths of the States will necessarily include seven of the Slave states. Their concurrence, if obtained, will give assurance of their severally adopting emancipation, at no very distant day, upon the new constitutional terms. This assurance would end the struggle now, and save the Union forever.

I do not forget the gravity which should characterize a paper addressed to the Congress of the nation by the Chief Magistrate of the nation. Nor do I forget that some of you are my seniors, nor that many of you have more experience than I, in the conduct of public affairs. Yet I trust that in view of the great responsibility resting upon me, you will perceive no want of respect to yourselves, in any undue earnestness I may seem to display.

Is it doubted, then, that the plan I propose, if adopted, would shorten the war, and thus lessen its expenditure of money and of blood? Is it doubted that it would restore the national authority and national prosperity, and perpetuate both indefinitely? Is it doubted that we here–Congress and Executive–can secure its adoption? Will not the good people respond to a united, and earnest appeal from us? Can we, can they, by any other means, so certainly, or so speedily, assure these vital objects? We can succeed only by concert. It is not "can *any* of us *imagine* better?" but "can we *all* do better?" Object whatsoever is possible, still the question recurs "can we do better?" The dogmas of the quiet past, are inadequate to the stormy present. The occasion is piled high with difficulty, and we must rise with the occasion. As our case is new, so we must think anew, and act anew. We must disenthrall our selves, and then we shall save our country.

Fellow-citizens, *we* cannot escape history. We of this Congress and this administration, will be remembered in spite of ourselves. No personal significance, or insignificance, can spare one or another of us. The fiery trial through which we pass, will light us down, in honor or dishonor, to the latest generation. We *say* we are for the Union. The world will not forget that we say this. We know how to save the Union. The world knows we do know how to save it. We–even *we here*–hold the power, and bear the responsibility. In *giving* freedom to the *slave,* we *assure* freedom to the *free*–honorable alike in what we give, and what we preserve. We shall nobly save, or meanly lose, the last best, hope of earth. Other means may succeed; this could not fail. The way is plain, peaceful, generous, just–a way which, if followed, the world will forever applaud, and God must forever bless.

December 1, 1862.   Abraham Lincoln

[DOCUMENT 5-12]
EMANCIPATION PROCLAMATION, JANUARY 1, 1863

Although Lincoln issued the preliminary Emancipation Proclamation in the wake of an apparent Union victory, by the time he had promised to issue the final proclamation, Union armies had suffered setbacks in Virginia and Mississippi. Some people were not even sure that Lincoln would keep his promise. Nevertheless, after shaking hands for several hours at a New Year's Day reception at the White House, Lincoln signed the following document, containing a text that differed in important ways from his July draft and September announcement.

By the President of the United States of America:
A Proclamation.

Whereas, on the twentysecond day of September, in the year of our Lord one thousand eight hundred and sixty two, a proclamation was issued by the President of the United States, containing, among other things, the following, towit:

"That on the first day of January, in the year of our Lord one thousand eight hundred and sixty-three, all persons held as slaves within any State or designated part of a State, the people whereof shall then be in rebellion against the United States, shall be then, thenceforward, and forever free; and the Executive Government of the United States, including the military and naval authority thereof, will recognize and maintain the freedom of such persons, and will do no act or acts to repress such persons, or any of them, in any efforts they may make for their actual freedom.

"That the Executive will, on the first day of January aforesaid, by proclamation, designate the States and parts of States, if any, in which the people thereof, respectively, shall then be in rebellion against the United States; and the fact that any State, or the people thereof, shall on that day be, in good faith, represented in the Congress of the United States by members chosen thereto at elections wherein a majority of the qualified voters of such State shall have participated, shall, in the absence of strong countervailing testimony, be deemed conclusive evidence that such State, and the people thereof, are not then in rebellion against the United States."

Now, therefore I, Abraham Lincoln, President of the United States, by virtue of the power in me vested as Commander-in-Chief, of the Army and Navy of the United States in time of actual armed rebellion against authority and government of the United States, and as a fit and necessary war measure for suppressing said rebellion, do, on this first day of January, in the year of our Lord one thousand eight hundred and sixty three, and in accordance with my purpose so to do publicly proclaimed for the full period of one hundred days, from the day first above mentioned, order and designate as the States and parts of States wherein the people thereof respectively, are this day in rebellion against the United States, the following, towit:

Arkansas, Texas, Louisiana, (except the Parishes of St. Bernard, Plaquemines, Jefferson, St. Johns, St. Charles, St. James, Ascension,

Assumption, Terrebonne, Lafourche, St. Mary, St. Martin, and Orleans, including the City of New-Orleans) Mississippi, Alabama, Florida, Georgia, South-Carolina, North-Carolina, and Virginia, (except the fortyeight counties designated as West Virginia, and also the counties of Berkley, Accomac, Northampton, Elizabeth-City, York, Princess Ann, and Norfolk, including the cities of Norfolk & Portsmouth); and which excepted parts are, for the present, left precisely as if this proclamation were not issued.

And by virtue of the power, and for the purpose aforesaid, I do order and declare that all persons held as slaves within said designated States, and parts of States, are, and henceforward shall be free; and that the Executive government of the United States, including the military and naval authorities thereof, will recognize and maintain the freedom of said persons.

And I hereby enjoin upon the people so declared to be free to abstain from all violence, unless in necessary self-defence; and I recommend to them that, in all cases when allowed, they labor faithfully for reasonable wages.

And I further declare and make known, that such persons of suitable condition, will be received into the armed service of the United States to garrison forts, positions, stations, and other places, and to man vessels of all sorts in said service.

And upon this act, sincerely believed to be an act of justice, warranted by the Constitution, upon military necessity, I invoke the considerate judgment of mankind, and the gracious favor of Almighty God.

In witness whereof, I have hereunto set my hand and caused the seal of the United States to be affixed.

Done at the City of Washington, this first day of January, in the year of our Lord one thousand eight hundred and sixty three, and of the Independence of the United States of America the eighty-seventh.

By the President: Abraham Lincoln
William H. Seward, Secretary of State.

[DOCUMENT 5-13]
TO JOHN A. MCCLERNAND, JANUARY 8, 1863

Eight days after he issued the Emancipation Proclamation, Lincoln reflected upon his decision in a letter to Major General John A. McClernand, an Illinois Democrat who was currently in command of a Union force currently in Arkansas.

Executive Mansion,

Major General McClernand   Washington, January 8. 1863.

My dear Sir Your interesting communication by the hand of Major Scates is received. I never did ask more, nor ever was willing to accept less, than for all the States, and the people thereof, to take and hold their places, and their rights, in the Union, under the Constitution of the United States. For this alone have I felt authorized to struggle; and I seek neither more nor less now. Still, to use a coarse, but an expressive figure, broken eggs can not be mended. I have issued the emancipation proclamation, and I can not retract it.

After the commencement of hostilities I struggled nearly a year and a half to get along without touching the "institution"; and when finally I conditionally determined to touch it, I gave a hundred days fair notice of my purpose, to all the States and people, within which time they could have turned it wholly aside, by simply again becoming good citizens of the United States. They chose to disregard it, and I made the peremptory proclamation on what appeared to me to be a military necessity. And being made, it must stand. As to the States not included in it, of course they can have their rights in the Union as of old. Even the people of the states included, if they choose, need not to be hurt by it. Let them adopt systems of apprenticeship for the colored people, conforming substantially to the most approved plans of gradual emancipation; and, with the aid they can have from the general government, they may be nearly as well off, in this respect, as if the present trouble had not occurred, and much better off than they can possibly be if the contest continues persistently.

As to any dread of my having a "purpose to enslave, or exterminate, the whites of the South," I can scarcely believe that such dread exists. It is too absurd. I believe you can be my personal witness that no man is less to be dreaded for undue severity, in any case.

If the friends you mention really wish to have peace upon the old terms, they should act at once. Every day makes the case more difficult. They can so act, with entire safety, so far as I am concerned.

I think you would better not make this letter public, but you may rely confidently on my standing by whatever I have said in it. Please write me if any thing more comes to light. Yours very truly

A. Lincoln

A New Birth
of Freedom,
1863

CHAPTER SIX

EMANCIPATION ESCALATED THE CIVIL WAR by broadening Union war aims; it also freed Lincoln to embrace the use of blacks as soldiers. As he explained to Tennessee's military governor, Andrew Johnson, he thought that the additional manpower might well prove decisive [Document 6-1]. "I believe it is a resource which, if vigorously applied now, will soon close the contest," he later told Ulysses S. Grant. "It works doubly, weakening the enemy and strengthening us."[1] The Confederate response, however, threatened to intensify the war still more. The Confederate Congress passed legislation that charged white Union officers of black regiments with inciting insurrection, subjecting them to the penalty of death if captured, while pledging to return to their masters captured black Union soldiers who had escaped from slavery. Some Confederate commanders and soldiers took matters into their own hands: before long reports filtered northward that black soldiers attempting to surrender at Milliken's Bend, Louisiana, on June 7, 1863, were instead killed by their Confederate captors, as was a white officer. In response, Lincoln issued an order promising to retaliate for any such incidents [Document 6-2]; however, the administration never acted on this pledge, most notably after Confederate soldiers attacking Fort Pillow, Tennessee, on April 12, 1864, slaughtered a number of black soldiers attempting to surrender. Instead, black soldiers sometimes retaliated in kind; as general-in-chief, Grant insisted that black prisoners receive the same treatment as their white counterparts, a policy that was partly responsible for the suspension of prisoner exchanges.

The use of black soldiers was one of several topics Lincoln addressed in a public letter to a gathering of war supporters in Springfield, Illinois, in September 1863 [Document 6-4]. He entrusted James C.

Conkling, an old lawyer friend and Republican, to share his sentiments with the audience. "You are one of the best public readers," he told Conkling, adding, "I have but one suggestion. Read it very slowly." Once more the president outlined his commitment to victory over the Confederacy, making clear why nothing else would do, and countered other objections to his policy. Although the crowd cheered the president's words, early newspaper accounts mangled it, causing Lincoln some anguish at seeing his handiwork "botched up."[2]

Committed to emancipation, Lincoln nevertheless knew that its legitimacy rested upon military necessity. As he explained to his treasury secretary, the antislavery advocate Salmon P. Chase, to expand the scope of the Emancipation Proclamation beyond that would lead to charges that he was, in fact, a military dictator–and it would also hurt his chances for reelection in 1864 [Document 6-5]. There were other ways to push for the destruction of slavery, however. In Tennessee, Andrew Johnson had excluded his state from the proclamation; now Lincoln pressed him to make sure that abolition would be part of the foundation of a reconstructed civil government there [Document 6-6]. Eventually, Tennessee's new constitution ended slavery, and the state was among the first to ratify the Thirteenth Amendment in 1865. In Louisiana, much of which was also excluded from the Emancipation Proclamation, the president, while maintaining that it was up to that state's unionists to shape a new state government, made it clear to General Nathaniel P. Banks, his man on the scene, that he would not support a reconstructed state government that did not end slavery [Documents 6-3 and 6-7]. He was much more flexible when it came to how best to make blacks part of free society, in part reflecting his own preferences for education and gradual change, and in part because he had not given much thought to the matter of post-emancipation society. For the moment, however, he left it up to Banks to work with unionists Benjamin Flanders, Michael Hahn, and Thomas J. Durant as well as military governor George F. Shepley, reminding the general that Congress as well as the president would pass on the result.

Perhaps Lincoln's clearest statement on how emancipation had transformed the meaning of the war is to be found in the Gettysburg Address [Document 6-8]. In response to a request for him to offer a "few appropriate remarks," Lincoln worked hard to give voice to thoughts that had circulated through his mind for several months. "How long ago is it?–eighty odd years–since on the Fourth of July for the first time in the history of the world a nation by its representatives, assembled and declared as a self-evident truth that 'all men are created equal,'" he had remarked in July 1863, adding, "Gentlemen, this is a glorious theme, and the occasion for a speech, but I am not prepared to make one worthy of the occasion."[3] Now he had his occasion, and he prepared for it, cheered by the knowledge that the Republicans had fared well in the 1863 fall elections. The result was indeed "worthy of the occasion."

1. Lincoln to Grant, August 9, 1863, Fehrenbacher, *Lincoln: Speeches and Writings,* 2:490.
2. Lincoln to Conkling, August 27 and September 3, 1863, Basler, *Collected Works,* 6:414, 430.
3. Response to a Serenade, July 7, 1863, Basler, *Collected Works,* 6:319–320.

[DOCUMENT 6-1]
TO ANDREW JOHNSON, MARCH 26, 1863

In 1862 Lincoln appointed Andrew Johnson military governor of Tennessee. Although Johnson had been a proslavery Democrat before the war, his staunch Unionism and hatred of secessionists led him to accept emancipation as a war measure—although it was not until 1865 that the peculiar institution was abolished in Tennessee. He visited Washington in March 1863 at the end of a long speaking tour through the North; there he lobbied for more soldiers to be sent to Tennessee.

Private
Hon. Andrew Johnson   Executive Mansion,
My dear Sir: Washington, March 26. 1863.
    I am told you have at least *thought* of raising a negro military force. In my opinion the country now needs no specific thing so much as some man of your ability, and position, to go to this work. When I speak of your position, I mean that of an eminent citizen of a slave-state, and himself a slave-holder. The colored population is the great *available* and yet *unavailed* of, force for restoring the Union. The bare sight of fifty thousand armed, and drilled black soldiers on the banks of the Mississippi, would end the rebellion at once. And who doubts that we can present that sight, if we but take hold in earnest? If you *have* been thinking of it please do not dismiss the thought. Yours truly
                                                        A. Lincoln

[DOCUMENT 6-2]
ORDER OF RETALIATION, JULY 30, 1863

Early in 1863, in response to the enlistment of blacks in the Union army, the Confederacy adopted a policy calling for the reenslavement of former slaves who became prisoners of war and proclaimed that white officers in command of black soldiers were subject to be tried on charges of inciting insurrection (a crime punishable by death). Some Confederate officers and soldiers carried retaliation a step further, executing black prisoners, most notably at Milliken's Bend, Louisiana, on June 7, 1863. After due consideration, Lincoln issued this order, although he drew back from acting in accordance with its provisions.

Executive Mansion, Washington D.C July 30. 1863

It is the duty of every government to give protection to its citizens, of whatever class, color, or condition, and especially to those who are duly organized as soldiers in the public service. The law of nations and the usages and customs of war as carried on by civilized powers, permit no distinction as to color in the treatment of prisoners of war as public enemies. To sell or enslave any captured person, on account of his color, and for no offence against the laws of war, is a relapse into barbarism and a crime against the civilization of the age.

The government of the United States will give the same protection to all its soldiers, and if the enemy shall sell or enslave anyone because of his color, the offense shall be punished by retaliation upon the enemy's prisoners in our possession.

It is therefore ordered that for every soldier of the United States killed in violation of the laws of war, a rebel soldier shall be executed; and for every one enslaved by the enemy or sold into slavery, a rebel soldier shall be placed at hard labor on the public works and continued at such labor until the other shall be released and receive the treatment due to a prisoner of war

Abraham Lincoln

[DOCUMENT 6-3]
TO NATHANIEL P. BANKS, AUGUST 5, 1863

Lincoln wrote Major General Nathaniel P. Banks in the wake of Banks's capture of Port Hudson, Louisiana, on July 9, 1863, five days after Ulysses S. Grant occupied Vicksburg, thus securing the Mississippi River. Although the president was eager for Banks to move westward into Texas as a show of force against French attempts to establish a new government in Mexico, he was also concerned about what would happen to the thousands of blacks liberated by Union military operations along the Mississippi River valley. Banks had shared with Massachusetts congressman George S. Boutwell the desire of Louisiana unionists to commence the task of constructing a loyal state government. Boutwell brought Banks's letter with him when he met the president on August 5, and the congressman reported back to Banks that Lincoln favored the idea provided that the men's plans included emancipation. In transmitting copies of the letter to Benjamin F. Flanders, Michael Hahn, and Thomas J. Durant, all leaders in the movement to establish a new state government, the president demonstrated that if he was not willing "to assume direction of the matter," he was perfectly willing to point others in the right direction.

Executive Mansion, Washington,
My dear General Banks   August 5, 1863.

Being a poor correspondent is the only apology I offer for not having sooner tendered my thanks for your very successful, and very valuable military operations this year. The final stroke in opening the Mississippi never should, and I think never will, be forgotten.

Recent events in Mexico, I think, render early action in Texas more important than ever. I expect, however, the General-in-Chief, will address you more fully upon this subject.

Governor Boutwell read me to-day that part of your letter to him, which relates to Louisiana affairs. While I very well know what I would be glad for Louisiana to do, it is quite a different thing for me to assume direction of the matter. I would be glad for her to make a new Constitution recognizing the emancipation proclamation, and adopting emancipation in those parts of the state to which the proclamation does not apply. And while she is at it, I think it would not be objectionable for her to adopt some practical system by which the two races could gradually live themselves out of their old relation to each other, and both come out better prepared for the new. Education for young blacks should be included in the plan. After all, the power, or element, of "contract" may be sufficient for this probationary period; and, by it's simplicity, and flexibility, may be the better.

As an anti-slavery man I have a motive to desire emancipation, which pro-slavery men do not have; but even they have strong enough reason to thus place themselves again under the shield of the Union; and to thus perpetually hedge against the recurrence of the scenes through which we are now passing.

Gov. Shepley has informed me that Mr. Durant is now taking a registry, with a view to the election of a Constitutional convention in Louisiana. This, to me, appears proper. If such convention were to ask my views, I could present little else than what I now say to you. I think the thing should be pushed forward, so that if possible, it's mature work may reach here by the meeting of Congress.

For my own part I think I shall not, in any event, retract the emancipation proclamation; nor, as executive, ever return to slavery any person who is free by the terms of that proclamation, or by any of the acts of Congress.

If Louisiana shall send members to Congress, their admission to seats will depend, as you know, upon the respective Houses, and not upon the President.

If these views can be of any advantage in giving shape, and impetus, to action there, I shall be glad for you to use them prudently for that object. Of course you will confer with intelligent and trusty citizens of the State, among whom I would suggest Messrs. Flanders, Hahn, and Durant; and to each of whom I now think I may send copies of this letter. Still it is perhaps better to not make the letter generally public.
Yours very truly   A. Lincoln
[Endorsement]
Copies sent to Messrs. Flanders, Hahn & Durant, each indorsed as follows.

The within is a copy of a letter to Gen. Banks. Please observe my directions to him. Do not mention the paragraph about Mexico.
Aug. 6. 1863.   A. Lincoln

[DOCUMENT 6-4]
To JAMES C. CONKLING, AUGUST 26, 1863

Starting in 1863, Lincoln took the opportunity of responding to invitations and resolutions by issuing public letters in an effort to outline administration policy. One such chance came when James C. Conkling, an old political associate, invited him to address a pro-Union rally at Springfield on September 3.

Hon. James C. Conkling   Executive Mansion,
My Dear Sir.   Washington, August 26, 1863.
Your letter inviting me to attend a mass-meeting of unconditional Union-men, to be held at the Capital of Illinois, on the 3d day of September, has been received.

It would be very agreeable to me, to thus meet my old friends, at my own home; but I can not, just now, be absent from here, so long as a visit there, would require.

The meeting is to be of all those who maintain unconditional devotion to the Union; and I am sure my old political friends will thank me for tendering, as I do, the nation's gratitude to those other noble men, whom no partizan malice, or partizan hope, can make false to the nation's life.

There are those who are dissatisfied with me. To such I would say: You desire peace; and you blame me that we do not have it. But how can we attain it? There are but three conceivable ways. First, to suppress the rebellion by force of arms. This, I am trying to do. Are you for it? If you are, so far we are agreed. If you are not for it, a second way is, to give up the Union. I am against this. Are you for it? If you are, you should say so plainly. If you are not for *force,* nor yet for *dissolution,* there only remains some imaginable *compromise.* I do not believe any compromise, embracing the maintenance of the Union, is now possible. All I learn, leads to a directly opposite belief. The strength of the rebellion, is its military—its army. That army dominates all the country, and all the people, within its range. Any offer of terms made by any man or men within that range, in opposition to that army, is simply nothing for the present; because such man or men, have no power whatever to enforce their side of a compromise, if one were made with them. To illustrate—Suppose refugees from the South, and peace men of the North, get together in convention, and frame and proclaim a compromise embracing a restoration of the Union; in what way can that compromise be used to keep Lee's army out of Pennsylvania? Meade's army can keep Lee's army out of Pennsylvania; and, I think, can ultimately drive it out of existence. But no paper compromise, to which the controllers of Lee's army are not agreed, can, at all, affect that army. In an effort at such compromise we should waste time, which the enemy would improve to our disadvantage; and that would be all. A compromise, to be effective, must be made either with those who control the rebel army, or with the people first liberated from the domination of that army, by the success of our own army. Now allow me to assure you, that no word or intimation, from that rebel army, or from any of the men controlling it, in relation to any peace compromise, has ever come to my knowledge or belief. All charges and insinuations to the contrary, are deceptive and groundless. And I promise you, that if any such proposition shall hereafter come, it shall not be rejected, and kept a secret from you. I freely acknowledge myself the servant of the people, according to the bond of service—the United States constitution; and that, as such, I am responsible to them.

But, to be plain, you are dissatisfied with me about the negro. Quite likely there is a difference of opinion between you and myself upon that subject. I certainly wish that all men could be free, while I suppose you do not. Yet I have neither adopted, nor proposed any measure, which is not consistent with even your view, provided you are for the Union. I suggested compensated emancipation; to which you replied you wished not to be taxed to buy negroes. But I had not asked you to be taxed to buy negroes, except in such way, as to save you from greater taxation to save the Union exclusively by other means.

You dislike the emancipation proclamation; and, perhaps, would have it retracted. You say it is unconstitutional—I think differently. I think the constitution invests its commander-in-chief, with the law of war, in time of war. The most that can be said, if so much, is, that slaves are property. Is there—has there ever been—any question that by the law of war, property, both of enemies and friends, may be taken when needed? And is it not needed whenever taking it, helps us, or hurts the enemy? Armies, the world over, destroy enemies' property when they can not use it; and even destroy their own to keep it from the enemy. Civilized belligerents do all in their power to help themselves, or hurt the enemy, except a few things regarded as barbarous or cruel. Among the exceptions are the massacre of vanquished foes, and non-combatants, male and female.

But the proclamation, as law, either is valid, or is not valid. If it is not valid, it needs no retraction. If it valid, it can not be retracted, any more than the dead can be brought to life. Some of you profess to think its retraction would operate favorably for the Union. Why better *after* the retraction, than *before* the issue? There was more than a year and a half of trial to suppress the rebellion before the proclamation issued, the last one hundred days of which passed under an explicit notice that it was coming, unless averted by those in revolt, returning to their allegiance. The war has certainly progressed as favorably for us, since the issue of the proclamation as before. I know as fully as one can know the opinions of others, that some of the commanders of our armies in the field who have given us our most important successes, believe the emancipation policy, and the use of colored troops, constitute the heaviest blow yet dealt to the rebellion; and that, at least one of those important successes, could not have been achieved when it was, but for the aid of the black soldiers. Among the commanders holding these views are some who have never had any affinity with what is called abolitionism, or with republican party politics; but who hold them purely as military opinions. I submit these opinions as being entitled to some weight against the objections, often urged, that emancipation, and arming the blacks, are unwise as military measures, and were not adopted, as such, in good faith.

You say you will not fight to free negroes. Some of them seem willing to fight for you; but, no matter. Fight you, then, exclusively to save the Union. I issued the proclamation on purpose to aid you in saving the Union. Whenever you shall have conquered all resistance to the Union, if I shall urge you to continue fighting, it will be an apt time, then, for you to declare you will not fight to free negroes.

I thought that in your struggle for the Union, to whatever extent the negroes should cease helping the enemy, to what extent it weakened the enemy in his resistance to you. Do you think differently? I thought that whatever negroes can be got to do as soldiers, leaves just so much less for white soldiers to do, in saving the Union. Does it appear otherwise to you? But negroes, like other people, act upon motives. Why should they do any thing for us, if we will do nothing for them? If they stake their lives for us, they must be prompted by the strongest motive—even the promise of freedom. And the promise being made, must be kept.

The signs look better. The Father of Waters again goes unvexed to the sea. Thanks to the great North-West for it. Nor yet wholly to them. Three hundred miles up, they met New-England, Empire, Key-Stone, and Jersey, hewing their way right and left. The Sunny South too, in more colors than one, also lent a hand. On the spot, their part of the history was jotted down in black and white. The job was a great national one; and let none be banned who bore an honorable part in it. And while those who have cleared the great river may well be proud, even that is not all. It is hard to say that anything has been more bravely, and well done, than at Antietam, Murfreesboro, Gettysburg, and on many fields of lesser note. Nor must Uncle Sam's Web-feet be forgotten. At all the watery margins they have been present. Not only on the deep sea, the broad bay, and the rapid river, but also up the narrow muddy bayou, and wherever the ground was a little damp, they have been, and made their tracks. Thanks to all. For the great republic—for the principle it lives by, and keeps alive—for man's vast future—thanks to all.

Peace does not appear so distant as it did. I hope it will come soon, and come to stay; and so come as to be worth the keeping in all future time. It will then have been proved that, among free men, there can be no successful appeal from the ballot to the bullet; and that they who take such appeal are sure to lose their case, and pay the cost. And then, there will be some black men who can remember that, with silent tongue, and clenched teeth, and steady eye, and well-poised bayonet, they have helped mankind on to this great consummation; while, I fear, there will be some white ones, unable to forget that, with malignant heart, and deceitful speech, they have strove to hinder it.

Still let us not be over-sanguine of a speedy final triumph. Let us be quite sober. Let us diligently apply the means, never doubting that a just God, in his own good time, will give us the rightful result. Yours very truly   A. Lincoln

[DOCUMENT 6-5]
TO SALMON P. CHASE, SEPTEMBER 2, 1863

Secretary of the Treasury Salmon P. Chase, an ardent antislavery leader, often took it upon himself to prod the president to embrace more radical measures against slavery—and envisioned himself as the president's successor in 1864. On August 29, 1863, the secretary pressed the president to modify the provision of the Emancipation Proclamation that excluded certain areas from falling under the proclamation, going so far as to hand Lincoln a draft of a document revoking the exceptions for certain areas. The day after Lincoln wrote this letter, Chase urged Francis H. Pierpont, governor of what passed for the loyal state of Virginia, to press Lincoln to revoke his decision to exclude portions of southeast Virginia from the proclamation on the grounds of military necessity, and drafted a letter for Pierpont to present as his own handiwork; Secretary of War Edwin M. Stanton agreed to join in the effort. Only on September 17 did Lincoln present the following letter to Chase; after some conversation he declared that he would not comply with Chase's request until after the elections of 1863—if then. Instead, Pierpont in 1864 steered through a new state constitution that abolished slavery.

Hon. S. P. Chase.   Executive Mansion,
My dear Sir: Washington, September 2. 1863.
    Knowing your great anxiety that the emancipation proclamation shall now be applied to certain parts of Virginia and Louisiana which were exempted from it last January, I state briefly what appear to me to be difficulties in the way of such a step. The original proclamation has no constitutional or legal justification, except as a military measure. The exemptions were made because the military necessity did not apply to the exempted localities. Nor does that necessity apply to them now any more than it did then. If I take the step must I not do so,

without the argument of military necessity, and so, without any argument, except the one that I think the measure politically expedient, and morally right? Would I not thus give up all footing upon constitution or law? Would I not thus be in the boundless field of absolutism? Could this pass unnoticed, or unresisted? Could it fail to be perceived that without any further stretch, I might do the same in Delaware, Maryland, Kentucky, Tennessee, and Missouri, and even change any law in any state? Would not many of our own friends shrink away appalled? Would it not lose us the elections, and with them, the very cause we seek to advance?

[DOCUMENT 6-6]
TO ANDREW JOHNSON, SEPTEMBER 11, 1863

Lincoln's efforts to encourage Andrew Johnson to move forward on reestablishing a state government in Tennessee proved abortive, for after the Union defeat at Chickamauga on September 19–20, 1863, Confederate forces threatened to recapture Knoxville and Chattanooga in East Tennessee. Note Lincoln's concern about his reelection prospects.

Private

Hon. Andrew Johnson: Executive Mansion,
My dear Sir: Washington, September 11, 1863.
    All Tennessee is now clear of armed insurrectionists. You need not to be reminded that it is the nick of time for re-inaugerating a loyal State government. Not a moment should be lost. You, and the co-operating friends there, can better judge of the ways and means, than can be judged by any here. I only offer a few suggestions. The re-inauguration must not be such as to give control of the State, and it's representation in Congress, to the enemies of the Union, driving it's friends there into political exile. The whole struggle for Tennessee will have been profitless to both State and Nation, if it so ends that Gov. Johnson is put down, and Gov. Harris is put up. It must not be so. You must have it otherwise. Let the reconstruction be the work of such men only as can be trusted for the Union. Exclude all others, and trust that your government, so organized, will be recognized here, as being the one of republican form, to be guarranteed to the state, and to be protected against invasion and domestic violence.
    It is something on the question of *time,* to remember that it can not be known who is next to occupy the position I now hold, nor what he will do.
    I see that you have declared in favor of emancipation in Tennessee, for which, may God bless you. Get emancipation into your new State

government–Constitution–and there will be no such word as fail for your case.

The raising of colored troops I think will greatly help every way.
Yours very truly   A. Lincoln

[DOCUMENT 6-7]
TO NATHANIEL P. BANKS, NOVEMBER 5, 1863

Three months after Lincoln wrote Banks on August 5, 1863 [Document 6-3], he urged the general to direct white Louisianans to commence the process of constructing a loyal state government.

                                                        Executive Mansion,
Major General Banks   Washington, Nov. 5. 1863.

Three months ago to-day I wrote you about Louisiana affairs, stating, on the word of Gov. Shepley, as I understood him, that Mr. Durant was taking a registry of citizens, preparatory to the election of a constitutional convention for that State. I sent a copy of the letter to Mr. Durant; and I now have his letter, written two months after, acknowledging receipt, and saying he is not taking such registry; and he does not let me know that he personally is expecting to do so. Mr. Flanders, to whom I also sent a copy, is now here, and he says nothing has yet been done. This disappoints me bitterly; yet I do not throw blame on you or on them. I do however, urge both you and them, to lose no more time. Gov. Shepley has special instructions from the War Department. I wish him–these gentlemen and others co-operating–without waiting for more territory, to go to work and give me a tangible nucleus which the remainder of the State may rally around as fast as it can, and which I can at once recognize and sustain as the true State government. And in that work I wish you, and all under your command, to give them a hearty sympathy and support. The instruction to Gov. Shepley bases the movement (and rightfully too) upon the loyal element. Time is important. There is danger, even now, that the adverse element seeks insidiously to pre-occupy the ground. If a few professedly loyal men shall draw the disloyal about them, and colorably set up a State government, repudiating the emancipation proclamation, and re-establishing slavery, I can not recognize or sustain their work. I should fall powerless in the attempt. This government, in such an attitude, would be a house divided against itself. I have said, and say again, that if a new State government, acting in harmony with this government, and consistently with general freedom, shall think best to adopt a reasonable temporary arrangement, in relation to the landless and homeless freed people, I do not object; but my word is out to be *for* and not *against* them on the question of their permanent freedom. I do not insist upon such temporary arrangement, but only say such would not be objectionable to me. Yours very truly

A. Lincoln

[DOCUMENT 6-8]
GETTYSBURG ADDRESS, NOVEMBER 19, 1863

In one of his two most famous public addresses, Lincoln reminds Americans that the struggle to preserve the Union is now also a struggle for equality—and yet he never mentioned the words "slavery" or "emancipation," preferring to make his point in somewhat more indirect fashion in speaking of "a new birth of freedom."

Address Delivered at the Dedication of the Cemetery at Gettysburg.

Four score and seven years ago our fathers brought forth on this continent, a new nation, conceived in Liberty, and dedicated to the proposition that all men are created equal.

Now we are engaged in a great civil war, testing whether that nation, or any nation so conceived and so dedicated, can long endure. We are met on a great battle-field of that war. We have come to dedicate a portion of that field, as a final resting place for those who here gave their lives that that nation might live. It is altogether fitting and proper that we should do this.

But, in a larger sense, we can not dedicate—we can not consecrate—we can not hallow—this ground. The brave men, living and dead, who struggled here, have consecrated it, far above our poor power to add or detract. The world will little note, nor long remember what we say here, but it can never forget what they did here. It is for us the living, rather, to be dedicated here to the unfinished work which they who fought here have thus far so nobly advanced. It is rather for us to be here dedicated to the great task remaining before us—that from these honored dead we take increased devotion to that cause for which they gave the last full measure of devotion—that we here highly resolve that these dead shall not have died in vain—that this nation, under God, shall have a new birth of freedom—and that government of the people, by the people, for the people, shall not perish from the earth.

November 19. 1863.   Abraham Lincoln

Revolution, Reconstruction, and Reelection, 1863–1864

CHAPTER SEVEN

ALTHOUGH LINCOLN HAD SHARED with others in private correspondence the principles he thought should guide the reconstruction of state governments in the South, it was not until December 1863 that he outlined them in his Proclamation of Amnesty and Reconstruction [Document 7-1]; in his third annual message [Document 7-2] he discussed the rationale behind the proclamation. The president sought to provide white southerners with an incentive to return to the Union by establishing relatively liberal conditions for the erection and presidential recognition of a new state constitution and government, although he held fast to his commitment to emancipation. By including recognition of various emancipation measures in the oath he required of white southerners who desired to participate in the process, he made it clear that they would have to acquiesce in the end of slavery. Nevertheless, by trying to make reconstruction as attractive as possible, Lincoln hoped his policy would erode support for the Confederacy; he also labored to achieve what he could as soon as he could, in case he lost his bid for reelection in 1864.

Lincoln expounded on emancipation and its consequences in several documents. To Alpheus Lewis, who was engaged in buying cotton grown on southern plantations, the president expressed his willingness to approve various reasonable working arrangements between recently freed blacks and white landowners [Document 7-3]. To Michael Hahn, who had just been elected governor of Louisiana, he made clear his desire for a limited form of black suffrage [Document 7-4]. This letter, coming as it did just after Lincoln had met with several Louisiana free blacks, suggested that he was now able to envision blacks as full and equal citizens; nevertheless, aware that traditionally states had decided who was entitled to vote, he left it to Hahn and white Louisianans to make the final decision (the state's 1864 constitution did not enfranchise blacks). As the president had told one Louisiana conservative, "I wish to avoid both the substance and appearance of dictation."[1] He continued to justify both emancipation and black enlistment as essential to Union victory. To Albert G. Hodges, a Kentucky newspaper editor, he reflected on how he had come to adopt emancipation as a war aim [Document 7-5]; some two weeks later he defended the enlistment of blacks in an address at Baltimore [Document 7-6], although he equivocated on how he would respond to the massacre of black soldiers at Fort Pillow [see introduction to Chapter Six].

Lincoln recognized that Congress had a voice in the process of reconstruction, for both houses could decide to refuse to seat representatives elected under his plan. A good number of congressional Republicans, worried that the president's lenient plans would enable Southern whites to shape emancipation according to conservative preferences and thus compromise black freedom, worked on framing an alternative plan that would guarantee that the reconstructed states would be controlled by trustworthy loyalists. Although the resulting legislation, named the Wade-Davis Bill after its cosponsors, Senator Benjamin F. Wade of Ohio and Representative Henry Winter Davis of Maryland, did not enfranchise blacks, it mandated emancipation by congressional fiat. The legislation went to Lincoln for his signature as the session closed; the president decided to issue a pocket veto by refusing to sign it. Several days later he explained his reasoning in a formal proclamation [Document 7-7]. Furious, Wade and Davis issued their own "manifesto" on August 5, charging that Lincoln was seeking to manipulate the reconstruction process to secure electoral votes for his reelection and asserted that in the matter of reconstruction Congress's authority was "paramount."

Although Wade and Davis overshot the mark when they claimed that Lincoln was seeking electoral votes from sham governments, the president was concerned about whether he would serve a second term. Without much difficulty he had fended off challenges to his renomination in June, but the failure of his new general-in-chief, Ulysses S. Grant, to achieve a decisive victory despite fighting a series of costly battles in the spring of 1864 sparked Democratic hopes to unseat the president. In an appeal to the racism of many Northern voters, Democrats charged that the president would not accept a negotiated peace that did not include emancipation as a precondition of reunion, thus rendering peaceful reunion impossible. Some of Lincoln's political advisers, correctly assuming that Confederate president Jefferson Davis would insist upon Confederate independence as a precondition to a peace settlement, urged Lincoln to counter the Democrats by dropping emancipation as part of reunion, thus simplifying the contest to one between union and disunion. Lincoln may have toyed with the idea, as the concluding sentence of his letter to Charles D. Robinson, a Wisconsin Democrat and newspaper editor, suggests [Document 7-8]. In the end, Lincoln probably did not mail this letter; ultimately, he rejected the idea of opening negotiations with Davis based solely on reunion.

Lincoln believed that he would be defeated in the fall presidential contest. So did the Democrats, who nominated George B. McClellan at the end of August. Within days, however, came the news that General William T. Sherman's armies had captured Atlanta. Finally Grant's plan of continuous and unremitting pressure all along the line had paid off; immediately the president's reelections prospects brightened. The president thought of using the opportunity to issue a rather strong statement in opposition to an armistice or the abandonment of emancipation [Document 7-9], but upon reflection he declined to do so. However, he cheered Maryland's ratification of a new state constitution that abolished slavery [Document 7-10], and a month later reflected on his reelection [Document 7-11] in the wake of a series of Union victories.

1. Lincoln to Thomas Cottman, December 15, 1863, Basler, *Collected Works,* 7:66–67.

[DOCUMENT 7-1]
PROCLAMATION OF AMNESTY AND RECONSTRUCTION, DECEMBER 8, 1863

In the following document Lincoln outlined his plan of reconstruction based upon the establishment of new state governments.

By the President of the United States of America:
A Proclamation.

Whereas, in and by the Constitution of the United States, it is provided that the President "shall have power to grant reprieves and pardons for offences against the United States, except in cases of impeachment;" and

Whereas a rebellion now exists whereby the loyal State governments of several States have for a long time been subverted, and many persons have committed and are now guilty of treason against the United States; and

Whereas, with reference to said rebellion and treason, laws have been enacted by Congress declaring forfeitures and confiscation of property and liberation of slaves, all upon terms and conditions therein stated, and also declaring that the President was thereby authorized at any time thereafter, by proclamation, to extend to persons who may have participated in the existing rebellion, in any State or part thereof, pardon and amnesty, with such exceptions and at such times and on such conditions as he may deem expedient for the public welfare; and

Whereas the congressional declaration for limited and conditional pardon accords with well-established judicial exposition of the pardoning power; and

Whereas, with reference to said rebellion, the President of the United States has issued several proclamations, with provisions in regard to the liberation of slaves; and

Whereas it is now desired by some persons heretofore engaged in said rebellion to resume their allegiance to the United States, and to reinaugurate loyal State governments within and for their respective States; therefore,

I, Abraham Lincoln, President of the United States, do proclaim, declare, and make known to all persons who have, directly or by implication, participated in the existing rebellion, except as hereinafter excepted, that a full pardon is hereby granted to them and each of them, with restoration of all rights of property, except as to slaves, and in property cases where rights of third parties shall have intervened, and upon the condition that every such person shall take and subscribe an oath, and thenceforward keep and maintain said oath inviolate; and which oath shall be registered for permanent preservation, and shall be of the tenor and effect following, to wit:

"I, ——, do solemnly swear, in presence of Almighty God, that I will henceforth faithfully support, protect and defend the Constitution of the United States, and the union of the States thereunder; and that I will, in like manner, abide by and faithfully support all acts of Congress passed during the existing rebellion with reference to slaves, so long and so far as not repealed, modified or held void by Congress, or by decision of the Supreme Court, and that I will, in like manner, abide by and faithfully support all proclamations of the President made during the existing rebellion having reference to slaves, so long and so far as not modified or declared void by decision of the Supreme Court. So help me God."

The persons excepted from the benefits of the foregoing provisions are all who are, or shall have been, civil or diplomatic officers or agents of the so-called confederate government; all who have left judicial stations under the United States to aid the rebellion; all who are, or shall have been, military or naval officers of said so-called confederate government above the rank of colonel in the army, or of lieutenant in the navy; all who left seats in the United States Congress to aid the rebellion; all who resigned commissions in the army or navy of the United States, and afterwards aided the rebellion; and all who have engaged in any way in treating colored persons or white persons, in charge of such, otherwise than lawfully as prisoners of war, and which persons may have been found in the United States service, as soldiers, seamen, or in any other capacity.

And I do further proclaim, declare, and make known, that whenever, in any of the States of Arkansas, Texas, Louisiana, Mississippi, Tennessee, Alabama, Georgia, Florida, South Carolina, and North Carolina, a number of persons, not less than one-tenth in number of the votes cast in such State at the Presidential election of the year of our Lord one thousand eight hundred and sixty, each having taken the oath aforesaid and not having since violated it, and being a qualified voter by the election law of the State existing immediately before the so-called act of secession, and excluding all others, shall re-establish a State government which shall be republican, and in no wise contravening said oath, such shall be recognized as the true government of the State, and the State shall receive thereunder the benefits of the constitutional provision which declares that "The United States shall guaranty to every State in this union a republican form of government, and shall protect each of them against invasion; and, on application of the legislature, or the executive, (when the legislature cannot be convened,) against domestic violence."

And I do further proclaim, declare, and make known that any provision which may be adopted by such State government in relation to the freed people of such State, which shall recognize and declare their permanent freedom, provide for their education, and which may yet be consistent, as a temporary arrangement, with their present condition as a laboring, landless, and homeless class, will not be objected to by the national Executive. And it is suggested as not improper, that, in constructing a loyal State government in any State, the name of the State, the boundary, the subdivisions, the constitution, and the general code of laws, as before the rebellion, be maintained, subject only to the modifications made necessary by the conditions hereinbefore stated, and such others, if any, not contravening said conditions, and which may be deemed expedient by those framing the new State government.

To avoid misunderstanding, it may be proper to say that this proclamation, so far as it relates to State governments, has no reference to States wherein loyal State governments have all the while been maintained. And for the same reason, it may be proper to further say that whether members sent to Congress from any State shall be admitted to seats, constitutionally rests exclusively with the respective Houses, and not to any extent with the Executive. And still further, that this proclamation is intended to present the people of the States wherein the national authority has been suspended, and loyal State governments have been subverted, a mode in and by which the national authority and loyal State governments may be re-established within said States, or in any of them; and, while the mode presented is the best the Executive can suggest, with his present impressions, it must not be understood that no other possible mode would be acceptable.

Given under my hand at the city, of Washington, the 8th. day of December, A.D. one thousand eight hundred and sixty-three, and of the independence of the United States of America the eighty-eighth.

Abraham Lincoln

By the President:

William H. Seward, Secretary of State.

[DOCUMENT 7-2]
THIRD ANNUAL MESSAGE, DECEMBER 8, 1863 (EXCERPT)

The president offered his reasons for issuing his proclamation of amnesty and reconstruction and presented an overview of the evolution of his emancipation policy in the following excerpt from his third annual message to Congress.

...When Congress assembled a year ago the war had already lasted nearly twenty months, and there had been many conflicts on both land and sea, with varying results.

The rebellion had been pressed back into reduced limits; yet the tone of public feeling and opinion, at home and abroad, was not satisfactory. With other signs, the popular elections, then just past, indicated uneasiness among ourselves, while amid much that was cold and menacing the kindest words coming from Europe were uttered in accents of pity, that we were too blind to surrender a hopeless cause. Our commerce was suffering greatly by a few armed vessels built upon and furnished from foreign shores, and we were threatened with such additions from the same quarter as would sweep our trade from the sea and raise our blockade. We had failed to elicit from European governments anything hopeful upon this subject. The preliminary emancipation proclamation, issued in September, was running its assigned period to the beginning of the new year. A month later the final proclamation came, including the announcement that colored men of suitable condition would be received into the war service. The policy of emancipation, and of employing black soldiers, gave to the future a new aspect, about which hope, and fear, and doubt contended in uncertain conflict. According to our political system, as a matter of civil administration, the general government had no lawful power to effect emancipation in any State, and for a long time it had been hoped that the rebellion could be suppressed without resorting to it as a military measure. It was all the while deemed possible that the necessity for it might come, and that if it should, the crisis of the contest would then be presented. It came, and as was anticipated, it was followed by dark and doubtful days. Eleven months having now passed, we are permitted to take another review. The rebel borders are pressed still further back, and by the complete opening of the Mississippi the country dominated by the rebellion is divided into distinct parts, with no practical communication between them. Tennessee and Arkansas have been substantially cleared of insurgent control, and influential citizens in each, owners of slaves and advocates of slavery at the beginning of the rebellion, now declare openly for emancipation in their respective States. Of those States not included in the emancipation proclamation, Maryland, and Missouri, neither of which three years ago would tolerate any restraint upon the extension of slavery into new territories, only dispute now as to the best mode of removing it within their own limits.

Of those who were slaves at the beginning of the rebellion, full one hundred thousand are now in the United States military service, about one-half of which number actually bear arms in the ranks; thus giving the double advantage of taking so much labor from the insurgent cause, and supplying the places which otherwise must be filled with so many white men. So far as tested, it is difficult to say they are not as good soldiers as any. No servile insurrection, or tendency to violence or cruelty, has marked the measures of emancipation and arming the blacks. These measures have been much discussed in foreign countries, and contemporary with such discussion the tone of public sentiment there is much improved. At home the same measures have been fully discussed, supported, criticised, and denounced, and the annual elections following are highly encouraging to those whose official duty it is to bear the country through this great trial. Thus we have the new reckoning. The crisis which threatened to divide the friends of the Union is past.

Looking now to the present and future, and with reference to a resumption of the national authority within the States wherein that authority has been suspended, I have thought fit to issue a proclamation, a copy of which is herewith transmitted. On examination of this proclamation it will appear, as is believed, that nothing is attempted beyond what is amply justified by the Constitution. True, the form of an oath is given, but no man is coerced to take it. The man is only promised a pardon in case he voluntarily takes the oath. The Constitution authorizes the Executive to grant or withhold the pardon at his own absolute discretion; and this includes the power to grant on terms, as is fully established by judicial and other authorities.

It is also proffered that if, in any of the States named, a State government shall be, in the mode prescribed, set up, such government shall be recognized and guarantied by the United States, and that under it the State shall, on the constitutional conditions, be protected against invasion and domestic violence. The constitutional obligation of the United States to guaranty to every State in the Union a republican form of government, and to protect the State, in the cases stated, is explicit and full. But why tender the benefits of this provision only to a State government set up in this particular way? This section of the Constitution contemplates a case wherein the element within a State, favorable to republican government, in the Union, may be too feeble for an opposite and hostile element external to, or even within the State; and such are precisely the cases with which we are now dealing.

An attempt to guaranty and protect a revived State government, constructed in whole, or in preponderating part, from the very element against whose hostility and violence it is to be protected, is simply absurd. There must be a test by which to separate the opposing elements, so as to build only from the sound; and that test is a sufficiently liberal one, which accepts as sound whoever will make a sworn recantation of his former unsoundness.

But if it be proper to require, as a test of admission to the political body, an oath of allegiance to the Constitution of the United States, and to the Union under it, why also to the laws and proclamations in regard to slavery? Those laws and proclamations were enacted and put forth for the purpose of aiding in the suppression of the rebellion. To give them their fullest effect, there had to be a pledge for their maintenance. In my judgment they have aided, and will further aid, the cause for which they were intended. To now abandon them would be not only to relinquish a lever of power, but would also be a cruel and an astounding breach of faith. I may add at this point, that while I remain in my present position I shall not attempt to retract or modify the emancipation proclamation; nor shall I return to slavery any person who is free by the terms of that proclamation, or by any of the acts of Congress. For these and other reasons it is thought best that support of these measures shall be included in the oath; and it is believed the Executive may lawfully claim it in return for pardon and restoration of forfeited rights, which he has clear constitutional power to withhold altogether, or grant upon the terms which he shall deem wisest for the public interest. It should be observed, also, that this part of the oath is subject to the modifying and abrogating power of legislation and supreme judicial decision.

The proposed acquiescence of the national Executive in any reasonable temporary State arrangement for the freed people is made with the view of possibly modifying the confusion and destitution which must, at best, attend all classes by a total revolution of labor throughout whole States. It is hoped that the already deeply afflicted people in those States may be somewhat more ready to give up the cause of their affliction, if, to this extent, this vital matter be left to themselves; while no power of the national Executive to prevent an abuse is abridged by the proposition.

The suggestion in the proclamation as to maintaining the political framework of the States on what is called reconstruction, is made in the hope that it may do good without danger of harm. It will save labor and avoid great confusion.

But why any proclamation now upon this subject? This question is beset with the conflicting views that the step might be delayed too long or be taken too soon. In some States the elements for resumption seem ready for action, but remain inactive, apparently for want of a rallying point–a plan of action. Why shall A adopt the plan of B, rather than B that of A? And if A and B should agree, how can they know but that the general government here will reject their plan? By the proclamation a plan is presented which may be accepted by them as a rallying point, and which they are assured in advance will not be rejected here. This may bring them to act sooner than they otherwise would.

The objections to a premature presentation of a plan by the national Executive consists in the danger of committals on points which could be more safely left to further developments. Care has been taken to so shape the document as to avoid embarrassments from this source. Saying that, on certain terms, certain classes will be pardoned, with rights restored, it is not said that other classes, or other terms, will never be included. Saying that reconstruction will be accepted if presented in a specified way, it is not said it will never be accepted in any other way.

The movements, by State of action, for emancipation in several of the States, not included in the emancipation proclamation, are matters of profound gratulation. And while I do not repeat in detail what I have hertofore so earnestly urged upon this subject, my general views and feelings remain unchanged; and I trust that Congress will omit no fair opportunity of aiding these important steps to a great consummation.

In the midst of other cares, however important, we must not lose sight of the fact that the war power is still our main reliance. To that power alone can we look, yet for a time, to give confidence to the people in the contested regions, that the insurgent power will not again over-run them. Until that confidence shall be established, little can be done anywhere for what is called reconstruction. Hence our chiefest care must still be directed to the army and navy, who have thus far borne their harder part so nobly and well. And it may be esteemed fortunate that in giving the greatest efficiency to these indispensable arms, we do also honorably recognize the gallant men, from commander to sentinel, who compose them, and to whom, more than to others, the world must stand indebted for the home of freedom disenthralled, regenerated, enlarged, and perpetuated.

Washington, December 8, 1863.

[DOCUMENT 7-3]
TO ALPHEUS LEWIS, JANUARY 23, 1864

What follows is the draft of a letter from Lincoln to Alpheus Lewis, who was engaged in cotton trading with Southern planters; Lincoln noted that the post-script on the draft was incorporated into the main text of the final letter. The letter reflects Lincoln's thoughts on how emancipation would reshape relationships on plantations in areas controlled by Union forces.

Alpheus Lewis, Esq.   Executive Mansion,
My dear Sir   Washington, January 23. 1864.
You have enquired how the government would regard and treat cases wherein the owners of plantations, in Arkansas, for instance, might fully recognize the freedom of those formerly slaves, and by fair contracts of hire with them, re-commence the cultivation of their plantations. I answer I should regard such cases with great favor, and should,

as the principle, treat them precisely as I would treat the same number of free white people in the same relation and condition. Whether white or black, reasonable effort should be made to give government protection. In neither case should the giving of aid and comfort to the rebellion, or other practices injurious to the government, be allowed on such plantations; and in either, the government would claim the right to take if necessary those of proper ages and conditions into the military service. Such plan must not be used to break existing leases or arrangements of abandoned plantations which the government may have made to give employment and sustenance to the idle and destitute people. With the foregoing qualifications and explanations, and in view of it's tendency to advance freedom, and restore peace and prosperity, such hireing and employment of the freed people, would be regarded by me with rather especial favor. Yours truly   A. Lincoln

P.S. To be more specific I add that all the Military, and others acting by authority of the United States, are to favor and facilitate the introduction and carrying forward, in good faith, the free-labor system as above indicated, by allowing the necessary supplies therefor to be procured and taken to the proper points, and by doing and forbearing whatever will advance it; *provided* that existing military and trade regulations be not transcended thereby. I shall be glad to learn that planters adopting this system shall have employed one so zealous and active as yourself to act as an agent in relation thereto.   A.L.

[DOCUMENT 7-4]
TO MICHAEL HAHN, MARCH 13, 1864

The occupation of New Orleans by Union forces in April 1862 provided the Lincoln administration with one of several opportunities to establish a new state government loyal to the United States. The president's impatience with the failure of Louisiana unionists to pursue such a course in 1862 contributed to his decision to issue the Emancipation Proclamation; in 1863 he had pushed for elections, and in December of that year he had outlined a more specific procedure for reestablishing loyal state governments. Yet Lincoln had excluded occupied Louisiana from the Emancipation Proclamation. What made Louisiana unusual was the large number of free blacks who lived in the state; in addition, many free and freed blacks had enlisted in the Union army. As the state's unionists finally commenced the process of constructing a new state government by electing a governor, Michael Hahn, and delegates to a constitutional convention, many black leaders wanted to make sure that they would not be excluded from the result this time. On March 12, 1864, two free men of color, Jean Baptiste Roudanez and Arnold Bertonneau, had visited the White House to present the president with a petition calling for the enfranchisement of blacks. Lincoln's reply was not encouraging. "I regret, gentlemen, that you are not able to secure all your rights," he remarked, "and that circumstances will not permit the government to confer them upon you." The next day Lincoln prepared the following letter, which Hahn circulated with delegates.

Private   Executive Mansion,
Hon. Michael Hahn   Washington,
My dear Sir: March 13. 1864.

   I congratulate you on having fixed your name in history as the first-free-state Governor of Louisiana. Now you are about to have a Convention which, among other things, will probably define the elective franchise. I barely suggest for your private consideration, whether some of the colored people may not be let in—as, for instance, the very intelligent, and especially those who have fought gallantly in our ranks. They would probably help, in some trying time to come, to keep the jewel of liberty within the family of freedom. But this is only a suggestion, not to the public, but to you alone. Yours truly   A. Lincoln

[DOCUMENT 7-5]
TO ALBERT G. HODGES, APRIL 4, 1864

On March 26, 1864, Lincoln met with Governor Thomas Bramlette of Kentucky, Archibald Dixon, a former senator for Kentucky, and Albert G. Hodges, editor of the Frankfort Commonwealth *to discuss the enlistment of Kentucky's blacks. During the conversation Lincoln, a Kentuckian by birth, offered his own views on slavery, emancipation, and black enlistment; Hodges later requested the president to put his words on paper. Hodges shared the letter with prominent Kentuckians. Lincoln knew that in effect he was preparing a position paper describing his understanding of what he could do as president concerning slavery; the final paragraph contains a series of reflections that found fuller expression eleven months later in his second inaugural address [Document 8-4].*

In addition to mentioning the actions he took in revoking the emancipation edicts of generals Frémont and Hunter, Lincoln makes reference to Secretary of War Simon Cameron's 1861 suggestion to arm blacks, which the secretary included in his annual report; Lincoln forced him to recall the publication and excise the suggestion.

A. G. Hodges, Esq   Executive Mansion,
Frankfort, Ky.   Washington, April 4, 1864.

My dear Sir: You ask me to put in writing the substance of what I verbally said the other day, in your presence, to Governor Bramlette and Senator Dixon. It was about as follows:

"I am naturally anti-slavery. If slavery is not wrong, nothing is wrong. I can not remember when I did not so think, and feel. And yet I have never understood that the Presidency conferred upon me an unrestricted right to act officially upon this judgment and feeling. It was in the oath I took that I would, to the best of my ability, preserve, protect, and defend the Constitution of the United States. I could not take the office without taking the oath. Nor was it my view that I might take an oath to get power, and break the oath in using the power. I understood, too, that in ordinary civil administration this oath even forbade me to practically indulge my primary abstract judgment on the moral question of slavery. I had publicly declared this many times, and in many ways. And I aver that, to this day, I have done no official act in mere deference to my abstract judgment and feeling on slavery. I did understand however, that my oath to preserve the constitution to the best of my ability, imposed upon me the duty of preserving, by every indispensable means, that government—that nation—of which that constitution was the organic law. Was it possible to lose the nation, and yet preserve the constitution? By general law life *and* limb must be protected; yet often a limb must be amputated to save a life; but a life is never wisely given to save a limb. I felt that measures, otherwise unconstitutional, might become lawful, by becoming indispensable to the preservation of the constitution, through the preservation of the nation. Right or wrong, I assumed this ground, and now avow it. I could not feel that, to the best of my ability, I had even tried to preserve the constitution if, to save slavery, or any minor matter, I should permit the wreck of government, country, and Constitution all together. When, early in the war, Gen. Fremont attempted military emancipation, I forbade it, because I did not then think it an indispensable necessity. When a little later, Gen. Cameron, then Secretary of War, suggested the arming of the blacks, I objected, because I did not yet think it an indispensable necessity. When, still later, Gen. Hunter attempted military emancipation, I again forbade it, because I did not yet think the indispensable necessity had come. When, in March, and May, and July 1862 I made earnest, and successive appeals to the border states to favor compensated emancipation, I believed the indispensable necessity for military emancipation, and arming the blacks would come, unless averted by that measure. They declined the proposition; and I was, in my best judgment, driven to the alternative of either surrendering the Union, and with it, the Constitution, or of laying strong hand upon the colored element. I chose the latter. In choosing it, I hoped for greater gain than loss; but of this, I was not entirely confident. More than a year of trial now shows no loss by it in our foreign relations, none in our home popular sentiment, none in our white military force,—no loss by it any how or any where. On the contrary, it shows a gain of quite a hundred and thirty thousand soldiers, seamen, and laborers. These are palpable facts, about which, as facts, there can be no cavilling. We have the men; and we could not have had them without the measure.

["]And now let any Union man who complains of the measure, test himself by writing down in one line that he is for subduing the rebellion by force of arms; and in the next, that he is for taking these hundred and thirty thousand men from the Union side, and placing them where they would be but for the measure he condemns. If he can not face his case so stated, it is only because he can not face the truth."

I add a word which was not in the verbal conversation. In telling this tale I attempt to compliment to my own sagacity. I claim not to have controlled events, but confess plainly that events have controlled me. Now, at the end of three years struggle the nation's condition is not what either party, or any man devised, or expected. God alone can claim it. Whither it is tending seems plain. If God now wills the removal of a great wrong, and wills also that we of the North as well as you of the South, shall pay fairly for our complicity in that wrong, impartial history will find therein new cause to attest and revere the justice and goodness of God. Yours truly

A. Lincoln

[DOCUMENT 7-6]
ADDRESS AT BALTIMORE, MARYLAND,
APRIL 18, 1864

During the Civil War the United States Sanitary Commission was one of several Union volunteer organizations that raised funds to buy clothes, personal supplies, and other items for soldiers; its representatives also investigated the condition of army camps and helped care for wounded and sick soldiers. One of the commission's favorite fund-raising devices was the sanitary fair; in March, 1864, reportedly responding to a request to contribute an autograph to an album for such a fair, Lincoln wrote, "I never knew a man who wished to be himself a slave. Consider if you know any good thing, that no man desires for himself." The following month, the president traveled to Baltimore to offer the following remarks at the opening of another fair; in remarking about the riot between soldiers of the 6th Massachusetts and a pro-secessionist mob on April 19, 1861, he did not add that as president-elect he had to make his way secretly through the city before dawn on February 23, 1861, in response to a reported plot to assassinate him—although he had included that story in a draft of his remarks.

On April 12, 1864, a Confederate force under the command of Nathan Bedford Forrest assaulted Fort Pillow, Tennessee, which was held by a garrison composed of black and white Union troops. The attackers killed a significant number of black soldiers who were attempting to surrender. Although General-in-Chief Ulysses S. Grant urged retaliation, Lincoln, despite the pledge he made to do just that the previous July [Document 6-2], declined to do so; a congressional investigation concluded that a massacre had indeed taken place.

Ladies and Gentlemen—Calling to mind that we are in Baltimore, we can not fail to note that the world moves. Looking upon these many people, assembled here, to serve, as they best may, the soldiers of the Union, it occurs at once that three years ago, the same soldiers could not so much as pass through Baltimore. The change from then till now, is both great, and gratifying. Blessings on the brave men who have wrought the change, and the fair women who strive to reward them for it.

But Baltimore suggests more than could happen within Baltimore. The change within Baltimore is part only of a far wider change. When the war began, three years ago, neither party, nor any man, expected it would last till now. Each looked for the end, in some way, long ere to-day. Neither did any anticipate that domestic slavery would be much affected by the war. But here we are; the war has not ended, and slavery has been much affected—how much needs not now to be recounted. So true is it that man proposes, and God disposes.

But we can see the past, though we may not claim to have directed it; and seeing it, in this case, we feel more hopeful and confident for the future.

The world has never had a good definition of the word liberty, and the American people, just now, are much in want of one. We all declare for liberty; but in using the same *word* we do not all mean the same *thing*. With some the word liberty may mean for each man to do as he pleases with himself, and the product of his labor; while with others the same word may mean for some men to do as they please with other men, and the product of other men's labor. Here are two, not only different, but incompatable things, called by the same name—liberty. And it follows that each of the things is, by the respective parties, called by two different and incompatable names—liberty and tyranny.

The shepherd drives the wolf from the sheep's throat, for which the sheep thanks the shepherd as a *liberator,* while the wolf denounces him for the same act as the destroyer of liberty, especially as the sheep was a black one. Plainly the sheep and the wolf are not agreed upon a definition of the word liberty; and precisely the same difference prevails to-day among us human creatures, even in the North, and all professing to love liberty. Hence we behold the processes by which thousands are daily passing from under the yoke of bondage, hailed by some as the advance of liberty, and bewailed by others as the destruction of all liberty. Recently, as it seems, the people of Maryland have been doing something to define liberty; and thanks to them that, in what they have done, the wolf's dictionary, has been repudiated.

It is not very becoming for one in my position to make speeches at great length; but there is another subject upon which I feel that I ought to say a word. A painful rumor, true I fear, has reached us of the massacre, by the rebel forces, at Fort Pillow, in the West end of Tennessee, on the Mississippi river, of some three hundred colored soldiers and white officers, who had just been overpowered by their assailants. There seems to be some anxiety in the public mind whether the government is doing it's duty to the colored soldier, and to the service, at this point. At the beginning of the war, and for some time, the use of colored troops was not contemplated; and how the change of purpose was wrought, I will not now take time to explain. Upon a clear conviction of duty I resolved to turn that element of strength to account; and I am responsible for it to the American people, to the christian world, to history, and on my final account to God. Having determined to use the negro as a soldier, there is no way but to give him all the protection given to any other soldier. The difficulty is not in stating the principle, but in practically applying it. It is a mistake to suppose the government is indiffe[re]nt to this matter, or is not doing the best it can in regard to it. We do not to-day *know* that a colored soldier, or white officer commanding colored soldiers, has been massacred by the rebels when made a prisoner. We fear it, believe it, I may say, but we do not *know* it. To take the life of one of their prisoners, on the assumption that they murder ours, when it is short of certainty that they do murder ours, might be too serious, too cruel a mistake. We are having the Fort-Pillow affair thoroughly investigated; and such investigation will probably show conclusively how the truth is. If, after all that has been said, it shall turn out that there has been no massacre at Fort-Pillow, it will be almost safe to say there has been none, and will be none elsewhere. If there has been the massacre of three hundred there, or even the tenth part of three hundred, it will be conclusively proved; and being so proved, the retribution shall as surely come. It will be matter of grave consideration in what exact course to apply the retribution; but in the supposed case, it must come.

[DOCUMENT 7-7]
PROCLAMATION CONCERNING RECONSTRUCTION, JULY 8, 1864

On July 2, 1864, Congress passed legislation outlining a plan for reconstructing loyal state governments in the South. Called the Wade-Davis Bill after its cosponsors, Senator Benjamin F. Wade of Ohio and Representative Henry Winter Davis of Maryland, the bill offered a marked contrast to the plan outlined by Lincoln in December 1863. It declared slavery abolished in the former Confederate states, required one-half of the eligible electorate in 1860 to take an oath of loyalty to the United States, and said that only those people who could swear to continuous loyalty to the Union throughout the conflict could participate in framing a new state constitution or hold office. Lincoln pocket-vetoed the bill and then issued the following proclamation.

By the President of the United States.
A Proclamation.

Whereas, at the late Session, Congress passed a Bill, "To guarantee to certain States, whose governments have been usurped or overthrown, a republican form of Government," a copy of which is hereunto annexed:

And whereas, the said Bill was presented to the President of the United States, for his approval, less than one hour before the *sine die* adjournment of said Session, and was not signed by him:

And whereas, the said Bill contains, among other things, a plan for restoring the States in rebellion to their proper practical relation in the Union, which plan expresses the sense of Congress upon that subject, and which plan it is now thought fit to lay before the people for their consideration:

Now, therefore, I, Abraham Lincoln, President of the United States, do proclaim, declare, and make known, that, while I am, (as I was in December last, when by proclamation I propounded a plan for restoration) unprepared, by a formal approval of this Bill, to be inflexibly committed to any single plan of restoration; and, while I am also unprepared to declare, that the free-state constitutions and governments, already adopted and installed in Arkansas and Louisiana, shall be set aside and held for nought, thereby repelling and discouraging the loyal citizens who have set up the same, as to further effort; or to declare a constitutional competency in Congress to abolish slavery in States, but am at the same time sincerely hoping and expecting that a constitutional amendment, abolishing slavery throughout the nation, may be adopted, nevertheless, I am fully satisfied with the system for restoration contained in the Bill, as one very proper plan for the loyal people of any State choosing to adopt it; and that I am, and at all times shall be, prepared to give the Executive aid and assistance to any such people, so soon as the military resistance to the United States shall have been suppressed in any such State, and the people thereof shall have sufficiently returned to their obedience to the Constitution and the laws of the United States,–in which cases, military Governors will be appointed, with directions to proceed according to the Bill.

In testimony whereof, I have hereunto set my hand and caused the Seal of the United States to be affixed

Done at the City of Washington this eighth day of July, in the year of Our Lord, one thousand eight hundred and sixty-four, and of the Independence of the United States the eighty-ninth.

By the President: Abraham Lincoln

William H. Seward, Secretary of State.

[DOCUMENT 7-8]
TO CHARLES D. ROBINSON, AUGUST 17, 1864

Scholars agree that Lincoln did not send the following letter, addressed to a pro-administration Democratic newspaper editor in Wisconsin; the last sentence nevertheless suggests that he at least pondered the advice offered by some of his advisers who suggested that he demonstrate a willingness to drop emancipation as a precondition to negotiations looking toward reunion. Robinson had urged such a step, claiming that the emancipation precondition "puts the whole question on a new basis, and takes us War Democrats off our feet, leaving us no ground to stand upon." The former governor of Wisconsin, Alexander W. Randall (now an assistant postmaster general) handed Robinson's letter to Lincoln on August 16. However, in the end Lincoln declined to accept the suggestion, telling Randall and a friend on August 19 that the War Democrats should have sup-

ported the war effort more energetically if they desired a victory without aboli-
tion, for it was impossible to win a war based upon the principle of conciliation
that allowed the Confederacy to draw upon the labor of slaves in its effort to
secure independence. To leave open the possibility of reenslaving black soldiers
was too awful a prospect to consider. "I should be damned in time & in eternity
for so doing," he exclaimed. "The world shall know that I will keep my faith to
friends & enemies, come what will." One of those most pleased by Lincoln's
decision was Frederick Douglass, who had told the president that very day that
any equivocation over emancipation "would be taken as a complete surrender of
your antislavery policy, and do you serious damage."

Lincoln had contributed to the dilemma he confronted when on July 18,
1864, in response to reports from newspaper editor Horace Greeley that Con-
federate commissioners at Niagara Falls, Canada, just across from New York,
were empowered to open peace negotiations, he wrote that he was willing to
consider any proposal "which embraces the restoration of peace, the integrity of
the whole Union, and the abandonment of slavery." Greeley was in error, for the
Confederates had no interest in negotiating peace (they were attempting to fuel
antiwar sentiment in the North); they published the letter to embarrass Lincoln
with War Democrats.

Hon. Charles D. Robinson   Executive Mansion,
My Dear Sir   Washington, August 17, 1864.

Your letter of the 7th. was placed in my hand yesterday by Gov. Randall.

To me it seems plain that saying re-union and abandonment of sla-very would be considered, if offered, is not saying that nothing *else* or *less* would be considered, if offered. But I will not stand upon the mere construction of language. It is true, as you remind me, that in the Greeley letter of 1862, I said: "If I could save the Union without freeing any slave I would do it; and if I could save it by freeing some, and leaving others alone I would also do that." I continued in the same letter as follows: "What I do about slavery and the colored race, I do because I believe it helps to save the Union. I shall do less whenever I shall be-lieve what I am doing hurts the cause; and I shall do more whenever I shall believe doing more will help the cause." All this I said in the utmost sincerity; and I am as true to the whole of it now, as when I first said it. When I afterwards proclaimed emancipation, and employed colored soldiers, I only followed the declaration just quoted from the Greeley letter that "I shall do *more* whenever I shall believe *doing* more will help the cause" The way these measures were to help the cause, was not to be by magic, or miracles, but by inducing the colored people to come bodily over from the rebel side to ours. On this point, nearly a year ago, in a letter to Mr. Conkling, made public at once, I wrote as follows: "But negroes, like other people, act upon motives. Why should they do anything for us if we will do nothing for them? If they stake their lives for us they must be prompted by the strongest motive—even the promise of freedom. And the promise, being made, must be kept." I am sure you will not, on due reflection, say that the promise being made, must be *broken* at the first opportunity. I am sure you would not desire me to say, or to leave an inference, that I am ready, whenever convenient, to join in re-enslaving those who shall have served us in consideration of our promise. As matter of morals, could such treachery by any possibility, escape the curses of Heaven, or of any good man? As matter of policy, to *announce* such a purpose, would ruin the Union cause itself. All recruiting of colored men would instantly cease, and all colored men now in our service, would instantly desert us. And rightfully too. Why should they give their lives for us, of full notice of our purpose to betray them? Drive back to the support of the rebellion the physical force which the colored people now give, and promise us, and neither the present, nor any coming administration, *can* save the Union. Take from us, and give to the enemy, the hundred and thirty, forty, or fifty thousand colored persons now serving us as soldiers, seamen, and laborers, and we can not longer maintain the contest. The party who would elect a President on a War & Slavery Restoration platform, would, of necessity, lose the colored force; and that force being lost, would be as powerless to save the Union as to do any other impossible thing. It is not a question of sentiment or taste, but one of physical force, which may be measured, and estimated. And by measurement, it is more than we can lose, and live. Nor can we, by discarding it, get a white force in place of it. There is a witness in every white mans bosom that he would rather go to the war having the negro to help him, than to help the enemy against him. It is not the giving of one class for another. It is simply giving a large force to the enemy, for *nothing* in return.

In addition to what I have said, allow me to remind you that no one, having control of the rebel armies, or, in fact, having any influence whatever in the rebellion, has offered, or intimated a willingness to, a restoration of the Union, in any event, or on any condition whatever. Let it be constantly borne in mind that no such offer has been made or intimated. Shall we be weak enough to allow the enemy to distract us with an abstract question which he himself refuses to present as a practical one? In the Conkling letter before mentioned, I said: "Whenever you shall have conquered all resistance to the Union, if I shall urge you to continue fighting, it will be an apt time *then* to declare that you will not fight to free negroes." I repeat this now. If Jefferson Davis wishes, for himself, or for the benefit of his friends at the North, to know what I would do if he were to offer peace and re-union, saying nothing about slavery, let him try me.

[DOCUMENT 7-9]
DRAFT OF LETTER TO ISAAC M. SCHERMERHORN, SEPTEMBER 12, 1864

Lincoln prepared the following letter to be delivered at a rally in support of the National Union ticket of Lincoln and Andrew Johnson; Republican leaders had adopted the new name in hopes of attracting support from War Democrats. Upon reflection, and recalling how earlier statements on war aims had entangled him in controversy, he decided not to send it, claiming somewhat disingenuously that he did not have the time to draft a letter, that it was not customary for an incumbent who was a candidate for re-election to compose such a letter, and that if he responded to this request he would be besieged by other solicitations for letters.

Isaac M. Schemerhorn   Executive Mansion,
My dear Sir.   Washington, Sept. 12. 1864.

Yours inviting me to attend a Union Mass Meeting at Buffalo is received. Much is being said about peace; and no man desires peace more ardently than I. Still I am yet unprepared to give up the Union for a peace which, so achieved, could not be of much duration. The preservation of our Union was *not* the sole avowed object for which the war was commenced. It was commenced for precisely the reverse object—*to destroy our Union.* The insurgents commenced it by firing upon the Star of the West, and on Fort Sumpter, and by other similar acts. It is true, however, that the administration accepted the war thus commenced, for the sole avowed object of preserving our Union; and it is not true that it has since been, or will be, prossecuted by this administration, for any other object. In declaring this, I only declare what I can know, and do know to be true, and what no other man can know to be false.

In taking the various steps which have led to my present position in relation to the war, the public interest and my private interest, have been perfectly parallel, because in no other way could I serve myself so well, as by truly serving the Union. The whole field has been open to me, where to choose. No place-hunting necessity has been upon me urging me to seek a position of antagonism to some other man, irrespective of whether such position might be favorable or unfavorable to the Union.

Of course I may err in judgment, but my present position in reference to the rebellion is the result of my best judgment, and according to that best judgment, it is the only position upon which any Executive can or could save the Union. Any substantial departure from it insures the success of the rebellion. An armistice—a cessation of hostilities—is the end of the struggle, and the insurgents would be in peaceable possession of all that has been struggled for. Any different policy in regard to the colored man, deprives us of his help, and this is more than we can bear. We can not spare the hundred and forty or fifty thousand now serving us as soldiers, seamen, and laborers. This is not a question of sentiment or taste, but one of physical force which may be measured and estimated as horse-power and Steam-power are measured and estimated. Keep it and you can save the Union. Throw it away, and the Union goes with it. Nor is it possible for any Administration to retain the service of these people with the express or implied understanding that upon the first convenient occasion, they are to be re-inslaved. It *can* not be; and it *ought* not to be.

[DOCUMENT 7-10]
TO HENRY W. HOFFMAN, OCTOBER 10, 1864

Lincoln found the time to prepare this letter, addressed to the chairman of the Maryland Unconditional Union Central Committee, knowing that it would be read on the eve of the popular vote to ratify the new state constitution, which abolished slavery. The document was ratified by less than 400 votes out of nearly 60,000 cast.

Hon. Henry W Hoffman   Executive Mansion, Washington,
My dear Sir: October 10, 1864.

A convention of Maryland has framed a new constitution for the State; a public meeting is called for this evening, at Baltimore, to aid in securing its ratification by the people; and you ask a word from me, for the occasion. I presume the only feature of the instrument, about which there is serious controversy, is that which provides for the extinction of slavery. It needs not to be a secret, and I presume it is no secret, that I wish success to this provision. I desire it on every consideration. I wish all men to be free. I wish the material prosperity of the already free which I feel sure the extinction of slavery would bring. I wish to see, in process of disappearing, that only thing which ever could bring this nation to civil war. I attempt no argument. Argument upon the question is already exhausted by the abler, better informed, and more immediately interested sons of Maryland herself. I only add that I shall be gratified exceedingly if the good people of the State shall, by their votes, ratify the new constitution. Yours truly   A. Lincoln

[DOCUMENT 7-11]
RESPONSE TO SERENADE, NOVEMBER 10, 1864

On November 8, 1864, Abraham Lincoln won reelection as President of the United States. That evening, a crowd gathered outside the White House to serenade the president with patriotic songs and cheers—thus offering him another chance to share his opinions with those assembled (as well as various newspaper reporters). Always concerned about his ability to speak effectively without preparing his remarks beforehand, the president took to composing his remarks beforehand; on November 10 he thus had the opportunity to respond to another group of well-wishers by offering the following remarks, which appear as if they had been composed in anticipation of a visit. "Martial music, the cheers of people, and the roar of cannon, shook the sky," recalled one observer, who reported that the crowd filled the grounds; upon making his appearance, Lincoln was greeted by "the maddest cheers from the crowd, and it was many minutes before the deafening racket permitted him to speak."

It has long been a grave question whether any government, not *too* strong for the liberties of its people, can be strong *enough* to maintain its own existence, in great emergencies.

On this point the present rebellion brought our republic to a severe test; and a presidential election occurring in regular course during the rebellion added not a little to the strain. If the loyal people, *united,* were put to the utmost of their strength by the rebellion, must they not fail when *divided,* and partially paralized, by a political war among themselves?

But the election was a necessity.

We can not have free government without elections; and if the rebellion could force us to forego, or postpone a national election, it might fairly claim to have already conquered and ruined us. The strife of the election is but human-nature practically applied to the facts of the case. What has occurred in this case, must ever recur in similar cases. Human-nature will not change. In any future great national trial, compared with the men of this, we shall have as weak, and as strong; as silly and as wise; as bad and good. Let us, therefore, study the incidents of this, as philosophy to learn wisdom from, and none of them as wrongs to be revenged.

But the election, along with its incidental, and undesirable strife, has done good too. It has demonstrated that a people's government can sustain a national election, in the midst of a great civil war. Until now it has not been known to the world that this was a possibility. It shows also how *sound,* and how *strong* we still are. It shows that, even among candidates of the same party, he who is most devoted to the Union, and most opposed to treason, can receive most of the people's votes. It shows also, to the extent yet known, that we have more men now, than we had when the war began. Gold is good in its place; but living, brave, patriotic men, are better than gold.

But the rebellion continues; and now that the election is over, may not all, having a common interest, re-unite in a common effort, to save our common country? For my own part I have striven, and shall strive to avoid placing any obstacle in the way. So long as I have been here I have not willingly planted a thorn in any man's bosom.

While I am deeply sensible to the high compliment of a re-election; and duly grateful, as I trust, to Almighty God for having directed my countrymen to a right conclusion, as I think, for their own good, it adds nothing to my satisfaction that any other man may be disappointed or pained by the result.

May I ask those who have not differed with me, to join with me, in this same spirit towards those who have?

And now, let me close by asking three hearty cheers for our brave soldiers and seamen and their gallant and skillful commanders.

With Malice Toward None, 1864–1865

LINCOLN'S REELECTION ensured the prosecution of the war to the finish on the basis of reunion with emancipation. In his fourth annual message [Document 8-1], he set forth the progress of the Union armies during the past year; before too long the news that William T. Sherman's army had reached Savannah, Georgia, on the Atlantic coast, provided another opportunity for celebration. Slavery had been abolished in Maryland and by the new state constitutions erected under Lincoln's reconstruction plan in Louisiana and Arkansas, while other states were making progress toward the same goal. Taking the election results as his cue, Lincoln now moved to make emancipation complete, national, and constitutional by urging Congress to pass a proposed amendment abolishing the peculiar institution. Such a measure had barely failed once before, but the president, noting that in any case the next Congress would surely approve an abolition amendment, called upon the last session of the Thirty-eighth Congress to pass it now. It did so on February 1, 1865; Lincoln celebrated the achievement that evening [Document 8-2].

Crumbling Confederate military fortunes also reduced the need to weaken the insurgents by wooing away supporters with the promises of a lenient peace in which the defeated could help shape the post-emancipation world. Lincoln suggested as much at the conclusion of his 1864 annual message. Nevertheless, there remained in him some sentiment for a gradual process of emancipation with some form of compensation to owners. In February 1865, after meeting a delegation of Confederate commissioners at Hampton Roads, Virginia, Lincoln, still willing to offer inducements for peace, framed a proposal looking toward compensation provided that the war end by April 1 and that the new Thirteenth Amendment be ratified by July 1 [Document 8-3]. He reasoned that the sum of money offered would actually cost the federal government less than continuing to wage war, and would inject much-needed capital into a region desperate for resources with which to rebuild their social and economic orders in a post-emancipation world. However, his cabinet members objected to the proposal and talked Lincoln out of making it public.

Lincoln took the opportunity of his second inaugural address [Document 8-4] to share with his audience his evolving understanding of the meaning of the war and the attitudes which should guide the process of reunion. Reconciliation was the order of the day; the president sought to mute the self-righteousness that often accompanied victory by reminding Northerners that God's purposes did not always coincide with their own. However, he took a much different tone—one which mixed humor with some sharp logic—in offering his observations on Confederate proposals to enlist blacks [Document 8-5].

At the end of March, Grant launched his final drive against Lee's army. Lincoln was on hand to watch the result. Richmond fell on April 3, 1865; the next day the president visited the city. In yet another effort to make white Southerners part of the process of ending the war, Lincoln unfolded a plan whereby the members of Virginia's state legislature would meet to take the state out of the war in accordance with his specified terms [Document 8-6]. Lee's surrender to Grant at Appomattox Court House four days later was far more effective in taking Virginia out of the war; it also saved Lincoln from criticism, including the charge that in effect he was recognizing the legitimacy of Confederate state governments. At the same time, Grant's terms—especially his pledge that the paroled Confederates would not be disturbed by federal authorities so long as they remained law-abiding hereafter—delighted the president, for they provided a foundation for the kind of peace he had advocated.

With the triumph of the Union made tangible at Appomattox, Lincoln took the opportunity of responding to yet another group of serenaders to share his thoughts on the peace to come—in carefully prepared remarks [Document 8-7]. Defending his past policy (and reminding listeners that all the members of his cabinet, including then-Secretary of the Treasury Salmon P. Chase, now heading the Supreme Court as chief justice, had agreed with it), Lincoln, setting aside the debate on whether the states in rebellion were now out of the Union, preferred to look ahead with an eye on the status of blacks in the postwar South. What to him was a "merely pernicious abstraction" was in fact a fairly important constitutional argument, for if one accepted that the former Confederate states had somehow lost or forfeited their place in the Union, Congress would then be empowered to set forth terms of readmission that might well conflict with Lincoln's approach. Anxious to retain the initiative in setting forth terms while avoiding destructive debate with congressional Republicans, the president preferred to set aside the issue of the current constitutional status of those states. Just as notable was his suggestion that the new state constitutions constructed by Southern governments might include a provision for allowing at least some blacks to vote–thus making public the advice he had previously offered in private to Louisiana's Michael Hahn [Document 7-4]. Finally, the president made it clear that with the advent of victory on the battlefield it was time to reassess the terms of reconstruction, for he no longer had to woo disaffected Confederates. New circumstances called for new approaches.

Not everyone in the assembled audience was happy with the president's remarks. The occasion called for celebration of the present, not contemplation of the future. One listener fumed as the president spoke. "That means nigger citizenship," snapped John Wilkes Booth, an actor and Confederate sympathizer. "Now, by God, I'll put him through. That is the last speech he will ever make." Three days later, he made good on his pledge. At 7:22 A.M. on the morning of April 15, 1865, Abraham Lincoln died from a gunshot wound to the head received the previous night while he was watching a play at a local theater.

[DOCUMENT 8-1]
FOURTH ANNUAL MESSAGE, DECEMBER 6, 1864 (EXCERPTS)

In his fourth annual message Lincoln reflected on recent military operations, notably General William T. Sherman's march through Georgia, and early efforts at reconstructing loyal state governments in the South before urging Congress to pass a constitutional amendment to abolish slavery. His haste was due in part to his concern about what would happen to slavery in areas of the Confederacy not yet touched by military operations once the war ended; an amendment would also take care of slavery in areas not covered by the Emancipation Proclamation or congressional legislation. In his observations concerning Reconstruction, he implied that with the end of the war he would have to reconsider his policy.

...The war continues. Since the last annual message all the important lines and positions then occupied by our forces have been maintained, and our arms have steadily advanced; thus liberating the regions left in rear, so that Missouri, Kentucky, Tennessee and parts of other States have again produced reasonably fair crops.

The most remarkable feature in the military operations of the year is General Sherman's attempted march of three hundred miles directly through the insurgent region. It tends to show a great increase of our relative strength that our General-in-Chief should feel able to confront and hold in check every active force of the enemy, and yet to detach a well-appointed large army to move on such an expedition. The result not yet being known, conjecture in regard to it is not here indulged.

Important movements have also occurred during the year to the effect of moulding society for durability in the Union. Although short of complete success, it is much in the right direction, that twelve thousand citizens in each of the States of Arkansas and Louisiana have organized loyal State governments with free constitutions, and are earnestly struggling to maintain and administer them. The movements in the same direction, more extensive, though less definite in Missouri, Kentucky and Tennessee, should not be overlooked. But Maryland presents the example of complete success. Maryland is secure to Liberty and Union for all the future. The genius of rebellion will no more claim Maryland. Like another foul spirit, being driven out, it may seek to tear her, but it will woo her no more.

At the last session of Congress a proposed amendment of the Constitution abolishing slavery throughout the United States, passed the Senate, but failed for lack of the requisite two-thirds vote in the House of Representatives. Although the present is the same Congress, and nearly the same members, and without questioning the wisdom or patriotism of those who stood in opposition, I venture to recommend the reconsideration and passage of the measure at the present session. Of course the abstract question is not changed; but an intervening election shows, almost certainly, that the next Congress will pass the measure if this does not. Hence there is only a question of *time* as to when the proposed amendment will go to the States for their action. And as it is to so go, at all events, may we not agree that the sooner the better? It is not claimed that the election has imposed a duty on members to change their views or their votes, any further than, as an additional element to be considered, their judgment may be affected by it. It is the voice of the people now, for the first time, heard upon the question. In a great national crisis, like ours, unanimity of action among those seeking a common end is very desirable—almost indispensable. And yet no approach to such unanimity is attainable, unless some deference shall be paid to the will of the majority, simply because it is the will of the majority. In this case the common end is the maintenance of the Union; and, among the means to secure that end, such will, through the election, is most clearly declared in favor of such constitutional amendment.

The most reliable indication of public purpose in this country is derived through our popular elections. Judging by the recent canvass and its result, the purpose of the people, within the loyal States, to maintain the integrity of the Union, was never more firm, nor more nearly unanimous, than now. The extraordinary calmness and good order with which the millions of voters met and mingled at the polls, give strong assurance of this. Not only all those who supported the Union ticket, so called, but a great majority of the opposing party also, may be fairly claimed to entertain, and to be actuated by, the same purpose. It is an unanswerable argument to this effect, that no candidate for any office whatever, high or low, has ventured to seek votes on the avowal that he was for giving up the Union. There have been much impugning of motives, and much heated controversy as to the proper means and best mode of advancing the Union cause; but on the distinct issue of Union or no Union, the politicians have shown their instinctive knowledge that there is no diversity among the people. In affording the people the fair opportunity of showing, one to another and to the world, this firmness and unanimity of purpose, the election has been of vast value to the national cause.

The election has exhibited another fact not less valuable to be known—the fact that we do not approach exhaustion in the most important branch of national resources—that of living men. While it is melancholy to reflect that the war has filled so many graves, and carried mourning to so many hearts, it is some relief to know that, compared with the surviving, the fallen have been so few. While corps, and divisions, and brigades, and regiments have formed, and fought, and dwindled, and gone out of existence, a great majority of the men who composed them are still living. The same is true of the naval service. The election returns prove this. So many voters could not else be found. The States regularly holding elections, both now and four years ago, to wit, California, Connecticut, Delaware, Illinois, Indiana, Iowa, Kentucky, Maine, Maryland, Massachusetts, Michigan, Minnesota, Missouri, New Hampshire, New Jersey, New York, Ohio, Oregon, Pennsylvania, Rhode Island, Vermont, West Virginia, and Wisconsin cast 3.982.011 votes now, against 3.870.222 cast then, showing an aggregate now of 3.982.011. To this is to be added 33.762 cast now in the new States of Kansas and Nevada, which States did not vote in 1860, thus swelling the aggregate to 4.015.773 and the net increase during the three years and a half of war to 145.551. A table is appended showing particulars. To this again should be added the number of all soldiers in the field from Massachusetts, Rhode Island, New Jersey, Delaware, Indiana, Illinois, and California, who, by the laws of those States, could not vote away from their homes, and which number cannot be less than 90.000. Nor yet is this all. The number in organized Territories is triple now what it was four years ago, while thousands, white and black, join us as the national arms press back the insurgent lines. So much is shown, affirmatively and negatively, by the election. It is not material to inquire *how* the increase has been produced, or to show that it would have been *greater* but for the war, which is probably true. The important fact remains demonstrated, that we have *more* men *now* than we had when the war *began;* that we are not exhausted, nor in process of exhaustion; that we are *gaining* strength, and may, if need be, maintain the contest indefinitely. This as to men. Material resources are now more complete and abundant than ever.

The national resources, then, are unexhausted, and, as we believe, inexhaustible. The public purpose to re-establish and maintain the national authority is unchanged, and, as we believe, unchangeable. The manner of continuing the effort remains to choose. On careful consideration of all the evidence accessible it seems to me that no attempt at negotiation with the insurgent leader could result in any good. He would accept nothing short of severance of the Union—precisely what we will not and cannot give. His declarations to this effect are explicit and oft-repeated. He does not attempt to deceive us. He affords us no excuse to deceive ourselves. He cannot voluntarily reaccept the Union; we cannot voluntarily yield it. Between him and us the issue is distinct, simple, and inflexible. It is an issue which can only be tried by war, and decided by victory. If we yield, we are beaten; if the Southern people fail him, he is beaten. Either way, it would be the victory and defeat following war. What is true, however, of him who heads the insurgent cause, is not necessarily true of those who follow. Although he cannot reaccept the Union, they can. Some of them, we know, already desire peace and reunion. The number of such may increase. They can, at any moment, have peace simply by laying down their arms and submitting to the national authority under the Constitution. After so much, the government could not, if it would, maintain war against them. The loyal people would not sustain or allow it. If questions should remain, we would adjust them by the peaceful means of legislation, conference, courts, and votes, operating only in constitutional and lawful channels. Some certain, and other possible, questions are, and would be, beyond the Executive power to adjust; as, for instance, the admission of members into Congress, and whatever might require the appropriation of money. The Executive power itself would be greatly diminished by the cessation of actual war. Pardons and remissions of forfeitures, however, would still be within Executive control. In what spirit and temper this control would be exercised can be fairly judged by the past.

A year ago general pardon and amnesty, upon specified terms, were offered to all, except certain designated classes; and, it was, at the same time, made known that the excepted classes were still within contemplation of special clemency. During the year many availed themselves of the general provision, and many more would, only that the signs of bad faith in some led to such precautionary measures as rendered the practical process less easy and certain. During the same time also special pardons have been granted to individuals of the excepted classes, and no voluntary application has been denied. Thus, practically, the door has been, for a full year, open to all, except such as were not in condition to make free choice—that is, such as were in custody or under constraint. It is still so open to all. But the time may come—probably will come—when public duty shall demand that it be closed; and that, in lieu, more rigorous measures than heretofore shall be adopted.

In presenting the abandonment of armed resistance to the national authority on the part of the insurgents, as the only indispensable condition to ending the war on the part of the government, I retract nothing heretofore said as to slavery. I repeat the declaration made a year ago, that "while I remain in my present position I shall not attempt to retract or modify the emancipation proclamation, nor shall I return to slavery any person who is free by the terms of that proclamation, or by any of the Acts of Congress." If the people should, by whatever mode or means, make it an Executive duty to re-enslave such persons, another, and not I, must be their instrument to perform it.

In stating a single condition of peace, I mean simply to say that the war will cease on the part of the government, whenever it shall have ceased on the part of those who began it.

December 6. 1864. Abraham Lincoln

[DOCUMENT 8-2]
RESPONSE TO SERENADE, FEBRUARY 1, 1865

Using the opportunity of yet another public serenade to express his views, Lincoln celebrated the passage of the Thirteenth Amendment. One newspaper reported his comments as follows:

The President said he supposed the passage through Congress of the Constitutional amendment for the abolishment of Slavery throughout the United States, was the occasion to which he was indebted for the honor of this call. [Applause.] The occasion was one of congratulation to the country and to the whole world. But there is a task yet before us—to go forward and consummate by the votes of the States that which Congress so nobly began yesterday. [Applause and cries—"They will do it," &c.] He had the honor to inform those present that Illinois had already to-day done the work. [Applause.] Maryland was about half through; but he felt proud that Illinois was a little ahead. He thought this measure was a very fitting if not an indispensable adjunct to the winding up of the great difficulty. He wished the reunion of all the States perfected and so effected as to remove all causes of disturbance in the future; and to attain this end it was necessary that the original disturbing cause should, if possible, be rooted out. He thought all would bear him witness that he had never shrunk from doing all that he could to eradicate Slavery by issuing an emancipation proclamation. [Applause.] But that proclamation falls far short of what the amendment will be when fully consummated. A question might be raised whether the proclamation was legally valid. It might be added that it only aided those who did not give themselves up, or that it would have no effect upon the children of the slaves born hereafter. In fact it would be urged that it did not meet the evil. But this amendment is a King's cure for all the evils. [Applause.] It winds the whole thing up. He would repeat that it was the fitting if not indispensable adjunct to the consummation of the great game we are playing. He could not but congratulate all present, himself, the country and the whole world upon this great moral victory.

[DOCUMENT 8-3]
PROPOSED MESSAGE TO CONGRESS, FEBRUARY 5, 1865

On February 2, 1865, Lincoln traveled to Hampton Roads, Virginia, to meet with three Confederate commissioners—Vice President Alexander H. Stephens, Assistant Secretary of War John A. Campbell (who had once served on the Supreme Court) and Senator R. M. T. Hunter. The president made it clear that a reunion based upon emancipation was his fundamental condition for peace; he would not otherwise end the fighting. However, Stephens later recalled that if Lincoln was inflexible when it came to the principle of emancipation, he was more malleable when it came to its implementation—which is supported by this document, which Lincoln prepared upon his return to Washington. However, when he presented it to his cabinet, everyone present expressed opposition; Lincoln dropped the idea.

Fellow citizens of the Senate, and House of Representatives.

I respectfully recommend that a Joint Resolution, substantially as follows, be adopted so soon as practicable, by your honorable bodies.

"Resolved by the Senate and House of Representatives, of the United States of America in congress assembled: That the President of the United States is hereby empowered, in his discretion, to pay four hundred millions of dollars to the States of Alabama, Arkansas, Delaware, Florida, Georgia, Kentucky, Louisiana, Maryland Mississippi, Missouri, North Carolina, South Carolina, Tennessee, Texas, Virginia, and West virginia, in the manner, and on the conditions following towit: The payment to be made in six per cent government bonds, and to be distributed among said States *pro rata* on their respective slave populations, as shown by the census of 1860; and no part of said sum to be paid unless all resistance to the national authority shall be abandoned and cease, on or before the first day of April next; and upon such abandonment and ceasing of resistance, one half of said sum to be paid in manner aforesaid, and the remaining half to be paid only upon the amendment of the national constitution recently proposed by congress, becoming valid law, on or before the first day of July next, by the action thereon of the requisite number of States"

The adoption of such resolution is sought with a view to embody it, with other propositions, in a proclamation looking to peace and reunion.

Whereas a Joint Resolution has been adopted by congress in the words following, towit

Now therefore I, Abraham Lincoln, President of the United States, do proclaim, declare, and make known, that on the conditions therein stated, the power conferred on the Executive in and by said Joint resolution, will be fully exercised; that war will cease, and armies be reduced to a basis of peace; that all political offences will be pardoned; that all property, except slaves, liable to confiscation or forfeiture, will be released therefrom, except in cases of intervening interests of third parties; and that liberality will be recommended to congress upon all points not lying within executive control.

[Endorsement]

Feb. 5. 1865

To-day these papers, which explain themselves, were drawn up and submitted to the Cabinet & unanamously disapproved by them.

A Lincoln

[D*OCUMENT* 8-4]
S*ECOND* I*NAUGURAL* A*DDRESS*, M*ARCH* 4, 1865

On March 4, 1865, Abraham Lincoln prepared to take the oath of office as President of the United States for the second time. He first delivered the following address; as he stepped forward to begin, the overcast skies above gave way to the sun. Perhaps this helped Lincoln to forget that he had just witnessed his new vice president, Andrew Johnson, ramble through his own remarks, the result of one too many glasses of whiskey to steady himself in the wake of sickness and nerves. What follows proved more worthy of the occasion: Lincoln himself expected it "to wear as well as—perhaps better than—any thing I have ever produced."

Fellow Countrymen:

At this second appearing to take the oath of the presidential office, there is less occasion for an extended address than there was at the first. Then a statement, somewhat in detail, of a course to be pursued, seemed fitting and proper. Now, at the expiration of four years, during which public declarations have been constantly called forth on every point and phase of the great contest which still absorbs the attention, and engrosses the energies of the nation, little that is new could be presented. The progress of our arms, upon which all else chiefly depends, is as well known to the public as to myself; and it is, I trust, reasonably satisfactory and encouraging to all. With high hope for the future, no prediction in regard to it is ventured.

On the occasion corresponding to this four years ago, all thoughts were anxiously directed to an impending civil-war. All dreaded it—all sought to avert it. While the inaugeral address was being delivered from this place, devoted altogether to *saving* the Union without war, insurgent agents were in the city seeking to *destroy* it without war—seeking to dissolve the Union, and divide effects, by negotiation. Both parties deprecated war; but one of them would *make* war rather than let the nation survive; and the other would *accept* war rather than let it perish. And the war came.

One eighth of the whole population were colored slaves, not distributed generally over the Union, but localized in the Southern part of it. These slaves constituted a peculiar and powerful interest. All knew that this interest was, somehow, the cause of the war. To strengthen, perpetuate, and extend this interest was the object for which the insurgents would rend the Union, even by war; while the government claimed no right to do more than to restrict the territorial enlargement of it. Neither party expected for the war, the magnitude, or the duration, which it has already attained. Neither anticipated that the *cause* of the conflict might cease with, or even before, the conflict itself should cease. Each looked for an easier triumph, and a result less fundamental and astounding. Both read the same Bible, and pray to the same God; and each invokes His aid against the other. It may seem strange that any men should dare to ask a just God's assistance in wringing their bread form the sweat of other men's faces; but let us judge not that we not be judged. The prayers of both could not be answered; that of neither has been answered fully. The Almighty has His own purposes. "Woe unto the world because of offences! for it must needs be that offences come; but woe to that man by whom the offence cometh!" If we shall suppose that American Slavery is one of those offences which, in the providence of God, must needs come, but which, having continued through His appointed time, He now wills to remove, and that He gives to both North and South, this terrible war, as the woe due to those by whom the offence came, shall we discern therein any departure from those divine attributes which the believers in a Living God always ascribe to Him? Fondly do we hope—fervently do we pray—that this mighty scourge of war may speedily pass away. Yet, if God wills that it continue, until all the wealth piled by the bond-man's two hundred and fifty years of unrequited toil shall be sunk, and until every drop of blood drawn with the lash, shall be paid by another drawn with the sword, as was said three thousand years ago, so still it must be said "the judgments of the Lord, are true and righteous altogether"

With malice toward none; with charity for all; with firmness in the right, as God gives us to see the right, let us strive on to finish the work we are in; to bind up the nation's wounds; to care for him who shall have borne the battle, and for his widow, and his orphan—to do all which may achieve and cherish a just, and a lasting peace, among ourselves, and with all nations....

[DOCUMENT 8-5]
SPEECH TO THE 140TH INDIANA REGIMENT, MARCH 17, 1865

Lincoln offered the following remarks to an Indiana regiment; they contain his observations upon Confederate proposals to arm slaves. The following text is taken from a newspaper transcript, which differs in minor ways from his handwritten draft.

FELLOW CITIZENS—It will be but a very few words that I shall undertake to say. I was born in Kentucky, raised in Indiana and lived in Illinois. (Laughter.) And now I am here, where it is my business to care equally for the good people of all the States. I am glad to see an Indiana regiment on this day able to present the captured flag to the Governor of Indiana. (Applause.) I am not disposed, in saying this, to make a distinction between the States, for all have done equally well. (Applause.) There are but few views or aspects of this great war upon which I have not said or written something whereby my own opinions might be known. But there is one—the recent attempt of our erring brethren, as they are sometimes called—(laughter)—to employ the negro to fight for them. I have neither written nor made a speech on that subject, because that was their business, not mine; and if I had a wish upon the subject I had not the power to introduce it, or make it effective. The great question with them was, whether the negro, being put into the army, would fight for them. I do not know, and therefore cannot decide. (Laughter.) They ought to know better than we. I have in my lifetime heard many arguments why the negroes ought to be slaves; but if they fight for those who would keep them in slavery it will be a better argument than any I have yet heard. (Laughter and applause.) He who will fight for that ought to be a slave. (Applause.) They have concluded at last to take one out of four of the slaves, and put them in the army; and that one out of the four who will fight to keep the others in slavery ought to be a slave himself unless he is killed in a fight. (Applause.) While I have often said that all men ought to be free, yet I would allow those colored persons to be slaves who want to be; and next to them those white persons who argue in favor of making other people slaves. (Applause.) I am in favor of giving an opportunity to such white men to try it on for themselves. (Applause.) I will say one thing in regard to the negro being employed to fight for them. I do know he cannot fight and stay at home and make bread too—(laughter and applause)—and as one is about as important as the other to them, I don't care which they do. (Renewed applause.) I am rather in favor of having them try them as soldiers. (Applause.) They lack one vote of doing that, and I wish I could send my vote over the river so that I might cast it in favor of allowing the negro to fight. (Applause.) But they cannot fight and work both. We must now see the bottom of the enemy's resources. They will stand out as long as they can, and if the negro will fight for them, they must allow him to fight. They have drawn upon their last branch of resources. (Applause.) And we can now see the bottom. (Applause.) I am glad to see the end so near at hand. (Applause.) I have said now more than I intended, and will therefore bid you goodby.

[DOCUMENT 8-6]
TO JOHN A. CAMPBELL, APRIL 5, 1865

At the end of March 1865, Lincoln traveled to Grant's headquarters at City Point, Virginia. Just over a week after his arrival, Union forces entered Richmond. So did Lincoln, on April 4. Soon thereafter he encountered John A. Campbell, one of the three Confederate commissioners for the Hampton Roads conference; Campbell, aware of the dimming prospects for Confederate independence, sounded out the president on how Virginia could reenter the Union. In response, Lincoln first offered this exposition of his terms; subsequent negotiations over the process whereby Virginia would abandon the Confederacy proved embarrassing to Lincoln and were rendered unnecessary when Robert E. Lee surrendered the Army of Northern Virginia to Grant at Appomattox Court House on April 9, 1865.

As to peace, I have said before, and now repeat, that three things are indispensable.

1. The restoration of the national authority throughout all the States.

2. No receding by the Executive of the United States on the slavery question, from the position assumed thereon, in the late Annual Message to Congress, and in preceding documents.

3. No cessation of hostilities short of an end of the war, and the disbanding of all force hostile to the government.

That all propositions coming from those now in hostility to the government; and not inconsistent with the foregoing, will be respectfully considered, and passed upon in a spirit of sincere liberality.

I now add that it seems useless for me to be more specific with those who will not say they are ready for the indispensable terms, even on conditions to be named by themselves. If there be any who are ready for those indispensable terms, on any conditions whatever, let them say so, and state their conditions, so that such conditions can be distinctly known, and considered.

It is further added that, the remission of confiscations being within the executive power, if the war be now further persisted in, by those opposing the government, the making of confiscated property at the least to bear the additional cost, will be insisted on; but that confiscations (except in cases of third party intervening interests) will be remitted to the people of any State which shall now promptly, and in good faith, withdraw it's troops and other support, from further resistance to the government.

What is now said as to remission of confiscations has no reference to supposed property in slaves.

[DOCUMENT 8-7]
SPEECH ON RECONSTRUCTION, APRIL 11, 1865

Word of Lee's surrender reached Washington on the evening of April 9, several hours after Lincoln had returned to the capital city. On the night of April 10, he was visited by the now-expected group of serenaders; Lincoln promised to treat them to a more considered set of remarks if they returned the following night, then requested that the band play "Dixie." When the crowd gathered on April 11, Lincoln appeared at a window on the second floor and read what follows by candlelight; his son Tad scampered about at his feet, collecting each page as his father dropped it, impatiently calling for "another."

It was the last speech Abraham Lincoln ever gave.

We meet this evening, not in sorrow, but in gladness of heart. The evacuation of Petersburg and Richmond, and the surrender of the principal insurgent army, give hope of a righteous and speedy peace whose joyous expression can not be restrained. In the midst of this, however, He, from Whom all blessings flow, must not be forgotten. A call for a national thanksgiving is being prepared, and will be duly promulgated. Nor must those whose harder part gives us the cause of rejoicing, be overlooked. Their honors must not be parcelled out with others. I myself, was near the front, and had the high pleasure of transmitting much of the good news to you; but no part of the honor, for plan or execution, is mine. To Gen. Grant, his skilful officers, and brave men, all belongs. The gallant Navy stood ready, but was not in reach to take active part.

By these recent successes the re-inauguration of the national authority—reconstruction—which has had a large share of thought from the first, is pressed much more closely upon our attention. It is fraught with great difficulty. Unlike the case of a war between independent nations, there is no authorized organ for us to treat with. No one man has authority to give up the rebellion for any other man. We simply must begin with, and mould from, disorganized and discordant elements. Nor is it a small additional embarrassment that we, the loyal people,

differ among ourselves as to the mode, manner, and means of reconstruction.

As a general rule, I abstain from reading the reports of attacks upon
myself, wishing not to be provoked by that to which I can not properly
offer an answer. In spite of this precaution, however, it comes to my
knowledge that I am much censured for some supposed agency in setting up, and seeking to sustain, the new State Government of Louisiana. In this I have done just so much as, and no more than, the public
knows. In the Annual Message of Dec. 1863 and accompanying Proclamation, I presented *a* plan of re-construction (as the phrase goes)
which, I promised, if adopted by any State, should be acceptable to,
and sustained by, the Executive government of the nation. I distinctly
stated that this was not the only plan which might possibly be acceptable; and I also distinctly protested that the Executive claimed no right
to say when, or whether members should be admitted to seats in Congress from such States. This plan was, in advance, submitted to the
then Cabinet, and distinctly approved by every member of it. One of
them suggested that I should then, and in that connection, apply the
Emancipation Proclamation to the theretofore excepted parts of Virginia and Louisiana; that I should drop the suggestion about apprenticeship for freed-people, and that I should omit the protest against my
own power, in regard to the admission of members to Congress; but
even he approved every part and parcel of the plan which has since
been employed or touched by the action of Louisiana. The new constitution of Louisiana, declaring emancipation for the whole State, practically applies the Proclamation to the part previously excepted. It does
not adopt apprenticeship for freed-people; and it is silent, as it could
not well be otherwise, about the admission of members to Congress.
So that, as it applies to Louisiana, every member of the Cabinet fully
approved the plan. The Message went to Congress, and I received many
commendations of the plan, written and verbal; and not a single objection to it, from any professed emancipationist, came to my knowledge,
until after the news reached Washington that the people of Louisiana
had begun to move in accordance with it. From about July 1862, I had
corresponded with different persons, supposed to be interested, seeking a reconstruction of a State government for Louisiana. When the
Message of 1863, with the plan before mentioned, reached New-Orleans, Gen. Banks wrote me that he was confident the people, with his
military co-operation, would reconstruct, substantially on that plan. I
wrote him, and some of them to try it; they tried it, and the result is
known. Such only has been my agency in getting up the Louisiana

government. As to sustaining it, my promise is out, as before stated. But, as bad promises are better broken than kept, I shall treat this as a bad promise, and break it, whenever I shall be convinced that keeping it is adverse to the public interest. But I have not yet been so convinced.

I have been shown a letter on this subject, supposed to be an able one, in which the writer expresses regret that my mind has not seemed to be definitely fixed on the question whether the seceded States, so called, are in the Union or out of it. It would perhaps, add astonishment to his regret, were he to learn that since I have found professed Union men endeavoring to make that question, I have *purposely* forborne any public expression upon it. As appears to me that question has not been, nor yet is, a practically material one, and that any discussion of it, while it thus remains practically immaterial, could have no effect other than the mischievous one of dividing our friends. As yet, whatever it may hereafter become, that question is bad, as the basis of a controversy, and good for nothing at all—a merely pernicious abstraction.

We all agree that the seceded States, so called, are out of their proper practical relation with the Union; and that the sole object of the government, civil and military, in regard to those States is to again get them into that proper practical relation. I believe it is not only possible, but in fact, easier, to do this, without deciding, or even considering, whether these states have been out of the Union, than with it. Finding themselves safely at home, it would be utterly immaterial whether they had ever been abroad. Let us all join in doing the acts necessary to restoring the proper practical relations between these states and the Union; and each forever after, innocently indulge his own opinion whether, in doing the acts, he brought the States from without, into the Union, or only gave them proper assistance, they never having been out of it.

The amount of constituency, so to to speak, on which the new Louisiana government rests, would be more satisfactory to all, if it contained fifty, thirty, or even twenty thousand, instead of only about twelve thousand, as it does. It is also unsatisfactory to some that the elective franchise is not given to the colored man. I would myself prefer that it were now conferred on the very intelligent, and on those who serve our cause as soldiers. Still the question is not whether the Louisiana government, as it stands, is quite all that is desirable. The question is "Will it be wiser to take it as it is, and help to improve it; or to reject, and disperse it?" "Can Louisiana be brought into proper practical relation with the Union *sooner* by *sustaining*, or by *discarding* her new State Government?"

Some twelve thousand voters in the heretofore slave-state of Louisiana have sworn allegiance to the Union, assumed to be the rightful political power of the State, held elections, organized a State government, adopted a free-state constitution, giving the benefit of public schools equally to black and white, and empowering the Legislature to confer the elective franchise upon the colored man. Their Legislature has already voted to ratify the constitutional amendment recently passed by Congress, abolishing slavery throughout the nation. These twelve thousand persons are thus fully committed to the Union, and to perpetual freedom in the State—committed to the very things, and nearly all the things the nation wants—and they ask the nations recognition, and it's assistance to make good their committal. Now, if we reject, and spurn them, we do our utmost to disorganize and disperse them. We in effect say to the white men "You are worthless, or worse—we will neither help you, nor be helped by you." To the blacks we say "This cup of liberty which these, your old masters, hold to your lips, we will dash from you, and leave you to the chances of gathering the spilled and scattered contents in some vague and undefined when, where, and how." If this course, discouraging and paralyzing both white and black, has any tendency to bring Louisiana into proper practical relations with the Union, I have, so far, been unable to perceive it. If, on the contrary, we recognize, and sustain the new government of Louisiana the converse of all this is made true. We encourage the hearts, and nerve the arms of the twelve thousand to adhere to their work, and argue for it, and proselyte for it, and fight for it, and feed it, and grow it, and ripen it to a complete success. The colored man too, in seeing all united for him, is inspired with vigilance, and energy, and daring, to the same end. Grant that he desires the elective franchise, will he not attain it sooner by saving the already advanced steps toward it, than by running backward over them? Concede that the new government of Louisiana is only to what it should be as the egg is to the fowl, we shall sooner have the fowl by hatching the egg than by smashing it? Again, if we reject Louisiana, we also reject one vote in favor of the proposed amendment to the national constitution. To meet this proposition, it has been argued that no more than three fourths of those States which have not attempted secession are necessary to validly ratify the amendment. I do not commit myself against this, further than to say that such a ratification would be questionable, and sure to be persistently questioned; while a ratification by three fourths of all the States would be unquestioned and unquestionable.

I repeat the question. "Can Louisiana be brought into proper practical relation with the Union *sooner* by *sustaining* or by *discarding* her new State Government?

What has been said of Louisiana will apply generally to other States. And yet so great peculiarities pertain to each state; and such important and sudden changes occur in the same state; and, withal, so new and unprecedented is the whole case, that no exclusive, and inflexible plan can safely be prescribed as to details and colatterals. Such exclusive, and inflexible plan, would surely become a new entanglement. Important principles may, and must, be inflexible.

In the present *"situation"* as the phrase goes, it may be my duty to make some new announcement to the people of the South. I am considering, and shall not fail to act, when satisfied that action will be proper.

Selected Bibliography

Lincoln's Works

Basler, Roy P., and others, eds. *The Collected Works of Abraham Lincoln.* 8 vols. plus index. New Brunswick, NJ, 1953–1955.

Basler, Roy P., ed. *The Collected Works of Abraham Lincoln: Supplement 1832–1865.* Westport, CT, 1974.

Basler, Roy P., and Christian O. Basler, eds. *The Collected Works of Abraham Lincoln: Second Supplement 1848–1865.* New Brunswick, NJ, 1990.

Fehrenbacher, Don E., ed. *Abraham Lincoln: Speeches and Writings.* 2 vols. New York, 1989.

Books on Lincoln

Boritt, Gabor. *Lincoln and the Economics of the American Dream.* Memphis, 1978.

——, ed. *The Historians' Lincoln: Pseudohistory, Psychohistory, and History.* Urbana, IL, 1988.

Cox, LaWanda. *Lincoln and Black Freedom: A Study in Presidential Leadership.* Columbia, SC, 1981.

Current, Richard N. *The Lincoln Nobody Knows.* New York, 1958.

——. *Lincoln and the First Shot.* Philadelphia, 1963.

Dennett, Tyler, ed. *Lincoln and the Civil War in the Diaries and Letters of John Hay.* New York, 1939.

Donald, David. *Lincoln Reconsidered: Essays on the Civil War Era.* Revised edition: New York, 1956.

——. *Lincoln.* New York, 1995.

Fehrenbacher, Don E. *Prelude to Greatness: Lincoln in the 1850s.* Stanford, CA, 1962.

Fehrenbacher, Don E., and Virginia Fehrenbacher, comp. and ed. *Recollected Words of Abraham Lincoln.* Stanford, CA, 1996.

Franklin, John Hope. *The Emancipation Proclamation*. Revised Edition. Wheeling, IL, 1995 [1963].

Hesseltine, William B. *Lincoln's Plan of Reconstruction*. Tuscaloosa, AL, 1960.

Johannsen, Robert W. *Lincoln, the South and Slavery*. Baton Rouge, 1991.

Lewis, Lloyd. *Myths After Lincoln*. New York, 1929.

McCrary, Peyton. *Abraham Lincoln and Reconstruction: The Louisiana Experiment*. Princeton, NJ, 1978.

Neely, Mark E., Jr. *The Abraham Lincoln Encyclopedia*. New York, 1982.

——. *The Last Best Hope of Earth: Abraham Lincoln and the Promise of America*. Cambridge, MA, 1993.

Nicolay, John G., and John Hay. *Abraham Lincoln: A History*. 10 vols.: New York, 1890.

Oates, Stephen B. *With Malice Toward None: The Life of Abraham Lincoln*. New York, 1977.

——. *Abraham Lincoln: The Man Behind the Myths*. New York, 1984.

Paludan, Phillip Shaw. *The Presidency of Abraham Lincoln*. Lawrence, KS, 1994.

Quarles, Benjamin. *Lincoln and the Negro*. New York, 1962.

Randall, James G. *Lincoln the President*. 4 vols. (volume 4 with Richard N. Current). New York, 1945–1955.

Thomas, Benjamin P. *Abraham Lincoln*. New York, 1952.

Thomas, John L., ed. *Abraham Lincoln and the American Political Tradition*. Amherst, MA, 1986.

Williams, T. Harry. *Lincoln and the Radicals*. Madison, WI, 1941.

——. *Lincoln and His Generals*. New York, 1952.

Zarefsky, David. *Lincoln, Douglas, and Slavery: In the Crucible of Public Debate*. Chicago, 1990.

Index

203